The Autobiography of Margaret Oliphant

The Autobiography
of
Margaret Oliphant

The Complete Text

Edited and introduced by
ELISABETH JAY

Oxford New York
OXFORD UNIVERSITY PRESS
1990

Oxford University Press, Walton Street, Oxford OX2 6DP

Oxford New York Toronto
Delhi Bombay Calcutta Madras Karachi
Petaling Jaya Singapore Hong Kong Tokyo
Nairobi Dar es Salaam Cape Town
Melbourne Auckland

and associated companies in
Berlin Ibadan

Oxford is a trade mark of Oxford University Press

British Library Cataloguing in Publication Data
Oliphant, Mrs. 1828–1897
The autobiography of Margaret Oliphant : the complete text.
1. Fiction in English. Oliphant, Mrs, 1828–1897
I. Title   II. Jay, Elisabeth
823.8
ISBN 0–19–818615–0

Library of Congress Cataloging in Publication Data
Oliphant, Mrs. (Margaret), 1828–1897.
[Autobiography and letters of Mrs. M.O.W. Oliphant]
The autobiography of Margaret Oliphant : the complete text /
edited and introduced by Elisabeth Jay.
p.   cm.   Includes bibliographical references (p. 179).
1. Oliphant, Mrs. (Margaret), 1828–1897—Biography.   2. Oliphant, Mrs. (Margaret),
1828–1897—Correspondence.   3. Novelists, Scottish—19th century—Biography.
4. Novelists, Scottish—19th century—Correspondence.
I. Jay, Elisabeth.   II. Title.
PR5114.A3   1990   823'.8—dc20   90–6723
ISBN 0–19–818615–0

Typeset by Colset Private Ltd.
Printed in Great Britain by
Bookcraft (Bath) Ltd.
Midsomer Norton, Avon

Acknowledgements

I am grateful to Mrs Oliphant's heirs, Messrs Danvers and James Valentine, for their permission to print hitherto unpublished portions of the *Autobiography* which remain in copyright. I should also like to express my thanks for the exceptionally courteous help I have received from the staff of the National Library of Scotland and to acknowledge the permission I have received to reprint the manuscript now in this Library's possession.

Contents

Introduction

Margaret Oliphant Wilson Oliphant, whose curious name derived from marrying a cousin on her mother's side of the family, was born on 4 April 1828 in Wallyford, Midlothian, and died in Wimbledon on 25 June 1897. Her first attempt at writing took the form of a novel written in her teens to secure 'some amusement and occupation for myself' while striving to overcome depression after a broken engagement and acting as the silent nurse and attendant her mother's serious illness required. The image is prophetic. Over the next fifty years Oliphant was to write some ninety-eight novels, fifty or more short stories, more than four hundred articles, numerous travel books and several biographies, while functioning as the mainstay of a family whose ever-widening circle and increasingly importunate demands she satisfied and, on occasion, distanced by means of her literary career. The final lines of her autobiographical manuscript, written after the death in adulthood of her two remaining children, also focus attention upon the intimate and complex relationship between the writing and the need that generated it.

> And now here I am all alone.
> I cannot write any more.

Experience had discouraged her from seeking support and solace from men. Her father seems to have been a detached, uncompanionable figure, totally overshadowed by her capable mother, to whom she was devoted. Despite being nine years younger than either of her two brothers, Oliphant provided for her elder brother Frank and his children upon his bankruptcy and subsequent mental collapse, and for the exiled life of the younger brother 'Willie' who declined into chronic alcoholism. Her husband's death after only seven years of marriage left her abroad, in debt, and with the three of her six children who had survived infancy to support. It is difficult, even with the full text of her autobiography, to construct a full picture of her marriage to her cousin Frank, which had so brief a span to survive many of the strains normal to the early years of married life, when money was short, childbearing an almost annual event, and the new relationship had to be negotiated in a strange environment under the additional strain of her parents coming to London with the sole aim of being near her. The strong emotional tie that existed between mother and daughter seems to have been a source of irritation and jealousy to Frank, especially since the bond seemed to have been cemented by a sense of the inadequacy of all the male figures in the Wilson family. Frank had therefore to carve out for himself the roles of husband and father while also trying to establish himself in business as a stained-glass window artist. Frank's naïvety in business affairs was something Oliphant could probably have forgiven, but the wound that never completely healed was Frank's failure to share with her his medical specialist's grim diagnosis of advanced tuberculosis. In retrospect she blamed herself for lack of sympathy, but also contrasted his petulant self-absorption with the heroic fortitude of her mother during her final illness. Above all the lack of trust and concern hurt, and many an apparently happily married couple in Oliphant's novels is resolved into two individuals harbouring thoughts that would astound or grieve the other. Though she set her face firmly against remarriage, partly on account of her conviction of reunion in heaven, it is remarkable that in her moments of deepest grief she seems only to think of the children already taken from her and her mother's welcoming presence, not of her husband. As the years passed and friends and dependants unknown to Frank came into being it is scarcely to be wondered at that the tenth of her life spent in marriage receded in importance.

When two of Oliphant's former dependants, her niece Denny, and her distant cousin Annie Coghill, came to publish her autobiographical manuscript in 1899, they had become so accustomed to her shaping powers as family provider, professional writer and businesswoman that they were astonished and disappointed, for 'it had no beginning: scraps had been written at long intervals and by no means consecutively'. So they attempted to redeem their relative's startling lapse by assembling the 'bits' and 'fragments' of which Oliphant herself spoke, into the narrative line they believed would prove acceptable to the market.

Yet they could not escape the anxiety 'that the needful fitting together has not been quite smoothly done', that the manuscript displayed a certain obstinate resistance to the literary template they wished to impose upon it. The reordering and suppressions involved in their editorial process wrenched the form a step away from the autobiographical impulse that had engendered it and a step nearer to the biographical record expressly forbidden by Oliphant upon her death-bed. Moreover, in their desire to 'gratify the many readers who have for so long a stretch of years regarded her as a friend', these two women in effect colluded with the constraints imposed upon women and women writers by the cultural assumptions enshrined in the market. Such a generalized accusation requires more specific illustration. Here then is the portrait of Oliphant that Annie Coghill offered to readers before they embarked upon the truncated autobiography.

[W]hatever sufferings might be lying in wait to seize upon her solitary hours, there was almost always a pleasant welcome and talk of the very best to be found in her modest drawing-room. If the visitors were congenial, her charm of manner awoke, her simple fitness of speech clothed every subject with life and grace, her beautiful eyes shone (they never sparkled), and the spell of her exquisite womanliness made a charmed circle around her.

This blueprint for feminine behaviour stresses decorum and restraint, the ability to give life to the charmed circle without insisting upon her own presence as its creative force. The passage, with its culminating tribute to 'the very atmosphere about her which was "pure womanly" ', constitutes the editors' hidden agenda. If Oliphant is to be presented as a social creature brought to life by her response to the needs of others, then the inner voice heard during those solitary hours, especially when raised against the demands imposed upon her by others, will have to be muted or altogether stifled.

The cuts that her editors made, which amounted to well over a quarter of the original manuscript, were of two sorts, though both might be seen to have their origin in their concern for this womanly image. There were small excisions of barbed comments, potentially embarrassing to the living, that seemed at odds with the qualities of charm and grace privileged in the prefatory account. The major and continuous portions of unpublished material, however, were all of a piece and written in each case immediately after the deaths in 1864, 1890 and 1894 of her three surviving children at the ages of 10, 33 and 34 respectively. These outpourings of grief, written in her 'solitary hours', form a painfully direct attempt to log the daily agony of recollection, desolation and theological speculation. They have no immediately imagined audience beyond God or her own consciousness; none the less they attain a literary stature beyond the purely personal. However intense the grief the cadences of her lucid style never deserted her and these *journal intime* passages share with the more public recollections the mark of the self-consciously professional writer feeling her way to appropriate form. At every stage of this diverse enterprise Oliphant compared her venture with the matter and mode revealed in the autobiographical literature that she read and reviewed. The process of recording her reactions to her daughter Maggie's death in the opening pages of the journal opened her eyes to the innovative nature of Tennyson's *In Memoriam*, which she had previously been inclined to judge harshly as a vehicle for philosophy rather than a spontaneous and bitter cry of pain (*Blackwood's Magazine*, February 1856). Now she recognized it as a model enabling the complex intertwining of reflection and emotion. Tennyson 'has done it already far better than I can', she wrote a few weeks after her daughter's death; nevertheless he had taught her how to 'put the long musings of my agony into words', and as she reread this section toward the end of her life she wondered whether it might not have its own place in the literature of bereavement.

It is important to make this point about the literariness of the *Autobiography* if only to dispel the long-held notion that this fragmented self-disclosure is merely a naïve compilation of diary, chronicle and anecdote, eliciting compassion for a series of personal tragedies. Even those among Oliphant's readers who had been comparably schooled in grief were impressed by the poignance with which this particular story was told. Virginia Woolf in the course of a polemical dismissal of Oliphant's novels as a kind of literary prostitution which 'smeared your mind and dejected your imagination' found herself surprised into the admission that the autobiography was, on the other hand, 'a most genuine and moving piece of work'

(*Three Guineas*, 1938). Woolf had herself experienced the profoundly disturbing effects of the shockingly premature deaths of a mother, a step-sister and a brother. Moreover she had a standard of literary comparison in her father Leslie Stephen's intimate memoir of two marriages, compiled as a record for his children and known in the family as the Mausoleum Book. Although the praise 'most genuine' might seem to come uncomfortably close to the accusation of ingenuousness, the *Autobiography* is, after all, remembered as 'a piece of work', a literary artefact.

For the self that Oliphant presents in the *Autobiography* is a deliberate creation; accustomed as a novelist to examining her characters as they appeared both to themselves and to the outside world, this dual perspective emerges in the half-mocking way in which she views her relations with the world around her. Indeed one critic has sardonically described her picture of herself as a woman whose talent had been circumscribed by the demands of her family as 'one of her better fictional efforts', seeing in it a desire to disguise the fact that she was a competent professional writer who had achieved the limited best of which she was capable (W. Evans Mosier, 'Mrs Oliphant's Literary Criticism', Ph.D. thesis, Northwestern University, 1967). The criticism misfires in confusing fiction with falsehood. There is a degree of deliberate self-marginalization in Oliphant's picture of herself as 'a fat, little commonplace woman, rather tongue-tied', living, half by choice and half by force of circumstance, a life remote from the literary coteries of London. This account ignores her friendship and acquaintance with many of the literary giants of her day, the fact that she frequented, if less frequently, the salons that were a source of inspiration to that intrepid social investigator, Henry James, and the type of wry confession found in a letter to her nephew Frank, telling him that although she did not particularly care for the way in which she had been 'made much of' at a Balliol College ball, doubtless she would have cared had she not received this attention (27 June 1879, National Library of Scotland Acc. 5793/2). Her repeated assertions of social awkwardness neglect her considerable gifts as a hostess capable, for instance, of organizing an open-air party on the island of Runnymede on 19 June 1877 to celebrate the twenty-fifth anniversary of her connection with the publishing firm of Blackwoods, an event which in itself suggests a sense of her own worth in the creative partnership.

Her own concept of her self-effacing manner was markedly at odds with other people's assessments. James spoke of 'her sharp and handsome physiognomy'. Annie Thackeray, one of her closest friends, was forced to admit that she could be 'cold in manner and tart in speech', while J. M. Barrie, searching for the words in which to convey her combined simplicity and hauteur, described her as 'the *grande dame* at one moment, almost a girl, it might be, the next'.

Barrie's appreciation of the apparently contradictory elements in her nature may help us to appreciate the problems Oliphant encountered in her autobiographical writing. As she sought to transcribe her mother's character she realized the inadequacy of fictional tools for such a purpose.

How little one realises the character or individuality of those who are most near and dear. It is with difficulty even now that I can analyse or make a character of her. She herself is there, not any type or variety of humankind. (p. 21)

The ensuing picture of her mother does, in part, rely upon her novelist's sense of physical presence, setting and illustrative anecdote to illuminate a psychological portraiture, but there are abundant qualifications and a sense of the inefficacy of the many superlatives she employs to convey 'this varying, this unknown and uncircumscribed spirit' (V. Woolf, 'Modern Fiction', *The Common Reader*, 1925).

One reason for Woolf's involuntary praise of the *Autobiography* may have been that it most nearly approached the condition to which she believed that fiction should aspire, 'so that, if a writer were a free man and not a slave, if he could write what he chose not what he must, if he could base his work upon his own feeling and not upon convention, there would be no plot, no comedy, no tragedy, no love interest or catastrophe in the accepted style'. Considered in the light of this paradigm it becomes possible to see the fragmentary dislocations of the *Autobiography* not merely as accidents of protracted composition, but as an experiment in narrative strategy.

While writing the first portion of the *Autobiography* in 1864 Oliphant had been reading Elizabeth Gaskell's *Life of Charlotte Brontë* and had concluded that, although her own novels might not have the emotional strength of Brontë's, yet she knew herself to have a 'fuller conception of life'. She recognized that 'the love between men and women, the marrying and giving in marriage, occupy in fact, so small a portion of either existence or thought', but market forces and crushing domestic financial problems contrived to prevent her fully exploiting this vision in her fiction. In her personal writing, however, she was free to strive for a mode compatible with the sense that her life did not fall into conventional rhetorical patterns. An innate elasticity of temperament, she ruefully lamented, meant that her life must always fall short of the dignity of tragedy. As a professional critic she became increasingly interested in the autobiographical and biographical genres (biography was to become her own preferred literary mode) and her second major bout of self-inscription was prompted by her dissatisfaction with two accounts of the lives of fellow writers that had recently appeared: J. W. Cross's *Life of George Eliot* (1883) and Anthony Trollope's posthumously published *Autobiography* (1883). Both records shocked her by the way in which the animus of the life had been, or was represented as having been, committed to or shaped by the demands of the writer's art. Her own energies, she felt, as she deconstructed her life, had been more widely dispersed.

Read against recent scholarship on the autobiographical genre prompted by gender studies, Oliphant's case is peculiarly interesting. She felt herself precluded from the domestic and professional advantages accorded to male writers, whose sense of progress and achievement could be measured in attaining such public goals as secure editorial positions. Yet when she compared herself with women writers she constantly stressed the burden of business and domestic decisions, traditionally assumed to be male prerogatives, that had been forced upon her. In her case the confusion of gender-defined roles intensified the anxiety of authorship experienced by so many nineteenth-century women writers, who experienced the need to justify their public persona against the traditional expectations of female behaviour and practice fostered by their upbringing. Although the pressing financial needs consequent upon early widowhood had served to legitimate the pleasure she took in writing, she began to perceive that a sanction derived from external circumstances did not speak to her inner sense of failure. By 1885, indeed, insisting upon the claims of motherhood as paramount began to be an index of failure: her sons, now twenty-four and twenty-eight, had not been coaxed from the nest and lived a life of indolent parasitism. Forced, therefore, into the acknowledgement that 'at the end of all things the work is almost the only thing—is it not?—in which there is satisfaction' (*Autobiography and Letters*, p. 360), she found, when she examined her writing without the benefit of her accustomed alibi, that she could not be sure her work would have been of a higher standard if she had been free of family responsibilities.

Stung by her sons' indifference and her sense of the inadequacy of either motherhood or literary reputation as a self-defining image, Oliphant resorted to writing as the epistemological tool she knew best to discover 'the thread' lying hidden 'below the surface' events of her life. The strong private need to assert her sense of self as more than a product of arbitrary external forces is, in part, suggested by the choice of Sunday evenings for this activity. Her religious upbringing would have accustomed her to the weekly opportunity provided by a private journal for self-assessment and detecting God's guiding hand in the course of daily life. Once again, however, Oliphant's desire to be true to her perception of life's apparent plotlessness led her to push against the limiting structures provided by providential explanations. Here, as in her novels, she cries out against a God whose dispositions are harsh and unfathomable and against simple-minded tracing of the ways of Providence. Increasingly she was inclined to postpone the divine revelation of purpose and meaning to the after-life—a belief which in her novels led to a marked repudi-ation of that favourite Victorian device, the final chapter in which order and happiness are reimposed. Bringing 'unconsidered moments of happiness' to consciousness, re-creating the impulses and needs that had driven her life, was all that remained possible in the way of self-definition, and it was in this deliberate privileging of small domestic memories and intimate friendships, over against the myths of progress achieved in a public arena often favoured by male autobiographies of the period, that constituted the poignant origin-ality of the work. The fragments, this autobiography asserts, are the meaning and the pattern of a woman's life.

The deaths of her two sons deprived Oliphant of the will to live and consequently of her interest in the experimental process of self-re-creation. The closing portion, begun in 1894, deliberately returns us to the formula of the more public memoir designed to secure an inheritance for her unmarried niece. Nevertheless the attempt to con-centrate upon 'making pennyworths of myself' sometimes defeated her, and she would find herself drifting back into the old habit of musing, pointless and painful though she now found it, or into the more subtle process of refracted autobiography observable in anecdotes and portraits that present her own case obliquely. The tenor of her life, moreover, obstinately refused to conform to the popular demand she perceived for tales of happy and successful lives, and her artistic instinct revolted against the shapeless proliferation she condemned in so many contemporary memoirs. It is perhaps unsurprising that Oliphant's editors failed to recognize the broken cadence with which the *Autobiography* ends as its wholly appropriate conclusion, expressing the agony of a continued physical existence severed from all that had made her life of interest to her. It may be easier for a later generation accustomed to the disjunctive modes of modernism to appreciate the narrative strategy of this experimental text.

The pious but misguided efforts made to rearrange her fractured narrative into the cleaner lines of a conventional memoir resulted, however, in the erection of a desolate Victorian folly. Shorn of its more incisive pieces and deprived of its more personal passages the edifice swiftly achieved the status of a period piece, a self-confirming monument to the courageous struggles of a woman who had chosen writing as the only means available to her of earning the family living. Oliphant undoubtedly played her own part in her rapid fall from critical favour. Like Trollope she probably suffered from her own self-depreciation in a posthumously published autobiography, but literary politics too contributed. Her stock-in-trade, the three-volume novel, was as she was aware, fast being superseded by the single volume, whose form invited a different style and may even have produced a different readership. Whereas three-deckers made ideal family entertainment, allowing serial reading and subsequent discussion by parents and children, the single volume might well accommodate material not considered suitable for adolescent perusal. In 1898, the year after her death, Mudie's circulating library still carried eighty-nine of her titles in its annual catalogue, but Mudie's no longer called the tune with publishers, nor did their expensive subscription any longer attract the ever-expanding and more diverse market of readers. Cheap editions of Oliphant's novels continued to appear in the early years of the new century, but neither the format nor the concerns of her fiction appealed to a post-war generation. The general reader had always formed her assumed

xvi   INTRODUCTION

audience and so it is less surprising that the tide of literary fashion
turned more swiftly against her work than against that of less
'popular' authors. The fact that several of her obituary notices made
the point that her appeal as a novelist had been as great to men as it
was to women may indicate sensitivity to a new critical landscape
dominated by male clubland. Liberated from the towering shadow
thrown by George Eliot's long domination of the literary scene, a
distinctly misogynistic tone was emerging and could be clearly
detected in the remarks of male novelists who had recently suffered at
the hands of Oliphant, who, as regular reviewer for *Blackwood's
Magazine*, had enjoyed uninterrupted power in the critical establishment. Henry James remarked in his obituary: 'I should almost
suppose in fact that no woman had ever, for half a century, had her
personal "say" so publicly and irresponsibly' (*Notes and Novelists*,
1914, p. 358) and Thomas Hardy, who in 1882 had welcomed 'direct
communication with a writer I have known in spirit so long' felt free
by 1912 to dismiss her criticisms as 'the screaming of a poor lady in
Blackwood' (*Collected Letters*, ed. R. L. Purdy and M. Millgate,
i. 107, and Postscript to the Preface of *Jude the Obscure*).

   Oliphant's own sense that she had taken 'a fuller conception of life'
than many women writers may have militated against her as an early
candidate for resurrection by the feminist presses of our own day.
Within the last two or three years there has been a flurry of interest in
her work, but because it is difficult to obtain access to her entire
œuvre (most of her novels seem to have been pulped) and even more
time-consuming to read every title, publishers have for the most part
relied upon reprinting the 'Chronicles of Carlingford' series in which
she recognized that she had exploited a best-selling formula, or those
novels such as *Kirsteen* (1890) which retained critical favour among
the obituarists of the 1890s. It is still difficult for the general reader to
obtain a clear picture of the professional acumen with which she
responded to the changing market in her fifty years as a novelist, or of
the range of her work and interests which embraced both the super-
natural and the quietly traced tale of domestic suffering or triumph.
Throughout her work Oliphant cast a wry eye upon the comparative
lots of men and women and the subtleties of the human temperament, which often submits against its own better judgement to the
orthodoxies society imposes. For society, as she often remarked,
looked after its own, and virtue all too frequently had a way of

becoming its own reward in the socially inferior position of the single woman. Such a view of life was not without its consequences for her writing and some of those novels which appear most completely to collude with the moral and stylistic conventions of the day do so only after a subtly subversive examination of many of the age's most treasured assumptions. The way in which her worthy but blinkered executors felt free to reshape her remains according to their own conventional pieties is merely one indicator of how easily much of her writing could be misconstrued as hack work produced in response to the prevailing fashions. Restoring the full text of her autobiography provides one way for the modern reader to catch more easily the distinctive timbre of the individual voice which ran through so much of her work.

A Note on the Text

The first edition of *The Autobiography and Letters of Mrs M. O. W. Oliphant Arranged and Edited by Mrs Harry Coghill* was published in Edinburgh and London by William Blackwood and Sons in 1899. Two further 'editions' appeared in the same year. The second 'edition' employed the same type as the first but effected a number of minor corrections. The 'third edition revised' abbreviated the text of both the Autobiography and the Letters and omitted the first attempt at a bibliography of Oliphant's novels and contributions to *Blackwood's Magazine* appended to the first 'edition'.

A photographic reprint of the first edition with an introduction by Q. D. Leavis was published in 1974 by Leicester University Press in their Victorian Library series. In 1988 the University of Chicago Press republished the Autobiography alone with a foreword by L. Langbauer.

This edition of the Autobiography is based not upon previously published versions but upon the manuscript itself. The vast number of Oliphant letters lodged in various collections suggests that it would be more appropriate to await a new selection rather than to reprint those included in the first published edition. Recent bibliographical scholarship has revealed the woeful inadequacy of the bibliography appended to the first edition and readers are advised instead to consult *Margaret Oliphant (1828–1897): A Bibliography compiled by J. S. Clarke* (Victorian Research Guides 11, University of Queensland, 1986), which is so far limited to a consideration of her fictional output.

The manuscript upon which this new text is based is now lodged in the archives of the National Library of Scotland (Acc. 5793/9; MS 23218/9). It consists of two volumes, the first in a small hardbound book, covered in marbled paper, with a leather spine and corners and bearing the marks of a missing metal clasp; the second in a red morocco binding. This text preserves the chronological sequence of composition rather than adopting the expedient of the 1899 editors who rearranged the entries to provide a chronology of the events of Oliphant's life.

The first volume shows evidence of a number of false starts: the opening pages have been torn out and the first entry, which has been half-erased, reads: '1849 23d of January, a Black Day, a day to be remembered'. The first phrase left to stand reads 'Sunday nights', but the first paragraph on the next page is heavily scored through. The decipherable part of the entry would appear to refer to the 'very doubtful experiment' of allowing her brother Willie to assume the authorship of four early novels.

The first substantial entry, with which the present text opens, must have been written between the writing of the early stories in the 'Chronicles of Carlingford' series in the early 1860s and her daughter Maggie's death in 1864. Oliphant's own dating, supplemented by occasional editorial clarification, is used to convey the sequence in which the remainder of the manuscript was composed.

The National Library of Scotland archives also contain a portion of manuscript 'Windsor, Ist. February 1885 . . . except little books of poetry half or more than half written by Daniel Wilson.' copied verbatim from Oliphant's manuscript by her niece Janet (Denny). This fair copy was presumably abandoned when it was decided to edit the manuscript more ruthlessly. The presence of the fair copy is an index to the problem inherent in transcribing Oliphant's hand. From early days it had been her practice to have a fair copy of her barely legible manuscripts prepared by a close relative. It would seem that it was also the task of the copyist to insert the appropriate punctuation wherever Oliphant had employed her favourite and much overworked form, the dash. The present editor has followed her copyists' practice in substituting standard punctuation when this seems practicable, and has replaced many of Oliphant's dashes by commas and full stops where appropriate. A comparison of the following exact transcription with the corresponding passage on p. 4 will give some idea of the editorial principles used:

I have not been resigned. I cannot feel resigned—my heart is sore as if it was an injury—God forgive me but I feel myself calling her my ewelamb as if it was to reproach Him who has taken her from me and has not spared—Oh my darling, my Maggie—I feel as if I could go down on my knees and pray for her not to forget her poor mother and as for the other prayers my heart seems crushed and stifled—when I went to read the chapter about the many mansions even then I seemed to be stifled again—Whatsoever . . .

Since the original editors of her autobiography were Oliphant's most experienced copyists and their work would, in the normal course of events, have been approved or discussed by Oliphant when she came to read her proofs, this edition has respected their punctuation decisions in the previously published portions.

Three of Oliphant's surviving diaries (NLS Acc. 5793/14,15,16; MSS 23214, 23215, 23216) contain passages written at the end of the year whose content and form seem closely related to the disclosures of the autobiographical volumes proper. These diary entries appear as appendices to the present text.

The National Library of Scotland is in the process of cataloguing these accessions and where possible I have provided the new catalogue number alongside the previous accession number.

A Chronology of Margaret Oliphant

1828   4 April: Margaret Oliphant Wilson born at Wallyford, Midlothian, youngest child of Francis W. Wilson (*c*.1788–1858), clerk, and Margaret Oliphant (*c*.1789–1854). Her two elder brothers are Francis (Frank) and William (Willie). During her first ten years the family move first to Lasswade, near Edinburgh, and then to Glasgow.

1838   Family move to Liverpool.

1845   Margaret suffers broken engagement.

1849   Publication of Margaret's first novel. She spends three months in London as housekeeper for Willie and there meets her cousin, Francis Wilson Oliphant (Frank).

1851   Margaret and her mother visit Edinburgh.

1852   Willie leaves his first ministerial post in Etal, Northumberland, and returns home, disgraced.
        4 May: Margaret marries her cousin Frank (1818–59), artist and stained-glass window designer, and moves to London. In August her parents and Willie move to London to be near her.

1853   21 May: Birth of daughter, Margaret Wilson Oliphant (Maggie).

1854   22 May: Birth of second daughter, Marjorie Isabella.
        17 September: Death of Margaret's mother.
        8 February: Death of Marjorie Isabella.

1855   November: Death of third child, a son, after only one day.

1856   16 November: Birth of fourth child, Cyril Francis (Tiddy or Tids).

1857   First signs of Frank Oliphant's tubercular condition.

1858   28 May: Death of fifth child, Stephen Thomas, aged nine weeks.

1859   Margaret, Frank, and the children leave for Italy hoping to improve Frank's health. Margaret's regular contributions to *Blackwood's Magazine* provide the family income.

        20 October: Frank dies in Rome.

        12 December: Birth of last child, Francis Romano (Cecco).

1860   February: Margaret and her children return to England to stay with her brother Frank and his family in Birkenhead. Summer spent in Fife. In October Margaret and her children move to Edinburgh.

1861   Begins *Chronicles of Carlingford* series. Moves to Ealing in October to be close to friends.

1863   Margaret and her children accompany friends to Italy.

1864   27 January: Eldest child, Maggie, dies in Rome; remainder of the year spent in Italy, Switzerland, and France.

1865   September: Returns from France to London. In December moves to Windsor for boys' schooling at Eton.

1866   Annie Louisa Walker (future Mrs H. Coghill, editor of *Autobiography*), becomes Margaret's housekeeper and secretary.

1868   Brother Frank suffers financial ruin. Margaret takes in his two eldest children and sends Frank junior to Eton when his parents go abroad.

1870   Margaret's recently widowed brother Frank returns to England, apparently having suffered a nervous breakdown. He and his two youngest children, Margaret Oliphant (Madge) and Janet Mary (Denny) become wholly dependent upon Oliphant.

1875   July: Margaret's brother Frank dies.

        August: Madge and Denny sent to school in Germany.

        October: Tiddy goes up to Balliol College, Oxford, and Margaret's nephew Frank, a qualified engineer, sails for India.

1879   Madge and Denny return from Germany in the spring, Madge to train as a wood-engraver and Denny to attend boarding-school in Windsor. In October their brother Frank dies in India.

1884   Tiddy leaves for Ceylon to be private secretary to the Governor, but soon returns in poor health. In the summer Margaret enjoys her first mystical experience, in St Andrews.

1885   Margaret's brother Willie dies in Rome where he had been supported by her for quarter of a century.

1890   Margaret, accompanied by her sons and Madge, travels to Jerusalem in the spring for research purposes. In November her eldest son, Tiddy, dies.

1893   July: Madge marries William Valentine, jute manufacturer.

1894   In October Margaret's last surviving child, Cecco, dies. Denny changes her name by Deed Poll to Oliphant.

1896   April: Final move to Wimbledon.

1897   25 June: Margaret Oliphant Wilson Oliphant dies.

THE AUTOBIOGRAPHY

To return to the idea with which I started that it was better when I steadily made up my mind in Edinburgh to enter without any props upon my natural lonely life—I am not so sure that it was a good idea after all. This was the time when I got into the last deeps with my work. That time when John Blackwood sent me back paper after paper and driven half desperate I dashed at the first story of the Chronicles of Carlingford and wrote it in two or three days feeling as if it was my last chance. It was the turning-point.* How sore and wounded and humbled and unsatisfied I was—what hard work I had to keep the tears within my eyes that time when they told me they did not want any story from me, lest the hard men—who were very kind notwithstanding, and friendly and just—should see I was crying and think it an appeal to their sympathies. How much better off I am now than then. I remember going down the hill to Fettes Row with my heart swelling and moved to a kind of anguish of resistance and determination not to be overcome. I had not a soul to tell my trouble to or console me. I had to put all the anxious young heart into my work. How well I recollect the wind that blew in my face going down the hill and how it dried the unshed tears and I said to myself, 'The tear that gathered in his eye, He left the mountain breeze to dry'* and the children's dear little faces when I got home who knew nothing about my trouble. It was bitter at the time, but it is not bitter to look back upon. I seem to think more kindly of myself after all the follies I know of when I remember such a trial. Poor heart of mine—it has had a good deal to go through one time and another—but I was not beaten that time after all and from that time as it happened to the giant who recovered strength every time he touched the earth,* my fall was good for me and gave me a new start. Since then, but never mind what has come and gone since, always a little more experience and some hours very fanciful and some internal struggles which there is no comfort in recalling, but no harm to speak of.* And now perhaps commences a graver era, more guarded and cautious than the past—if experience ever teaches—which, however, I have already concluded it does not.

Rome, 1864.

A graver era, God help me, but I did not know when I wrote the words that I was coming to lay my sweetest hope, my brightest anticipations for the future, with my darling, in her father's grave.* Oh this terrible, fatal, miserable Rome! I came here rich and happy, with my blooming daughter, my dear bright child, whose smiles and brightness everybody noticed, and who was sweet as a little mother to her brothers. There was not an omen of evil in any way. Our leaving of home, our journey, our life here, have all been among the brightest passages of my life; and my Maggie looked the healthiest and happiest of all the children, and ailed nothing and feared nothing,—nor I for her. Four short days made all the difference, and now here I am with my boys thrown back again out of the light into the darkness, into the valley of the shadow of death. My dearest love never knew nor imagined that she was dying; no shadow of dread ever came upon her sweet spirit. She got into heaven without knowing it, and God have pity upon me, who have thus parted with the sweetest companion, on whom unconsciously, more than on any other hope of life, I have been calculating. I feared from the first moment her illness began, and yet I had a kind of underlying conviction that God would not take my ewe-lamb,* my woman-child from me.

I have not been resigned. I cannot feel resigned, my heart is sore as if it was an injury. God forgive me, but I feel myself calling her my ewe-lamb as if it was to reproach Him who has taken her from me and has not spared. Oh my darling, my Maggie. I feel as if I could go down on my knees and pray for her not to forget her poor mother and as for the other prayers, my heart seems crushed and stifled. When I went to read the chapter about the many mansions,* even then I seemed to be stifled again. Whatsoever you shall ask in my name seemed to come to me like a mockery. I ask myself why, why, and I cannot find any answer. I had but one woman-child and she was just beginning to sympathize with me, to comfort me, and at this dear moment, her little heart expanding, her little mind growing, her sweet life blossoming day by day, God has taken her away out of my arms and refuses to hear my cry and prayer. My heart feels dead. I only have a sense of my loss now and then and when I see the other girls, when I think of all the mothers round me who are happy in their children, my heart cries out against God's will. Now I have to go limping and anxious through the world all the days of my life. If the brothers are spared to grow up I shall have no-one to help me to make a bright home for them, nobody to make brightness possible to me. God forgive me for repining. I have still my two dear precious boys, and I cry out to Him like a savage creature to spare them, to spare them, to let me die first and to leave them alive. Oh God forgive me and help me. O God convey to me a sense of my darling's happiness, a feeling that she will not forget me and that I shall find her again, and have pity upon a poor heartbroken creature who does not know what she is saying. Now that they are passed I realize at least how happy I have been these two years back. I have plagued myself with fanciful unhappiness and suffered foolish griefs of my own making, but I have been happy, happy, and all has been well with me. I know it now when grief has come back and when instead of my sweet, living, loving child I have but a curl of the dear hair and another name upon the marble out at Testaccio.* Those curls I was so proud at were never more beautiful than when they were all rippling back with the gold string through them from her dear head as she lay ill, and when they lay all peaceful and still with her white wreath of hyacinths and snowdrops, she was as lovely as the angel she is. Oh my child, my child. Perhaps if I had stayed at home and not come here, but what is the good of saying perhaps. It was rotting Rome that did it and I must not think of God as if he were lying in wait for me to take such terrible vengeance on me. They were so well when they were here before that I had no alarms for them and she was so well until the very moment her illness came on. What can I say? I will go softly all the days of my life* until it please God to take me where I have so much treasure. God send it even tonight, but I must live if I can for my dear little boys whom our dear Lord in his mercy preserve and bless. Oh Father in heaven. Oh Saviour of men, spare the two who are left. Let them lay me in my grave for Christ's sake. They don't need me as my

Maggie would have done and now she, my darling, needs me no
more. One thing is a little comfort to me to think she had a happy life
and never lacked any pleasure I could give her. When I think of the
Sunday nights, how she used to get on my knees with her arms close
clasped round me, it is too much to bear. I think my darling enjoyed
these moments more than her little pleasures. God bless her for ever
and ever and bring me to Him soon, soon for his mercy and goodness
sake.

The hardest moment in my present sad life is the morning, when
I must wake up and begin the dreary world again. I can sleep
during the night, and I sleep as long as I can; but when it is
no longer possible, when the light can no longer be gainsaid,
and life is going on everywhere, then I, too, rise up to bear my burden. How different it used to be! When I was a girl I remember
the feeling I had when the fresh morning light came round. Whatever grief there had been the night before, the new day triumphed
over it. Things must be better than one thought, must be well,
in a world which woke up to that new light, to the sweet dews
and sweet air which renewed one's soul. Now I am thankful for the
night and the darkness, and shudder to see the light and the day
returning.

The Principal* calls 'In Memoriam'* an embodiment of the spirit
of this age, which he says does not know what to think, yet thinks
and wonders and stops itself, and thinks again; which believes and
does not believe, and perhaps, I think, carries the human yearning
and longing farther than it was ever carried before. Perhaps my
own thoughts are much of the same kind. I try to realise heaven to
myself, and I cannot do it. The more I think of it, the less I am able to
feel that those who have left us can start up at once into a heartless
beatitude without caring for our sorrow. Do they sleep until the
great day? Or does time so cease for them that it seems but a matter
of hours and minutes till we meet again? God who is Love cannot
give immortality and annihilate affection; that surely, at least,
we must take for granted—as sure as they live they live to love us.
Human nature in the flesh cannot be more faithful, more tender,
than the purified human soul in heaven. Where, then, are they,
those who have gone before us? Some people say around us, still
seeing, still knowing all that occupies us; but that is an idea I cannot entertain either. It would not be happiness but pain to be
beside those we love yet unable to communicate with them,

unable to make ourselves known. Where are you, oh my child, my child. I have tried to follow her in imagination, to think of her delight and surprise when from the fever, wandering and languour of her bed she came suddenly into the company of angels and the presence of the Lord. But then, the child was but a child and death is but a natural event; it changed her surroundings, her capabilities, but it could not change the little living soul. Did she not stop short there and say, 'Where is Mamma?' did not the separation overwhelm her? This thought of very desolation. Did she not think of the sad horror, the heart that was breaking for her? God knows. All this is fanciful, perhaps wrong, but I cannot help it. They neither marry nor give in marriage* our Lord said, but if heaven was ignorant of the bonds of nature it surely would be no heaven for the spirits of men. Do they dwell in families, in long succession of kindred and race. Was my mother called to receive the child who was her baby as well as mine? Oh if one could but know, if anyhow even in a dream I could but for a moment see my Maggie with the family in heaven, if I could but have a glimpse of her, a word from her how it would comfort my heart. But no, this is the trial of faith which is precious.* I don't think I ever realized that trial so fully before. If I could see her even for a moment it would be no longer faith—now the faith must be absolute. She is with God, she is in his hands. I know nothing, cannot even imagine anything. Can I trust her with Him? Can I trust Him that He has done what was best for her, that He has her safe, that there has been no mistake, no error, but only his purpose in all, and that he is keeping her now in the position most happy for her, that even my own human judgement, when enlightened, will approve as the best? This is the question that He puts to me and keeps putting to me through all these weary nights and days. This the faith He demands of me. I used to think faith meant only believing in Our Saviour which is but the dearest easiest beginning. It never was any difficulty to me to believe in Him. Does he not prove himself above all criticisms and questions?—I cannot but think so. In Him, the one thing certain in this terrible problem of human existence, I believe, as in the only light which throws a little illumination on the darkness. That is not the agonizing faith that God demands of me. It is to believe in the face of all appearances to the contrary, in opposition to my knowledge of myself, against the aching and yearning of my heart, that in this and all He does He has done well. It is to trust Him that it has not been done unadvisedly, that there is a reason for it greater than all the manifest human reasons which were against it. No man would have inflicted such a blow upon me, from my least intimate friends. Such a man as John Blackwood—mourns over the loss of my companion. None of them but would have taken the trouble on themselves, made exertions to save my darling to me after all my other troubles. God is more merciful than man,* but He has not spared. He hateth nothing he has made.* He does not grieve willingly nor afflict the children of men; from all this must I believe He had a reason. What reason? I cannot tell. I cannot imagine. My misery makes my heart harder not softer. I grudge and wonder at the happiness of others. I am not the better for my grief. Still I know this is the trial of my faith. God knows, though I do not, God demands of me this proof of trust in him. Oh Father Almighty. I strive against thee. I reproach thee, I do not submit, but my reasons and my heart alike confess that thou must know thine own purpose best. That thou canst not have sent without reason a calamity so terrible, that somehow it must be well. Maggie, my darling, though you are but a child, you know better than your poor mother. Oh if I could but see you, could but hear of you, only for a moment. My heart yearns for sight rather than faith. But vain, vain are all the yearnings of the heart. It is not yet six weeks that she has gone from me and already new habits, new arrangements are rising over the vacant place. The place that has known her knows her no more* and I must go though my darling has stopped short in the way. I cannot stop and go no further. I must go on to places, among people who know not of her, the awful routine of life has commenced again. I have no longer any power of revival, any new hope to rise in my heart. That does not matter. I must go on. I must endure. It is the lot God has appointed to me, and as this hard lot cannot come wantonly or by chance, there is but one alternative. It must be well. He knows his own reasons. This is the trial of your faith which is more precious than gold that perisheth. I cannot help thinking sometimes if from that sick-bed He had raised her up again to life and strength how much good it would have done me, how thankful, how humble, how pitiful I would have been in my great joy—so it appears to me. If I could have filled up that grave which was waiting for her with any sacrifice, my own health, my powers such as they are, any, the most costly offering. If I could have kept her still and worked for her and her brothers, not easily and with credit as I do now, but tilling with my hands in poverty and care. Oh how I should have welcomed the alternative. But God gave me no alternative, not even time to be familiar with the thought.

The world is changed, and my life is darkened; and all that I can do is to take desperate hold of this one certainty, that God cannot have done it without reason. I can get no farther. Sometimes such a longing comes upon me to go and seek somebody, as I used to go to Frank* to the studio in the old times. But I have nobody now: my friends are very sorry for me; but there is nobody in the world who has a right to share my grief, to whom my grief belongs, as it does to myself—and that is what one longs for. Sympathy is sweet, but sympathy is for lighter troubles. When it is a grief that rends one asunder, one's longing is for the other—the only other whose heart is rent asunder by the same stroke. For me, I have all the burden to bear myself. My brother Frank writes very kindly, speaking as if it were his sorrow too; but oh, do I not know he will go back among his unbroken family, and feel all the more glad in his heart for the contrast of my affliction, and thank God the more! I don't blame him. I would, perhaps, have done the same. Here is the worst of all. I am alone. I am a woman. I have nobody to stand between me and the roughest edge of grief. All the terrible details have to come to me. I have to bear the loss, the pang unshared. My boys are too little to feel it, and there is nobody else in the world to divide it with me. O Lord, Thou wouldest not have done it but for good reason! Stand by the forlorn creature who fainteth under Thy hand, but whom Thou sufferest not to die.

Albano, March 13

I keep on always upbraiding and reproaching God. I can't help thinking of the question somebody once asked a grieving woman, Have you not yet forgiven God? I feel like that myself. So many burdens as I have, so much to do, so little help in this hard way of life, he might have left me my little band of children unbroken. By then the perfect number, and oh my firstborn, my only daughter, my Maggie. How He sows children broadcast about this world, how they swarm untaught, uncared for by the score in these Italian villages, living in beggary and wretchedness. Oh my Lord why didst thou grudge to me the one blossom of womankind that I thought my own.

In the days of Job when affliction was considered a direct punishment for sin and in later days when people had taken up the idea, I know not on what foundation that it was the faithful, the righteous who were tried with unceasing troubles, it must have been easier to accept the judgements of God—but what can one say? I am neither better nor worse than my brother Frank who has never known a trouble in his family—I am neither better nor worse than my dear friend who is so much happier, so much more blessed than I, but I am smitten and they are spared—why is it?—God has put upon me a great many things to do—Frank left me *not* only with my children to work for, but with many encumbrances to clear off—and W. is entirely dependent both for his living and for such guidance as is possible upon me*—I have been wilful and extravagant in many things but I have not shrunk from any of my duties—I have faced the burden and borne it and never tried to put off any part of it upon the shoulders of others—God help me—does this make me think that I had a right to demand from him that divine cordial of happiness which I have been enjoying for these years past, but which now he has deprived me of? If I feel so is that not enough to show how needful was the blow—but God is not like man—He sees our foolishness—he pities us as a father his children*—so must I come round again to the one misused unfailing answer—God must ever have a reason—The reason must have been sufficient since it pleased Him.

I was reading of Charlotte Brontë the other day, and could not help comparing myself with the picture more or less as I read. I don't suppose my powers are equal to hers—my work to myself looks perfectly pale and colourless beside hers—but yet I have had far more experience and, I think, a fuller conception of life.* I have learned to take perhaps more a man's view of mortal affairs,—to feel that the love between men and women, the marrying and giving in marriage, occupy in fact so small a portion of either existence or thought. When I die I know what people will say of me: they will give me credit for courage (which I almost think is not courage but insensibility), and for honesty and honourable dealing; they will say I did my duty with a kind of steadiness, not knowing how I have rebelled and groaned under the rod. Scarcely anybody who cares to speculate further will know what to say of my working power and my own conception of it; for, except one or two, even my friends will scarcely believe how little possessed I am with any thought of it all,—how little credit I feel due to me, how accidental most things have been, and how entirely a matter of daily labour, congenial work, sometimes now and then the expression of my own heart, almost always the work most pleasant to me, this has been. I wonder if God were to try me with the loss of this gift, such as it is, whether I should feel it much? If I could live otherwise I do not think I should. If I could move about the house, and serve my children with my own hands, I know I should be happier. But this is vain talking; only I know very well that for years past neither praise nor blame has quickened my pulse ten beats that I am aware of. This insensibility saves me some pain, but it must also lose me a great deal of pleasure.

Capri.

I have not written anything for several weeks that I could help writing—Letters have come to be a pain and trouble to me—I wrote almost eagerly at first because the utterance was something like crying; it relieved me and exhausted me and exhaustion is a great blessing when trouble is great. I even went so far as to write to Mr Maurice* who had sent me some words of kindness, asking him if he knew any explanation of this terrible enigma God had given me to read—a vain question to ask of anyone. He writes to me as they all write to me—and failing of anything else, tells me that he thinks it is my work in the world to tell truths which are not likely to be welcome to my contemporaries and that this is a baptism of fire—this is the last desperate shift of human consolation. It is kindly as well as solemnly meant—meant to comfort me and stimulate me and warm me. What can anyone say to me—I know it is vain to accept any explanation, any light upon this darkness. Nobody on earth can tell me any more than I can tell myself, though I ask night and day why God has bereaved my life. He has done so that is all—and what I have to do is to take up my cross and endure—as for teaching anybody God knows I have nothing to teach—I may put the long musings of my agony into words, but Tennyson has done it already far better than I can—and how can I who sit in darkness show any light to my neighbours. And then they say God will give me compensation. Thus people speak in their perplexity and sympathy, not knowing what to say. This is why I have no more heart to write letters—one or two I have written with a kind of vague, foolish hope that some true word of comfort might come to me in reply, but after the pitying, troubled letters I get how can I go on further—I cannot believe that it is because I am beloved more than others, that I am afflicted more than others. Our Lord who surely had it been true would have given that explanation did not say so when he was asked about those on whom the tower fell.* If God does not love us all I do not see what is the good of submitting to this heavy yoke of life, and encountering its horrible chances. His dealings are unequal beyond all doubt or question—I can trust Him through all my doubts that somehow it is right, but I cannot shut my eyes to this strange inequality nor can I persuade myself that they are specially beloved who are specially afflicted. The only explanation I can make out to myself for my own grief is that I am myself but a secondary person in it. The first and original question must have been between my darling herself and her Maker. It is hard to think of her as an individual for herself, my dear little almost dependent child, but God knows best. Between Him and the child was the first question. He has arranged it as was best for her, knowing all things as her mother would not know—I am but second in this matter. Had she lived to be married or to sustain any of the great changes of life I must, when the time had come, have stood back and refrained from interfering with her happiness even if to do so had made an end of my own. Early, very early, and more absolutely than would have been possible had she lived, the same sacrifice has been demanded of me. I have made it with wild outcries of reluctance, with groans of pain, with remonstrances against God's will. For me it is hard and terrible, a rending asunder of my life—but I must make up my mind to the loss which her happiness as ordained by God exacts from me. One tries to get a new aspect of this never-ceasing, ever-present loss which will make it less horrible, less blank and bitter. My Maggie, if you had lived to be some man's love and wife and had gone away with him to the end of the world would I your mother have stood in the way of your happiness? God forbid—And how can I tell what bright life, what sweet existence is opening upon you now. I am stranded upon this desolate shore, but you are away upon your voyage in the region which God saw most meet for you. I think if I could have but one word, one token, one glimpse of her I would be content. But now comes in the question which is between God and me—What He demands of me is that I should trust to Him entirely for her welfare, and though my heart is breaking I will, I will.

For it is all so strange. She was my compensation for the solitude of my life. My boys, God bless them, if they are spared must go away from me, must leave me. My daughter would have been at least for all the sweet years of her youth my constant companion by night and day. Now in this innermost chamber of the heart which no man except a husband can enter and he but a little, I am alone always, alone in the world for ever. Help me, Oh help me Lord. I am a poor helpless woman without any strength and thou hast snatched away the props on which I leant. Stand by me and grant me a little patience till I die.

[Here the manuscript breaks, to be resumed on the opposite page in 1885. Some time after 1894 when both of the sons to whom she had hoped to entrust the manuscript were dead, she inserted a slip of paper which opens with a remark that helps to explain why her literary executors felt free to cut the material restored in the present edition: 'Whether anything should be taken from the preliminary pages, Denny, with the help of perhaps Cousin Annie, or some other friend (none so capable) whom she can trust, must decide. My musings at this dreadful moment when my firstborn was taken from me might perhaps give a sense of fellowship to other mourners—I know not.' She copied out the first five sentences of the text below and then wrote, 'I had intended to copy out and enlarge all of this, but this is enough for the thing it is. I will add something here and there.']

                                        Windsor, 1st February 1885.

Twenty-one years have passed since I wrote what is on the opposite page. I have just been reading it all with tears; sorry, very sorry for that poor soul who has lived through so much since. Twenty-one years is a little lifetime. It is curious to think that I was not very young, nearly thirty-six, at that time, and that I am not very old, nearly fifty-seven, now. Life though it is short, is very long, and contains so much. And one does not, to one's consciousness, change as one's outward appearance and capabilities do. Doesn't Mrs Somerville* say that, so far from feeling old, she was not always quite certain (up in the seventies) whether she was quite grown up! I entirely understand the feeling, though I have had enough, one

would think, to make one feel old. Since the time when that most
unexpected, most terrible blow overtook me in Rome—where her
father had died four years before—I have had trials which, I say it
with full knowledge of all the ways of mental suffering, have been
harder than sorrow. I have lived a laborious life, incessant work,
incessant anxiety, and in the last nine years or so pangs of disappointment and misery beyond description,* anguish that has no comfort in
it, nor even the feeling that God's hand is in it, for though he permits
it alas, yet He is not the creator of wrong doing. Nor can I say, 'It is
thy will', as I did in other calamities. And yet so strange, so
capricious is this human being, that I would not say I have had an
unhappy life. I have said this to one or two friends who know faintly
without details what I have had to go through, and astonished them.
(Sara,* for instance, who thinks that no one has ever sustained so
great a sorrow as her own, and C. R., whose tempestuous life has
known a great many pains and sacrifices too.*) Sometimes I am
miserable—always there is in me the sense that I may have active
cause to be so at any moment—always the gnawing pangs of anxiety,
and deep, deep dissatisfaction beyond words, and the sense of
helplessness, which of itself is despair. And yet there are times when
my heart jumps up in the old unreasonable way, and I am,—yes,
happy—though the word seems so inappropriate—without any cause
for it, with so many causes the other way. I wonder whether this is
want of feeling, or mere temperament and elasticity, or if it is a
special compensation—'Werena my heart licht I wa' deed'*—Grizel
Hume must have had the same.

I have been tempted to begin writing by George Eliot's life*—with
that curious kind of self-compassion which one cannot get clear of. I
wonder if I am a little envious of her? I always avoid considering
formally what my own mind is worth. I have never had any theory
on the subject. I have written because it gave me pleasure, because
it came natural to me, because it was like talking or breathing, besides
the big fact that it was necessary for me to work for my children.
That, however, was not the first motive, so that when I laugh inquir-
ies off and say that it is my trade, I do it only by way of eluding the
question which I have neither time nor wish to enter into. Anthony
Trollope's talk about the characters in his books* astonished me
beyond measure, and I am totally incapable of talking about anything
I have ever done in that way. As he was a thoroughly sensible genu-

ine man, I suppose he was quite sincere in what he says of them,—or was it that he was driven into a fashion of self-explanation which belongs to the time, and which I am following now though in another way? I feel that my carelessness of asserting my claim is very much against me with everybody. It is so natural to think that if the work-man himself is indifferent about his work, there can't be much in it that is worth thinking about. I am not indifferent, yet I should rather like to forget it all, to wipe out all the books, to silence those compli-ments about my industry, &c., which I always turn off with a laugh. I suppose this is really pride, with a mixture of Scotch shyness, and a good deal of that uncomprehended, unexplainable feeling which made Mrs Carlyle* reply with a jibe, which meant only a whimsical impulse to take the side of opposition, and the strong Scotch sense of the absurdity of a chorus of praise, but which looks so often like detraction and bitterness, and has now definitely been accepted as such by the public in general. I don't find words to express it ade-quately, but I feel it strenuously in my own case. When people com-ment upon the number of books I have written, and I say that I am so far from being proud of that fact that I should like at least half of them forgotten, they stare—and yet it is quite true; and even here I could no more go solemnly into them, and tell why I had done this or that, than I could fly. They are my work, which I like in the doing, which is my natural way of occupying myself, which are never so good as I meant them to be. And when I have said that, I have said all that it is in me to say.

I don't quite know why I should put this all down. I suppose because George Eliot's life has, as I said above, stirred me up to an involuntary confession. How I have been handicapped in life! Should I have done better if I had been kept, like her, in a mental greenhouse and taken care of? This is one of the things it is perfectly impossi-ble to tell. In all likelihood our minds and our circumstances are so arranged that, after all, the possible way is the way that is best; yet it is a little hard sometimes not to feel with Browning's Andrea,* that the men who have no wives, who have given themselves up to their art, have had an almost unfair advantage over us who have been given perhaps more than one Lucrezia to take care of. And to feel with him that perhaps in the after-life four square walls in the New Jerusalem may be given for another trial! I used to be intensely impressed in the Laurence Oliphants* with that curious freedom from human ties which I have never known; and that they felt it possible to make up their minds to do what was best, without any sort of *arrière pensée*, without having to consider whether they could or not. Curious freedom! I have never known what it was. I have always had to think of other people, and to plan everything—for my own pleasure, it is true, very often, but always in subjection to the necessity which bound me to them. On the whole, I have had a great deal of my own way, and have insisted upon getting what I wished, but only at the cost of infinite labour, and of carrying a whole little world with me wherever I moved. I have not been able to rest, to please myself, to take the pleasures that have come in my way, but have always been forced to go on without a pause. When my poor brother's family fell upon my hands,* and especially when there was question of Frank's education, I remember that I said to myself, having then perhaps a little stirring of ambition, that I must make up my mind to think no more of that, and that to bring up the boys for the service of God was better than to write a fine novel, supposing even that it was in me to do so. Alas! the work has been done; the education is over; my good Frank, my steady, good boy, is dead—and the rest—. It seemed rather a fine thing to make that resolution (though in reality I had no choice); but now I think that if I had taken the other way, which seemed the less noble, it might have been better for all of us. I might have done better work. I should in all probability have earned nearly as much for half the production had I done less; and I might have had the satisfaction of knowing that there was something laid up for them and for my old age; while they might have learned habits of work which now seem beyond recall. Who can tell? I did with much labour what I thought the best, and there is only a might have been on the other side.

In this my resolution which I did make, I was after all, only following my instincts, it being in reality easier to me to keep on with a flowing sail, to keep my household and make a number of people comfortable at the cost of incessant work, and an occasional great crisis of anxiety, than to live the self-restrained life which the greater artist imposes upon himself.

What casuists we are on our own behalf!—this is altogether self-defence. And I know I am giving myself the air of being *au fond* a finer sort of character than the others. I may as well take the little satisfaction to myself, for nobody will give it to me. No one even will mention me in the same breath with George Eliot. And that is just. It is a little justification to myself to think how much better off she was,—no trouble in all her life as far as appears, but the natural one of her father's death—and perhaps coolnesses with her brothers and sisters, though that is not said. And though her marriage, so called, is not one that most of us would have ventured on, still it seems to have secured her a caretaker and worshipper unrivalled—little nasty body though he looked, and hideous in nastiness as his previous story was.*

I think she must have been a dull woman with a great genius distinct from herself, something like the gift of the old prophets, which they sometimes exercised with only a dim sort of perception what it meant. But this is a thing to be said only with bated breath, and perhaps further thought on the subject may change my mind soon. She took herself with tremendous seriousness, that is evident, and was always on duty, never relaxing, her letters ponderous beyond description—and those to the Hennell party giving one the idea of a mutual improvement society for the exchange of essays.

Let me be done with this—I wonder if I will ever have time to put a few autobiographical bits down before I die. I am in very little danger of having my life written. No one belonging to me has energy enough to do it, or even to gather the fragments for some one else and that is all the better in this point of view—for what could be said of me? George Eliot and George Sand* make me half inclined to cry over my poor little unappreciated self—'Many love me (*i.e.*, in a sort of a way), but by none am I enough beloved.'* These two bigger women did things which I have never felt the least temptation to do—but how very much enjoyment they seem to have got out of their life, how much more praise and homage and honour! I would not buy their fame with their disadvantages, but I do feel very small, very obscure, beside them, rather a failure all round, never securing any strong affection, and throughout my life, though I have had all the usual experiences of woman, never impressing anybody,—what a droll little complaint!—why should I? I acknowledge frankly that there is nothing in me—a fat, little, commonplace woman, rather tongue-tied—to impress any one; and yet there is a sort of whimsical injury in it which makes me sorry for myself.

Feb. 8th.

Here, then, for a little try at the autobiography. I ought to be doing some work, getting on a little in advance for to-morrow, which gives a special zest to doing nothing:[1] to doing what has no need to be done—and Sunday evenings have always been a time to *fantasticare*, to do what one pleased; and I have dropped out of the letter I used to do on these occasions, having—which, by the way, is a little sad when one comes to think of it—no one to write to, of anything that is beneath the surface. Curious! I had scarcely realised it before. Now for a beginning.

I remember nothing of Wallyford, where I was born, but opened my eyes to life, so far as I remember, in the village of Lasswade, where we lived in a little house, I think, on the road to Dalkeith. I recollect the wintry road ending to my consciousness in a slight ascent with big ash-trees forming a sort of arch; underneath which I fancy was a toll-bar, the way into the world appropriately barred by that turnpike. But no, that was not the way into the world; for the world was Edinburgh, the coach for which, I am almost sure, went the other way through the village and over the bridge to the left hand, starting from somewhere close to Mr Todd the baker's shop, of which I have a faint and kind recollection. It was by that way that Frank came home on Saturday nights to spend Sunday at home, walking out from Edinburgh (about six miles) to walk in again on Monday in the dark winter mornings. I recollect nothing about the summer mornings when he set out on that walk, but remember vividly like a picture the Monday mornings in winter; the fire burning cheerfully and candles on the breakfast-table, all dark but with a subtle sense of morning, though it seemed a kind of dissipation to be up so long before the day. I can see myself, a small creature seated on a stool by the fire, toasting a cake of dough which was brought for me by the baker with the prematurely early rolls, which were for Frank. (This dough was the special feature of the morning to me, and I suppose I had it only on these occasions.) And my mother, who never seemed to sit down in the strange, little, warm, bright picture, but to hover about the table pouring out tea, supplying everything he wanted to her boy (how proud, how fond of him!—her eyes liquid and

---

[1] This is exactly what Sir Walter says in his Diary, only published in 1890, so I was like him in this without knowing it.

bright with love as she hovered about); and Frank, the dearest of companions so long—then long separated, almost alienated, brought back
again at the end to my care to linger out his life here, and die old and
suffering and deteriorated, he and I so far apart. How bright he was
then, how good always to me, how fond of his little sister!—impatient
by moments, good always. And he was a kind of god to me—my
Frank, as I always called him. I remember once weeping bitterly over
a man singing in the street, a buttoned-up, shabby-genteel man,
whom, on being questioned why I cried, I acknowledged I thought
like my Frank. That was when he was absent, and my mother's
anxiety reflected in a child's mind went, I suppose, the length of
fancying that Frank too might have to sing in the street. (He would
have come off very badly in that case, for he did not know one tune
from another, much less could he sing a note!) How well I recollect
the appearance of the man in his close-buttoned black coat, with his
dismal song, and the acute anguish of the thought that Frank might
have come to that for anything I knew. Frank, however, never gave
very much anxiety; it was Willie , poor Willie, who was our sore and
constant trouble—Willie, who lives still in Rome, as he has done for
the last two-or three-and-twenty years—nearly a quarter of a century—among strangers who are kind to him, wanting nothing, I
hope, yet also having outlived everything. I shrank from going to see
him when I was in Italy, which was wrong; but how can I return to
Rome, and how could he have come to me?—poor Willie! the hand-
somest, brightest of us all, with eyes that ran over with fun and laughter—and the hair which we used to say he had to poll, like Absalom*
so many times a-year. Alas!

What I recollect in Lasswade besides the Monday morning
aforesaid is not much. I remember standing at the smithy with
brother Willie, on some occasion when the big boy was very
unwillingly charged with his little sister to take somewhere or
other,—standing in the dark, wondering at the sparks as they flew up
and the dark figures of the smith and his men; and I remember
playing on the road opposite the house, where there was a low wall
over which the Esk and the country beyond could be seen (I think),
playing with two little kittens, who were called Lord Brougham and
Lord Grey. It must have been immediately after the passing of the
Reform Bill,* and I suppose this was why the kittens bore such
names. We were all tremendously political and Radical, my mother

especially and Frank. Likewise I recollect with the most vivid clearness on what must have been a warm still summer day, lying on my
back in the grass, the little blue speedwells in which are very distinct
before me, and looking up into the sky. The depths of it, the blueness
of it, the way in which it seemed to move and fly and avoid the gaze
which could not penetrate beyond that profound unfathomable
blue,—the bliss of lying there doing nothing, trying to look into it,
growing giddy with the effort, with a sort of vague realisation of the
soft swaying of the world in space! I feel the giddiness in my brain
still, and the happiness, as if I had been the first discoverer of that
wonderful sky. All my little recollections are like pictures to which
the meaning, naturally, is put long afterwards. I did not know the
world moved or anything about it, being under six at most; but I can
feel the sensation of the small head trying to fix that great universe,
and in the effort growing dizzy and going round.

We left Lasswade when I was six, my father's business taking him
to Glasgow,* to the misery of my mother, who was leaving her boys
behind her. My father is a very dim figure in all that phantasmagoria.
I had to be very quiet in the evenings when he was at home, not to
disturb him; and he took no particular notice of me or of any of us.
My mother was all in all. How she kept everything going, and
comfortably going, on the small income she had to administer, I can't
tell; it seems like a miracle, though of course we lived in the utmost
obscurity and simplicity, she herself doing the great part of all that
was done in the house. I was the child of her age—not her old age, but
the sentiment was the same. She had lost three children one after
another—one a girl about whom I used to make all sorts of dream-
romances, to the purport that Isabella had never died at all, and was
brought back in this or that miraculous way to make my mother and
myself supremely happy. I was born after that period of misery, and
brought back life to my mother's heart. She was of the old type of
Scotch mothers, not demonstrative, not caressing, but I know now
that I was a kind of idol to her from my birth. My clothes were all
made by her tender hands, finer and more beautifully worked than
ever child's clothes were; my under garments fine linen and trimmed
with little delicate laces, to the end that there might be nothing
coarse, nothing less than exquisite, about me; that I might grow up
with all the delicacies of a woman's ideal child.

But she was very quick in temper notwithstanding this, and was very far from spoiling me. I was not petted nor called by sweet names. But I know now that my mere name meant everything to her. I was her Maggie—what more could mortal speech find to say? How little one realises the character or individuality of those who are most near and dear. It is with difficulty even now that I can analyse or make a character of her. She herself is there, not any type or variety of humankind. She was taller than I am, not so stout as I have grown. She had a sweet fresh complexion, and a cheek so soft that I can feel the sensation of putting mine against it still, and beautiful liquid brown eyes, full of light and fun and sorrow and anger, flashing and melting, terrible to look at sometimes when one was in disgrace. Her teeth projected when she had teeth, but she lost and never replaced them, which did not, I think, harm her looks very much—at least, not in my consciousness. I am obliged to confess that when I remember her first she wore a brown front!* according to the fashion of the time—which fashion she detested, and suddenly abandoning it one day, appeared with the most lovely white hair, which gave a charm of harmonious colour to her beautiful complexion and brown eyes and eyebrows, but which was looked upon with consternation by her contemporaries, who thought the change wickedness. She had grown very early grey like myself, but was at this period, I should think, about forty-five. She wore always a cap with white net quilled closely round her face, and tied under her chin with white ribbons; and in winter always a white shawl; her dress cut not quite to her throat, and a very ample white net or cambric handkerchief showing underneath. She had read everything she could lay hands upon all her life, and was fond of quoting Pope, so that we used to call her Popish in afterdays however, when I knew what Popish in this sense meant.

She had entered into everything that was passing all her life with the warmest energy and animation, as was her nature; was Radical and democratic and the highest of aristocrats all in one. She had a very high idea, founded on I have never quite known what, of the importance of the Oliphant family,[1] so that I was brought up with the sense of belonging (by her side) to an old, chivalrous, impoverished race. I have never got rid of the prejudice, though I don't think our

---

[1] It appears she was quite right in this and that her father was the representative of the Oliphants of Kellie, though fallen into poverty and obscurity.*

branch of the Oliphants was much to brag of. I would not, however, do anything to dispel the delusion, if it is one, for my mother's sake, who held it stoutly and without a doubt. Her father had been a prodigal, and I fear a profligate, whose wife had not been able to bear with him (my mother would have borne anything and everything for her children's sake, to keep their home intact), and her youth had been a troubled and partially dependent one,—dependent upon bourgeois relations on the other side,[1] whom it was a relief, I suppose, to the high-spirited girl to think as much inferior in race as they were in generosity and princeliness of nature which was hers. So far as that went she might have been a queen. She had also I am bound to admit it, a great contempt for my father's family of whom I never knew anything, but from whose side we got all our bad qualities. The Wilson constitution, as she once said, in a moment of fervour, being a compound of 'vitriol and vinegar'.

I understand the Carlyles, both he and she, by means of my mother as perhaps few people can do—or at least as few people appear able to do. She had Mrs Carlyle's wonderful gift of narrative, and she possessed in perfection that dangerous facility of sarcasm and stinging speech which Sir Walter attributes to Queen Mary.* Though her kindness was inexhaustible and her love boundless, yet she could drive her opponent of the moment half frantic with half-a-dozen words, and cut to the quick with a flying phrase. On the other side, there was absolutely nothing that she would not have done or endured for her own; and no appeal to her generosity was ever made in vain. She was a poor woman all her life, but her instinct was always to give. I have seen her take off a warm garment of her own (that is euphemistic, but to say the plain truth it was a flannel petticoat!) to give it to a poor woman. And she would have kept open house if she could have had her way, on heaven knows how little a-year. My father was in one way very different. He hated strangers; guests at his table were a bore to him. In his later days he would have nobody invited, or if guests came, retired and would not see them,—but he was not illiberal.

We lived for a long time in Liverpool, where my father had an office in the Custom-house.* I don't know exactly what, except that

---

[1] She took me to one of them when we went to Fife, which ignominiously made an end of my dreams of family, though they had nothing to do with the Oliphants, a fact I did not realise at the time.

he took affidavits—which was a joke in the house—having a special commission for that purpose. We lived for some time in the North End (no doubt a great deal changed now, and which I have known nothing about for thirty years and more), where there was a Scotch church, chiefly for the use of the engineers and their families who worked in the great foundries. One of the first things I remember here was great distress among the people, on what acount I cannot tell—I must have been a girl of thirteen or so, I think. A fund was raised for their relief, of which my father was treasurer, and both my brothers were drawn in to help. This was very momentous in our family, from the fact that it was the means of bringing Frank, up to this time everything that was good except in respect to the Church, to that last and crowning excellence. He got interested about the poor, and began to come with us to church, and filled my mother's cup with happiness. Willie, always careless, always kind, ready to do anything for anybody, but who had already come by some defeat in life which I did not understand, and who was at home idle, took the charge of administering this charity, and used to go about the poor streets with a cart of coal behind him and his pockets stuffed with orders for bread and provisions of all kinds. All this I remember, I think, more through my mother's keen half anguish of happiness and pride than through my own recollection. That he had done so poorly for himself was bitter, but that he did so well for the poor was sweet; oh! and such a vindication of the bright-eyed, sweet-tempered unfortunate, who never was anybody's enemy but his own—words which were more true in his case than in most others. And then Frank was busy in the good work too, and at last a member of the Church, and all was well. This is not to say that there were not domestic gusts at times.

When I was sixteen I began to have—what shall I say?—not lovers exactly, except in the singular—but one or two people about who revealed to me the fact that I too was like the girls in the poets. I recollect distinctly the first compliment, though not a compliment in the ordinary sense of the word, which gave me that bewildering happy sense of being able to touch somebody else's heart—which was half fun and infinitely amusing, yet something more. The speaker was a young Irishman, one of the young ministers that came to our little church, at that time "vacant". He had joined Frank and me on a walk, and when we were passing and looking at a very pretty

cottage on the slope of the hill at Everton, embowered in gardens and
shrubberies, he suddenly looked at me and said, 'It would be
Elysium.' I laughed till I cried at this speech afterwards, though at
the moment demure and startled. But the little incident remains to
me, as so many scenes in my early life do, like a picture suffused with
a soft delightful light: the glow in the young man's eyes; the lowered
tone and little speech aside; the soft thrill of meaning which was
nothing and yet much. Perhaps if I were not a novelist addicted to
describing such scenes, I might not remember it after—how long?
Forty-one years. What a long time! I could not have been sixteen.
Then came the episode of J.Y., which was very serious indeed. We
were engaged on the eve of his going away. He was to go to America
for three years and then return for me. He was a good, simple, pious,
domestic, kind-hearted fellow, fair-haired, not good-looking, not
ideal at all. He cannot have been at all clever, and I was rather. When
he went away our correspondence for some time was very full; then I
began to find his letters silly, and I suppose said as much. Then there
were quarrels, quarrels with the Atlantic between, then explanations,
and then dreadful silence. It is amusing to look back upon, but it was
not at all amusing to me then. My poor little heart was broken. I
remember another scene without being able to explain it: my
mother and myself walking home from somewhere—I don't know
where—after it was certain that there was no letter, and that all was
over. I think it was a winter night and rainy, and I was leaning on her
arm, and the blank of the silence, and the dark and the separation,
and the cutting off of all the dreams that had grown about his name,
came over me and seemed to stop my very life. My poor little heart
was broken. I was a little over seventeen, I think.

These were the only breaks in my early life. We lived in the most
singularly secluded way. I never was at a dance till after my marriage,
never went out, never saw anybody at home. Our pleasures were
books of all and every kind, newspapers and magazines, which
formed the staple of our conversation, as well as all our amusemer
In the time of my depression and sadness my mother had a bad
ness, and I was her nurse, or at least attendant. I had to sit for ho
by the bedside and keep quiet. I had no liking then for needlework
taste which developed afterwards, so I took to writing. There was i
particular purpose in my beginning except this, to secure some
amusement and occupation for myself while I sat by my mother's

bedside. I wrote a little book in which the chief character was an angelic elder sister, unmarried, who had the charge of a family of motherless brothers and sisters, and who had a shrine of sorrow in her life in the shape of the portrait and memory of her lover who had died young. It was all very innocent and guileless, and my audience—to wit, my mother and brother Frank—were highly pleased with it. (It was published long after by W. on his own account,* and very silly I think it is, poor little thing.) I think I was then about sixteen. Afterwards I wrote another very much concerned with the Church business, in which the heroine, I recollect, was a girl, who in the beginning of the story was a sort of half-witted undeveloped creature, but who ended by being one of those lofty poetical beings whom girls love. She was called, I recollect, Ibby, but why, I cannot explain. I had the satisfaction afterwards, when I came to my full growth, of burning the manuscript, which was a three-volume business. I don't think any effort was ever made to get a publisher for it.

We were living at the time in Liverpool, either in a house in Great Homer Street or in Juvenal Street—very classical in point of name but in nothing else. Probably neither of these places exists any longer—very good houses though, at least the last. I have lately described in a letter in the 'St James' Gazette' a curious experience of mine as a child while living in one of these places. It was in the time of the Anti-Corn Law agitation, and I was about fourteen. There was a great deal of talk in the papers, which were full of that agitation, about a petition from women to Parliament upon that subject, with instructions to get sheets ruled for signatures, and an appeal to ladies to help in procuring them. It was just after or about the time of our great charity, and I was in the way of going thus from house to house. Accordingly I got a number of these sheets, or probably Frank got them for me, and set to work. Another girl went with me, I believe, but I forget who she was. The town was all portioned out into districts under the charge of ladies appointed by the committee, but we flung ourselves upon a street, no matter where, and got our papers signed and put all the authorised agents comically out. Nobody could discover who we were. I took my sheets to the meeting of the ladies, and was much wondered at, being to the external eye a child, though to my own consciousness quite a grown-up person. The secretary of the association or committee, or whatever it was, was, I think, a Miss

Hayward; at all events her Christian name was Lawrencina, which she wrote L'cina. I admired her greatly, and admired her pretty handwriting and everything about her. I myself wrote abominably, resisting up to this time all efforts to teach me better; but the circulars and notes with Miss L'cina's pretty name developed in me a warm ambition. I began to copy her writing, and mended in my own from that day. It did not come to very much, the printers would say.

I was a tremendous politician in those days.

I forget when it was that we moved to Birkenhead—not, I think, till after the extraordinary epoch of the publication of my first book. From the time above spoken of I went on writing, and somehow, I don't remember how, got into the history of Mrs Margaret Maitland.* There had been some sketches from life in the story which, as I have said, I burned; but that was pure imagination. A slight reflection of my own childhood perhaps was in the child Grace, a broken bit of reflection here and there from my mother in the picture of Mrs Margaret. Willie, after many failures and after a long illness, which we were in hopes had purified him from all his defects, had gone to London to go through some studies at the London University and in the College called the English Presbyterian, to which in our warm Free Churchism we had attached ourselves. He took my MS. to Colburn, then one of the chief publishers of novels, and for some weeks nothing was heard of it, when one morning came a big blue envelope containing an agreement by which Mr Colburn pledged himself to publish my book on the half-profit system, accompanied by a letter from a Mr S.W. Fullom, full of compliments as to its originality, &c. I have forgotten the terms now, but then I knew them by heart. The delight, the astonishment, the amusement of this was not to be described. First and foremost, it was the most extraordinary joke that ever was. Maggie's story! My mother laughed and cried with pride and happiness and amazement unbounded. She thought Mr S.W. Fullom a great authority and a man of genius, and augured the greatest advantage to me from his acquaintance and that of all the great literary persons about him. This wonderful event must have come most fortunately to comfort the family under new trouble; for things had again gone wrong with poor Willie—he had fallen once more into his old vice and debt and misery. He had still another term in London before he finished the course of study he was engaged in; and when the time came for his return I was sent with him to take care of him. It was almost the first time I had ever been separated from my mother. One visit of two or three weeks to the Hasties of Fairy Knowe, which had its part too in my little development, had been my only absence from home; and how my mother made up her mind to this three months' parting I do not know, but for poor Willie's sake everything was possible. We had lodgings near Burton Crescent in a street where our cousins, Frank and Tom Oliphant, were in the same house. We had the parlour, I remember, where I sat in the mornings when Willie was at his lectures. Afterwards he came in and I went out with him to walk. We used to walk through all the curious little passages leading, I believe, to Holborn, and full of old bookshops, which were our delight. And he took me to see the parks and various places—though not those to which I should suppose now a girl from the country would be taken. The bookshops are the things I remember best. He was as good as he could be, docile and sweet-tempered and never rebellious; and I was a little dragon watching over him with remorseless anxiety. I discovered, I remember, a trifling bill which had not been included when his debts were paid, and I took my small fierce measures that it should never reach my mother's ears, nor trouble her. I ordained that for two days in the week we should give up our mid-day meal and make up at the evening one, which we called supper, for the want of it. On these days, accordingly, he did not come home, or came only to fetch me, and we went out for a long walk, sustaining ourselves with a bun until it should be time to come home to tea. He agreed to this ordinance without a murmur—my poor, good, tender-hearted, shipwrecked Willie; and the little bill was paid and never known of at home.

Curiously enough, I remember little of the London sights or of any impression they made upon me. We knew scarcely anybody. Mrs Hamilton, I think, the sister of Edward Irving's wife* and a relation, took a little notice of us, but she was almost the only individual I knew. And my heart was too full of my charge to think much of the cousin up-stairs with whom my fate was soon to be connected. We had known scarcely anything of each other before. We were new acquaintances, though relations. He took me, I remember, to the National Gallery, full of expectation as to the effect the pictures would have upon me. And I—was struck dumb with disappointment. I had never seen any pictures. I can't tell what I expected to see—something that never was on sea or shore.* My ideal of absolute ignorance was far too high-flown, I suppose, for anything human. I was horribly disappointed, and dropped down from untold heights of imagination to a reality I could not understand. I remember, in the humiliation of my downfall, and in the sense of my cousin's astonished disappointment at my want of appreciation, fixing upon a painting—a figure of the Virgin in a Crucifixion, I think by Correggio, but I am quite vague about it—as the thing I liked best. I chose that as Wordsworth's little boy put forth the weathercock at Kilve*—in despair at my own incapacity to admire. I remember also the heads of the old Jews in Leonardo's Christ in the Temple. The face of the young Redeemer with its elaborate crisped hair shocked me with a sense of profanity, but the old heads I could believe in. And that was all I got out of my first glimpse into the world of art. I cannot recollect whether it was then or after, that an equally great disillusionment in the theatre befell me. The play was 'Twelfth Night,' and the lovely beginning of that play—

'That strain again! it had a dying fall'

—was given by a nobody in white tights lying on a sofa and balancing a long leg as he spoke. The disgust, the disenchantment, the fury remain in my mind now. Once more I came tumbling down from my ideal and all my anticipations. Mrs Charles Kean was Viola, and she was middle-aged and stout!* I was more than disappointed, I was angry and disgusted and cast down. What was the good of anything if that was all that Shakespeare and the great Masters could come to?

I remember after this a day at Greenwich and Woolwich, and the sight of the Arsenal, though why that should have made an impression on my memory, heaven knows! I remember the pyramids of balls, and some convicts whose appearance gave me a thrill of horror,—I think they were convicts, though why convicts should be at Woolwich I can't tell—perhaps it was a mistake. And then Mr Colburn kindly—I thought most kindly, and thanked him *avec effusion*—gave me £150 for 'Margaret Maitland.' I remember walking along the street with delightful elation, thinking that, after all, I was worth something—and not to be hustled aside. I remember, too, getting the first review of my book in the twilight of a wintry dark afternoon, and reading it by the firelight—always half-amused at the thought that it was *me* who was being thus discussed in the newspapers. It was the 'Athenæum,'* and it was on the whole favourable. Of course this event preceded by a couple of months the transaction with Mr Colburn. I think the book was in its third edition before he offered me that £150. I remember no reviews except that one of the 'Athenæum,' nor any particular effect which my success produced in me, except that sense of elation. I cannot think why the book succeeded so well.* When I read it over some years after, I felt nothing but shame at its foolish little polemics and opinions. I suppose there must have been some breath of youth and sincerity in it which touched people, and there had been no Scotch stories for a long time. Lord Jeffrey, then an old man and very near his end, sent me a letter of sweet praise, which filled my mother with rapture and myself with an abashed gratitude.* I was very young. Oddly enough, it has always remained a matter of doubt with me whether the book was published in 1849 or 1850. I thought the former; but Geraldine Macpherson, whom I met in London for the first time a day or two before it was published, declared it to be 1850, from the fact that *that* was the year of her marriage. If a woman remembers any date, it must be the date of her marriage!* so I don't doubt Geddie was right. Anyhow, if it was 1850, I was then only twenty-two, and in some things very young for my age, as in others perhaps older than my years. I was wonderfully little moved by the business altogether. I had a great pleasure in writing, but the success and the three editions had no particular effect upon my mind. For one thing, I saw very few people. We had no society. My father had a horror of strangers, and would never see any one who came to the house, which was a continual wet blanket to my mother's cordial, hospitable nature; but she had given up struggling long before my time, and I grew up without any idea of the pleasures and companions of youth. I did not know them, and therefore did not miss them; but I daresay this helped to make me—not indifferent, rather unconscious, of what might in other circumstances have 'turned my head.' My head was as steady as a rock. I had nobody to praise me except my mother and Frank, and their applause—well, it was delightful, it was everything in the world—it was life,—but it did not count. They were part of me, and I of them, and we were all in it. After a while it came to be the custom that I should every night 'read what I had written' to them before I went to bed. They were very critical sometimes, and I felt while I was reading whether my little audience was with me or not, which put a good deal of excitement into the performance. But that was all the excitement I had.

I began another book called 'Caleb Field,'* about the Plague in London, the very night I had finished 'Margaret Maitland.' I had been reading Defoe, and got the subject into my head. It came to one volume only, and I took a great deal of trouble about a Nonconformist minister who spoke in antitheses very carefully constructed. I don't think it attracted much notice, but I don't remember. Other matters, events even of our uneventful life, took so much more importance in life than these books—nay, it must be a kind of affectation to say that, for the writing ran through everything. But then it was also subordinate to everything, to be pushed aside for any little necessity. I had no table even to myself, much less a room to work in, but sat at the corner of the family table with my writing-book, with everything going on as if I had been making a shirt instead of writing a book. Our rooms in those days were sadly wanting in artistic arrangement. The table was in the middle of the room, the centre round which everybody sat with the candles or lamp upon it. My mother sat always at needle-work of some kind, and talked to whoever might be present, and I took my share in the conversation, going on all the same with my story, the little groups of imaginary persons, these other talks evolving themselves quite undisturbed. It would put me out now to have some one sitting at the same table talking while I worked—at least I would think it put me out, with that sort of conventionalism which grows upon one. But up to this date, 1888, I have never been shut up in a separate room, or hedged off with any observances. My study, all the study I have ever attained to, is the little second drawing-room of my house, with a wide opening into the other drawing-room where all the (feminine) life of the house goes on; and I don't think I have ever had two hours undisturbed (except at night, when everybody is in bed) during my whole literary life. Miss Austen, I believe, wrote in the same way, and very much for the same reason; but at her period the natural flow of life took another form. The family were half ashamed to have it known that she was not just a young lady like the others, doing her embroidery. Mine were quite pleased to magnify me, and to be proud of my work, but always with a hidden sense that it was an admirable joke, and no idea that any special facilities or retirement was necessary. My mother, I believe, would have felt her pride and rapture much checked, almost humiliated, if she had conceived that I stood in need of any artificial aids of that or any other description. That would at once have made the work unnatural to her eyes, and also to mine. I think the first time I ever secluded myself for my work was years after it had become my profession and sole dependence—when I was living after my widow-hood in a relation's house, and withdrew with my book and my inkstand from the family drawing-room out of a little conscious ill-temper which made me feel guilty, notwithstanding that the retire-ment was so very justifiable! But I did not feel it to be so, neither did the companions from whom I withdrew.

After this period our poor Willie became a minister of the English Presbyterian Church, then invested with glory by the Free Church, its real parent, which in our fervid imagination we had by this time dressed up with all sorts of traditional glory. It, we flattered our-selves, was the direct successor of the two thousand seceders of 1661* (was that the date?). There had been a downfall, we allowed, into Unitarianism and indifference; but this was the real, and a very respectable, tradition. Willie went to a very curious little place in the wilds of Northumberland, called Etal, where my mother and I decided—with hopes strangely wild, it seems to me now, after all that had gone before—that he was at length to do well, and be as strenuous to his duty as he was gentle in temper and tender in heart. Poor Willie! It was a sort of show village with pretty flowery cottages and gardens, in a superior one of which he lived, or rather lodged, the income being very small and the position humble. It was, however, so far as my recollection goes, sufficiently like a Scotch parish to convince us that the church and parsonage were quite exotic, and the humble chapel the real religious centre of the place. A great number of the people were, I believe, Presbyterians, and the continuance of their worship and little strait ceremony undoubted from the time of the Puritans, though curiously enough the minister was known to his flock by the title of the priest. I don't in the least recollect what the place was like, yet a whiff of the rural air tinged with peat or wood, and of the roses with which the cottages were garlanded, and an impression of the subdued light through the greenish small windows half veiled in flowers, remains with me,—very sweet, homely, idyllic, like something in a pathetic country story of peace overshadowed with coming trouble. There was a shadow of a ruined castle in the background, I think Norham; but all is vague,—I have not the clear memory of what I saw in my youth that many people retain. I see a little collection of pictures, but the background is all vague. The only vehicle we could get to take us to Berwick was, I recollect, a cart, carefully arranged with straw-covered sacking to make us comfortable. The man who drove it was very anxious to be engaged and taken with us as 'Miss Wilson's coachman.' Why mine, or why we should have taken a rustic 'Jockey-to-the-fair' for a coachman, if we had wanted such an article, I don't know. I suppose there must have been some sort of compliment implied to my *beaux yeux*, or I should not have remembered this. We left Willie with thankful hearts, yet an ache of fear. Surely in that peaceful humble quiet, with those lowly sacred duties and all his goodness and kindness, he would do well! I don't remember how long it continued. So long as he kept up the closest correspondence, writing every second day and giving a full account of himself, there was an uneasy satisfaction at home. But there is always a prophetic ache in the heart when such calamity is on the way.

One day, without warning, except that his letters had begun to fail a little, my mother received an anonymous letter about him. She went off that evening, travelling all night to Edinburgh, which was the quickest way, and then to Berwick. She was very little used to travelling, and she was over sixty, which looked a great age then. I suppose the trains were slower in those days, for I know she got to Edinburgh only in the morning, and then had to go on by the other line to Berwick, and then drive six or more miles to Etal, where she found all the evil auguries fulfilled, and poor Willie fallen again helpless into that Slough of Despond. She remained a few miserable days, and then brought him back with her, finally defeated in the battle which he was quite unfit to wage. He must have been then, I think, about thirty-three, in the prime of strength and youth; but except for a wavering and uncertain interval now and then, he never got out of the mire nor was able to support himself again. I remember the horrible moment of his coming home. Frank and I went down, I suppose, to the ferry at Birkenhead to meet the travellers. We were all very grave—not a word of reproach did any one say, but to be cheerful, to talk about nothing, was impossible. We drove up in silence to Kenyon Terrace where we lived, asking a faint question now and then about the journey. I remember that Willie had a little dog called Brownie with him, and the relief this creature was, which did not understand being shut up in the carriage and made little jumps at the window, and had to be petted and restrained. Brownie brought a little movement, an involuntary laugh at his antics, to break the horrible silence—an angel could scarcely have done more for us. When we got home there was the settling down in idleness, the hopeless discussion of any wretched possibility there might be for him. The days and weeks and months in which he smoked and read old novels and the papers, and, most horrible of all, got to content himself with that life! The anguish in all our hearts looking at him, not knowing what to do, sometimes assailed by gusts of impatience, always closing down in the hopelessness of it; the incapacity to find or suggest anything, the dreary spectacle of that content is before me, with almost as keen a sense of the misery as if it had been yesterday. Alas—is it not yesterday? Life is full of dreadful repetitions.

I had been in the habit of copying out carefully, quite proud of my neat MS., all my books, now becoming a recognised feature of the family life. It struck us all as a fine idea that Willie might copy them for me, and retrieve a sort of fictitious independence by getting 10 per cent upon the price of them; and I really think he felt quite comfortable on this. Of course, the sole use of the copying was the little corrections and improvements I made in going over my work again.

It was after this that my cousin Frank came upon a visit. We had seen, and yet had not seen, a great deal of each other in London during the three months I had spent there with Willie; but my mind had been preoccupied with Willie chiefly, and a little with my book. When Frank made me the extraordinary proposal for which I was totally unprepared, that we should, as he said, build up the old Drumthwacket together, my only answer was an alarmed negative, the idea never having entered my mind. But in six months or so things changed. It is not a matter into which I can enter here.

In the spring of 1851 my mother and I were in Edinburgh, and there made the acquaintance of the Wilsons, our second cousins,—George Wilson being at that time Professor of something which meant chemistry, but was not called so. His mother was an exceedingly bright, vivacious, ugly, old lady, a universal devourer of books, and with that kind of scientific tendency which made her encourage her boys to form museums, and collect fossils, butterflies, &c. I forget how my mother and she got on, but I always liked her.

She was all culture, intellect, improvement of the mind and so forth, things which in words my mother scorned, being spontaneous to her fingers' ends, loving books because she loved them and not because they improved the mind. But the other Mrs Wilson was tempered too by a wholesome touch of humour, grimmer sarcasm, though not so keen, and she was not lovely, which my mother with her beautiful complexion and eyes always was—a great difference always, a great and fundamental injustice, no doubt, as people nowadays say.

George Wilson* was an excellent talker, full of banter and a kind of humour, full of ability, too, I believe, writing very amusing letters and talking very amusing talk, which was all the more credit to him as he was in very bad health, kept alive by the fact that he could eat, and so maintain a modicum of strength—enough to get on by. There were two daughters—Jessie and Jeanie—the younger of whom became my brother Frank's wife; and the eldest son, who was married, lived close by, and was then, I think, at the head (in a literary point of view) of the business of Messrs Nelson, reading for them and advising them about books, though I never could make out what books they published, except little books of poetry half or more than half written by Daniel Wilson. He very soon after this migrated to Canada, and became eventually President of University College, Toronto, and Sir Daniel in the end of his life.*

My mother at this time renewed acquaintance with Dr Moir of Musselburgh,* an old friend of hers, who had, I believe, attended me when, as a very small child, I fell into the fire, or rather against the bars of the grate, marking my arm in a way which it never recovered. This excellent man, whom everybody loved, was the Delta of 'Blackwood's Magazine,' and called everywhere by that name. He had written much gentle poetry, and one story à la Galt* called 'Mansie Wauch,' neither of which were good enough for him, yet got him a certain reputation, especially some pathetic verses about children he had lost, which went to the heart of every mother who had lost children, my own mother first and foremost. He had married a very handsome stately lady, a little conventional, but with an unfailing and ready kindness which often made her mannerisms quite gracious and beautiful. There was already a handsome daughter married, though under twenty, and many other fine, tall, well-bred handsome creatures, still in long hair and short skirts, growing up. I think I was left behind to pay a visit when my mother returned home, and then had a kind of introduction to Edinburgh literary society, in one case very important for myself. For in one expedition we made, Major Blackwood, one of the publishing firm, and brother of the editor of the 'Magazine,' was of the party; and my long connection with his family thus began. He was accompanied by a young man, a Mr Cupples,* of whom, except his name, I have no recollection, but who was the author of a sea-story then, I think, going on in 'Blackwood,' called the 'Green Hand,' and who, it was hoped, would be as successful as 'Tom Cringle' the author of the 'Cruise of the Midge,' who had been a very effective contributor twenty years before.* All I remember of him was that my cousin Daniel Wilson, who was also of the party, indignantly pointed out to me the airs which this young author gave himself, 'as if it was such a great thing to be a contributor to "Blackwood"!' I am afraid I thought it *was* a great thing, and had not remarked the young author's airs; but Daniel was of the opposite camp. Major Black- wood, who interested me most, was a mild soldierly man, with the gentlest manners and drooping eyelids, which softened his look, or so at least it appears to me at the end of so many years.

I remember that one of the places we visited was Wallyford, where was the house in which I was born, but of which I had no recollec- tion. It must have been a pleasant homely house,* with a projecting half turret enclosing the staircase, as in many houses in the Lothians, the passages and kitchen down-stairs floored with red brick, and a delightful large low drawing-room above, with five greenish win- dows looking out upon Arthur's Seat in the distance, and a ghost of Edinburgh. That room charmed me greatly, and in after days I used to think of becoming its tenant and living there, for the sake of the landscape and the associations and that pretty old room; but before I could have carried out such an idea, even had it been more real than a fancy, the pretty house was pulled down, and a square, aggressive, and very commonplace new farmhouse built in its place.

The consequence of my introduction to Major Blackwood was, that some time in the course of the following months I sent him the manuscript of my story 'Katie Stewart':* a little romance of my mother's family, gleaned from her recollections and descriptions. The scene of this story was chiefly laid in old Kellie Castle, which I was not then aware was the home of our own ancestors, from whom it had passed long before into the hands of the Erskines, Earls of

Kellie—with the daughter of which house Katie Stewart had been brought up. She was my mother's great-aunt, and had lived to a great age. She had seen Prince Charlie enter Edinburgh, and had told all her experiences to my mother, who told them to me, so that I never was quite sure whether I had not been Katie Stewart's contemporary in my own person. And this was her love-tale. I received proofs of this story on the morning of my wedding-day, and thus my connection with the firm of Blackwood began. They were fond of nick-names, and I was known among them by the name of 'Katie' for a long time, as I discovered lately (1896) in some old letters. I suppose they thought me so young and simple (as they say in these letters) that the girl's name was appropriate to me. I was not tall ('middle height' we called it in those days), and very inexperienced,—'so simple and yet self-possessed,' I am glad to say Major Blackwood reports of me. I was only conscious of being dreadfully *shy*.

We were married in Birkenhead on the 4th May 1852,—and the old home, which had come to consist of such incongruous elements, was more or less broken up. My brother Frank, discontented and wounded partly by my marriage, partly by the determination to abandon him and follow me to London, which my father and mother had formed, married too, hastily, but very successfully in a way as it turned out, and so two new houses were formed out of the partial ruins of the old. Had the circumstances been different—had they stayed in Birkenhead and I gone alone with my husband to London—some unhappiness might have been spared. Who can tell? There would have been other unhappiness to take its place. As it was there was plenty. They settled in a quaint little house in a place called Park Village, old-fashioned, semi-rustic, and pretty enough, with a long strip of garden stretching down to the edge of a deep cutting of the railway, where we used to watch the trains passing far below. The garden was gay with flowers, quantities of brilliant poppies of all colours I remember, which I liked for the colour and hated for the heavy ill odour of them, and the sensation as of evil flowers. Our house in Harrington Square was very near: it looked all happy enough but was not, for my husband and my mother did not 'get on' as people say. His mind was full of the foolish ideas about a mother-in-law, and thus, I fear, of a jealousy often touched with little darts of movements towards them which might have brought about something better had they been responded to. But they were not. My father sat passive, taking no notice, with his paper, not perceiving much I believe, and poor Willie, tucked in the study that had been made for him, copying for me, reading old books, smoking and something worse than smoking, while she, poor mother, poor bright, thwarted, wasted Love incarnate as she was, lived between her daughter, who was taken from her, and her son, who was an anguish to her. To think of this in the house that looked so tranquil in this life that might have been sweet tranquillity for once, parted from Frank, the other habitual companion, and with nothing but shame and misery in the thought of poor Willie, makes my heart ache, though she has been at rest so long. And this was the end of all her striving and hoping and working for us. I, for my part, was torn in two. I have gone through many sorrows since, but I don't know that any period of my life has ever contained more intolerable moments than those first years that should have been so happy. My child's birth made a momentary gleam of joy soon lost in angry clouds and then another year, Willie growing worse. The silent (not always silent) conflict over me growing stronger, coming to a horrible breach, which I was almost glad of because it kept those two, the nearest to me, from meeting, while I stole to her daily though she never crossed my doors. Thus she became ailing and concealed it, and kept alive—or at least kept her last illness off by sheer stress of will until my second child was born a year and a day after the first. There had been some reconciliation before that event for she was with me, but sank next day into an illness from which she never rose. She died in September 1854, suffering no attendance but mine, though she concealed from me how ill she was for a long time. I remember the first moment in which I had any real fear, speaking to the doctor with a sudden impulse, in the front of her door, all in a green shade with the waving trees, demanding his real opinion. I do not think I had any under-standing of the gravity of the circumstances. He shook his head, and I knew—the idea having never entered my mind before that she was to die. I recollect going away, walking home as in a dream, not able to go to her, to look at her, from whom I had never had a secret, with this secret in my soul that must be told least of all to her; and the sensation that here was something which would not lighten after a while as all my troubles had always done, and pass away. I had never come face to face with the inevitable before. I was well enough used to sounding all the depths of miserable thought and then with a spring getting up

from this very deep and seeing daylight again—but there was no daylight here—no hope—no getting over it. Then there followed a
struggle of a month or two, much suffering on her part and a long
troubled watch and nursing on mine. At the very end I remember the
struggle against overwhelming sleep, after nights and days in incessant anxiety, which made me so bitterly ashamed of the limits of
wretched nature. To want to sleep while she was dying seemed so
unnatural and horrible. I never had come within sight of death
before. And, oh me! when all was over, mingled with my grief there
was—how can I say it?—something like a dreadful relief. However
sad I might be the conflict was over—there were no longer two people
to please, but only one.

Within a few months after, my little Marjorie, my second child,
died on the 8th February; and then with deep shame and anguish I
felt what I suppose was another wretched limit of nature. My dearest
mother, who had been everything to me all my life, and to whom I
was everything; the companion, friend, counsellor, minstrel, story-
teller, with whom I had never wanted for constant interest, entertainment, and fellowship,— did not give me, when she died, a pang so
deep as the loss of the little helpless baby, eight months old. I miss
my mother till this moment when I am nearly as old as she was (sixty,
10th June 1888); I think instinctively still of asking her something,
referring to her for information, and I dream constantly of being a
girl with her at home. But at that moment her loss was nothing to me
in comparison with the loss of my little child.

I lost another infant after that, a day old. My spirit sank completely
under it. I used to go about saying to myself, 'A little while and ye
shall not see me,'* with a longing to get to the end and have all
safe—for my one remaining, my eldest, my Maggie seemed as if she
too must be taken out of my arms. People will say it was an animal
instinct perhaps. Neither of these little ones could speak to me or
exchange an idea or show love, and yet their withdrawal was like the
sun going out from the sky—life remained, the daylight continued,
but all was different. It seems strange to me now at this long
distance—but so it was.

The little glimpse of society I had during my married life in
London was not of a very elevating kind; or perhaps I—with my shyness and complete unacquaintance with the ways of people who gave
parties and paid incessant visits—was only unable to take any

pleasure in it, or get beyond the outside petty view, and the same strange disappointment and disillusion with which the pictures and the stage had filled me, bringing down my ridiculous impossible ideal to the ground. I have tried to illustrate my youthful feelings about this several times in words.* I had expected everything that was superlative,—beautiful conversation, all about books and the finest subjects, great people whose notice would be an honour, poets and painters, and all the sympathy of congenial minds, and the feast of reason and the flow of soul. But it is needless to say I found none of these things. We went 'out,' not very often, to parties where there was always a good deal of the literary element, but of a small kind, and where I found everything very commonplace and poor, not at all what I expected. I never did myself any justice, as a certain little lion-hunter, a Jewish patroness of the arts, who lived somewhere in the region about Harley Street, said. That is to say, I got as quickly as I could into a corner and stood there, rather wistfully wishing to know people, but not venturing to make any approach, waiting till some one should speak to me; which much exasperated my aspiring hostess, who had picked me up as a new novelist, and meant me to help to amuse her guests, which I had not the least idea how to do. I fear I must have been rather exasperating to my husband, who was more given to society than I, and tried in vain (as I can now see) to form me and make me attend to my social duties, which even in such a small matter as returning calls I was terribly neglectful of—out of sheer shyness and gaucherie, I think; for I was always glad and grateful when anybody would insist on making friends with me, as a few people did. There was an old clergyman, Mr Laing,* who did, I remember, and more or less his wife—he especially. He liked me, I think, and complimented me by saying he did not like literary ladies—a sort of thing people are rather disposed to say to me. And Lance (the painter of fruits and flowers and still life), who was a wit in his way, was also a great friend of mine. He dared me to put him in a book, and I took him at his word and did so, making a very artless representation, and using some of his own stories; so that everybody recognised the sketch, which was done in mere fun and liking, and pleased him very much—the only actual bit of real life I ever took for a book. It was in 'Zaidee,' I think.*

Among my literary acquaintances was the Mr Fullom who had read for old Colburn my first book, and whose acquaintance as an eminent literary man and great notability we had all thought at home it would be such a fine thing to make. He turned out a very small personage indeed, a fat solemn man, with a common little wife, people whom it was marvellous to think of as connected with anything that pretended to be intellectual. He wrote a book called 'The Marvels of Science,' a dull piece of manufacture, for which by some wonderful chance he received a gold medal, *Für Kunst*, from the King of Hanover. I think I see him moving solemnly about the little drawing-room with this medal on his breast, and the wife following him. He soon stalked away into the unknown, and I saw him no more. I forget how I became acquainted with the S. C. Halls, who used to ask me to their parties, and who were literary people of the most prominent and conventional type, rather satisfying to the sense on the whole, as the sort of thing one expected.* Mrs Hall had retired upon the laurels got by one or two Irish novels, and was surrounded by her husband with the atmosphere of admiration, which was the right thing for a 'fair' writer. He took her very seriously, and she accepted the *rôle*, though without, I think, any particular setting up of her own standard. I used to think and say that she looked at me inquisitively, a little puzzled to know what kind of humbug I was, all being humbugs. But she was a kind woman all the same; and I never forget the sheaf of white lilies she sent us for my child's christening, for which I feel grateful still. He was certainly a humbug of the old mellifluous Irish kind—the sort of man whose specious friendlinesses, and compliments, and 'blarney' were of the most innocent kind, not calculated to deceive anybody but always amusing. He told Irish stories capitally.

They had the most wonderful collection of people at their house, and she would stand and smile and shake hands, till one felt she must stiffen so, and had lost all consciousness who anybody was. He on his side was never tired, always insinuating, jovial, affectionate. It was at their house, I think, that we met the Howitts*—Mary Howitt, a mild, kind delightful woman, who frightened me very much, I remember, by telling me of many babies whom she had lost through some defective valve in the heart, which she said was somehow connected with too much mental work on the part of the mother,—a foolish thing, I should think, yet the same thing occurred twice to myself. It alarmed and saddened me terribly—but I liked her greatly. Not so her husband, who did not please me at all. For a short time we met them everywhere in our small circle, and then they too disappeared, going abroad, I think. There was a great deal about spiritualism (so called) in the air at this time—its first development in England,—and the Howitts' eldest daughter was an art medium producing wonderful scribble-scrabbles, which it was the wonder of wonders to find her mother, so full of sense and truth, so genuine herself, full of enthusiasm about.*

I remember a day at the Halls, which must have been in the summer of 1853. They had then a pretty house at Addleston, near Chertsey. My husband and I travelled down by train in company with a dark, dashing person, an American lady, whom, on arriving at the station, we found to be going to the Halls too. She and I were put into their brougham to drive there, while the gentlemen walked; and she did what she could in a patronising way to find out who I was. She thought me, I supposed, the poor little shy wife of some artist, whom the Halls were being kind to, or something of that humble kind. She turned out to be a literary person of great pretensions, calling herself Grace Greenwood, though that was not her real name,—and I was amused to find a paragraph about myself, as 'a little homely Scotchwoman,' in the book which she wrote when she got back.* Two incidents of this entertainment remain very clear in my memory. One was, that being placed at table beside Mr Frost, the academician,* who was deaf and very gentle and kind, I was endeav- uring with many mental struggles to repeat to him something that d produced a laugh, and which his wistful look had asked to under- d, when suddenly one of those hushes which sometimes come a large company occurred, and my voice came out distinct—to wn horrified consciousness, at least—a sound of terror and e to me. The other was, that Gavan Duffy,* one of the recent rebels, and my husband began to discuss, I suppose, national cteristics, or what they believed to be such, when the Irishman ioned gravely and with some heat that the frolic and the wit usu- attributed to his countrymen were a mere popular delusion, while the Scotchman with equal earnestness repudiated the caution and prudence ascribed to his race; which was whimsical enough to be remembered.

Another recollection of one of the Halls' evening parties in town at a considerably later period rises like a picture before me. They were fond of every kind of lion and wonder, great and small. Rosa

Bonheur,* then at the height of her reputation, was there one
evening, a round-faced, good-humoured woman, with hair cut short
and divided at one side like a man's and indeed not very distinct in
the matter of sex so far as dress and appearance went. There was
there also a Chinese mandarin in full costume, smiling blandly upon
the company, and accompanied by a missionary, who had the charge
of him. By some means or other the Chinaman was made to sing what
we were informed was a sentimental ballad, exceedingly touching
and romantic. It was like nothing so much as the howl of a dog, one of
those grave pieces of canine music which my poor old Newfoundland
used to give forth when his favourite organgrinder came into the
street. (Merry's performance was the most comical thing imaginable.
There was one organ among many which touched his tenderest
feelings. When it appeared once a-week, he rushed to it, seated
himself beside the man, listened till rapture and sentiment were
wound up to the highest pitch, and then, lifting his nose and his voice
to heaven,—sang. There could be no doubt that the dear dog was
giving forth all the poetry of his being in that appalling noise,—his
emotion, his sentiment, his profound seriousness were indisputable,
while any human being within reach was overwhelmed and helpless
with laughter.) The Chinaman sang exactly like Merry, with the
same effect. Rosa Bonheur, I suppose was more civil than *nous autres*,
and her efforts to restrain the uncontrollable laugh were super-
human. She almost swallowed her handkerchief in the effort to
conceal it. I can see her as in a picture, the central figure, with her
bushy short hair, and her handkerchief in her mouth. All my recollections are like pictures, not continuous, only a scene detached and
conspicuous here and there.

Miss Mulock* was another of the principal figures perceptible in
the somewhat dimmed panorama of that far-off life. Her friends the
Lovells lived in Mornington Crescent, which was close to our little
house in Harrington Square,—all in a remote region near Regent's
Park, upon the Hampstead Road, where it seems very strange to me
we should ever have lived, and which, I suppose, is dreadfully shabby
and out-of-the-way. Perhaps it was shabby then, one's ideas change
so greatly. Miss Mulock lived in a small house in a street a little
farther off even in the wilds than ours. She was a tall young woman
with a slim pliant figure, and eyes that had a way of fixing the eyes of
her interlocutor in a manner which did not please my shy fastidious-

ness. It was embarrassing, as if she meant to read the other upon whom she gazed,—a pretension which one resented. It was merely, no doubt, a fashion of what was the 'intense' school of the time. Mrs Browning did the same thing the only time I met her,* and this to one quite indisposed to be read. But Dinah was always kind, enthusiastic, somewhat didactic and apt to teach, and much looked up to by her little band of young women. She too had little parties, at one of which I remember Miss Cushman, the actress, in a deep recitative, without any apparent tune in it, like the voice of a skipper at sea I thought it, giving forth Kingsley's song of 'The Sands of Dee.' I was rather afraid of the performer, though long afterwards she came to see me in Paris when I was in much sorrow, and her tenderness and feeling gave me the sensation of suddenly meeting a friend in the darkness, of whose existence there I had no conception. There used to be also at Miss Mulock's parties an extraordinary being in a wheeled chair, with an imperfect face (as if it had been somehow left unfinished in the making), a Mr Smedley,* a terrible cripple, supposed to be kept together by some framework of springs and supports, of whom the story was told that he had determined, though the son of a rich man, to maintain himself, and make himself a reputation, and had succeeded in doing both, as the writer—of all things in the world—of sporting novels. He was the author of 'Lewis Arundel' and 'Frank Fairleigh,' both I believe athletic books, and full of feats of horsemanship and strength; which was sufficiently pathetic—though the appearance of this poor man somewhat frightened me too.

Mr Lovell, the father of one of Miss Mulock's chief friends, the portly and sententious Secretary of an Insurance Company was the author of 'The Wife's Secret,' a play lately revived, and which struck me when I saw it as one of the most conventional and unreal possible, very curious to come out of that sober city man.* All the guests at these little assemblies were something of the same kind. One looked at them rather as one looked at the figures in Madame Tussaud's, wondering if they were waxwork or life—wondering in the other case whether the commonplace outside might not cover a painter or a poet or something equally fine—whose ethereal qualities were all invisible to the ordinary eye.

What I liked best in the way of society was when we went out occasionally quite late in the evening, Frank and I, after he had left off work in his studio, and went to the house of another painter uninvited, unexpected, always welcome,—I with my work. Alexander Johnstone's house* was the one to which we went most. I joined the wife in her little drawing-room, while he went up-stairs to the studio. (They all had the drawing-room proper of the house, the first-floor room, for their studios.) We women talked below of our subjects, as young wives and young mothers do—with a little needle-work and a little gossip. The men above smoked and talked their subjects, investigating the picture of the moment, going over it with advice and criticism; no doubt giving each other their opinions of other artists and other pictures too. And then we supped, frugally, cheerfully, and if there was anything of importance in the studio the wives went up to look at it, or see what progress it had made since the last time, after supper. And then we walked home again. They paid us a return visit some days after of just the same kind. If I knew them now, which I no longer do, I would ask them to dinner, and they me, and most likely we would not enjoy it at all. But those simple evenings were very pleasant. Our whole life was upon very simple lines at this period: we dined in the middle of the day, and our little suppers were not of a kind to require elaborate preparation if another pair came in unexpectedly. It was true society in its way. Nothing of the kind seems possible now.

Sunday 9 November 1890

It was very early in this day, rather on Saturday night, that God has taken away my Tiddy, God keep him. Oh, if I could but follow my boy in thought where he is yours, if I could but feel how it is, if not where he is. I am not afraid of my God. O my, my father almighty, I am not afraid of thee. Thou wilt cradle him in thy arms. Thou wilt comfort him as one whom his mother comforteth. He has sinned, he has sinned, and done evil in thy sight.* His life has failed, his future in this world was without hope. Lord of Lords thou art holding him awful in thy arms before he begins the sweet, the better life. The way in which he will not err—Oh my father I am content that it is best, that thou hast done what is best for him. I've again, I know, been thinking and thinking in anguish what will he do when I die, and now the question is solved. I have been permitted to do everything for him, to wind up his young life, to accept the thousand and thousand disappointments and thoughts of what might have been. It is only heartache that cries out, not my judgement. Lord thou will set him straight in this narrow life. It will no longer be possible to err, and his heart was still sound though his flesh was weak.

He was the most delightful child that ever was born, the light of the home which he came into healthy and strong when his father was just beginning to be ill. He was not three when my husband died—but when the child saw me cry as I came out of his father's sickroom, when I had been doing all I could to look cheerful he would come up to my knee, and look up into my face and smile; he would not cry but smile, to cheer me, God bless my darling child.

All his childhood was delightful and there never was any boy more bright. At Eton he had the happiest and brightest career, not a fault but lightheartedness, before he left. When he was grown up, sometimes I used to say he was Chaucer's Squire in person, 'singing he was, or floyting all the day. He was as fresh as are the flowers in May.' All that comes back to my sorrow. Oh how sweet my boy was, how kind and tender and ever bright—his voice always singing, his heart always gay. Cecco told not long ago a story of the two together which went very much to my heart though I knew little what was coming. They were coming down from Strathtyrum* down the dark avenue and afraid, the two little boys together and Tiddy sang 'Lead kindly light' to cheer them. The two little figures in the dark.

And then Oxford with its clouds—when I awoke again to that anxiety which has been the burden of my life—and years, sad years after, anxiety for ever, always anxiety. He never did so much harm as many more did and came out of it in the end all right. Perhaps my constant coming in to him, avid to make up and preserve him from any evil consequences did harm, God knows. We are so foolish we know so little. Perhaps I did not take the right way with him. At all events that is all over. God knows which is the right way and now will take it unencumbered by any contradictions of humanity. I have a feeling that He will force us on—that we must make our choice and do our own will there—at least there God will not compel us to be good. But now all is different—the fatal desire has been worked out and punished, oh much and sorely here—my darling boy never had badness in his heart. He never could speak of a good deed or a generous effort without the water in his eyes—he responded to any kind thought—he harmed nobody.

Here this day I set up my pattern of memorial.* All this year I have thought he was just our Lord's age when He began his ministry and that this would bring him a blessing. —Oh my God was this the only blessing possible to my son for thy son's sake. God bless my Cyril, my Tiddy, my darling—I think of him, or rather I try to think of him as resting a little in his father's arms, and wondering at the calm and peace, before he knows the new life.

Not farewell my dearest, not farewell—I will soon be with you again. Sunday 9 November—in another week, on Sunday, the day he was born, he would have been 34.

Davos.

On Sunday the 16th I was travelling here thro' the dark mountains with Cecco and Denny and so the birthday passed. In the middle of the day at our lunch my Cecco said, 'If all had been well we would have been drinking Tiddy's health. It might not be fit to do that now, but let us drink to our meeting with him' and we did so solemnly. This is how we are to take our sorrow, never to avoid his name. From the time of her death till now I have never named Maggie's name. I have avoided it and called her my child, my darling, never that familiar sound named. But Cecco will not have it so with his brother. He speaks of him constantly and I am training myself to do it too—nay, I think I can do it without difficulty—as yet. But my first feeling of a kind of awful satisfaction and consent to God's will is hard to keep up in the face of nature that mourns for her children and will not be comforted because they are not.*

And yet it is all true. Life was becoming an impossible thing. The self denial that would have made all right was what he could not do. Oh so small a thing it seems, so easy to be done, yet impossible and the other way so terrible, the rending asunder of all things. Did he ever believe, I wonder, that it was so serious, or only, with the heedlessness of his nature, that today would be as yesterday, and nothing more?

November 19.

This day last week we laid him in the grave, crowned with sunshine and with flowers. I thought all through that I could almost see him, and Frank with him,* looking on—interested, not the least sad—not thinking of me or any one, just looking on, two heavenly youths—and this kept me strangely up and strangely calm. His old master, whom he loved, Dr Hornby and Mr Donaldson, his old schoolfellow, and

Mr Blake, whom he liked, stood all through at the head of the grave, reading the service*—he would have liked it so, and perhaps he came to look on and see it done. But I don't wish him to be hanging about us in our dreary human way. I don't want him to think of me. I never was jealous of his love, never but happy and glad to think he could have friends better and more near him than I. I am not jealous of the girl who thinks he loved her—Did he love her: or was no love strong enough to rouse the languour of his being? Did he find that he had thrown away his life in that last spasm and anguish when he called upon God—God alone? God, above the beginning and end of all things, only can know. He called upon God and they say our Lord Jesus, though I did not know that,—Did he know then for the moment suddenly, what was coming? I cannot bear that he should have had even that little time of mortal distress—I would rather he had not known at all—but woken in God's arms and known no death— but to all the rest it seems a comfort that he should have cried to his Father. Oh Father, I never doubted, never feared what thy reception of him would be, a perfect pity, perfect love—to punish if need was, but what is punishment when all misunderstanding is over, and he knows now as he is known.* And all this is only a week ago, the flowers not faded on his grave, everything done in love and honour, his little book* left behind him to prove even more than the truth and his name sweet. Oh it is well, it is well. There was no way but this.

And I go away to my poor work, my writing of novels, my trivial little conversations and realization of the shadow life into which I dare not put all my experiences, nor disclose my heart. What tragedy of all is so bitter and terrible as to have to say of a human creature, nobly endowed, beautifully formed, made for everything that was good, that before he had reached the crown of human strength it had come to be that there was no way but this—

And the better life beyond, thank God, the way where he will not err, the path which is in the full light of the Father's countenance, where, please God, he is walking now, no thought of burials or death in him or about him. Amen. God bless my dearest boy for ever and ever and give him joy and a blessed career.

Saturday 22

A fortnight since his last hours, I feel that it would be a little comfort to me to write the history down of the week that ended everything for this world. On Tuesday afternoon, while Cecco and I were sitting in the drawing room, he came in saying he felt very unwell. We were both stricken with alarm at once, fearing the one dreadful thing: his face was heavy and swollen and sad, as it was on the former occasion.* I got him to go to bed. He was evidently much alarmed himself, and thought for a time it was going to pass over, but just when the others were sitting down to dinner the attack came, only slight, only once and passed off to my great thankfulness. I thought there would be the usual night of confused guilt and all well next day. Next day he continued confused, dozing continually, and the doctor spoke of a little congestion of the lung, and looked very grave, but did not try the temperature nor anything till Thursday night when it was 103, and I became very much frightened, but next morning it had fallen a little and on Saturday he was full of fun and I gave God thanks and thought all was well. During this whole time he was always confused and cloudy, speaking with difficulty with long pauses between the words—twice he complained, 'I can't speak'—but he seemed to understand well enough. Once when I asked him if he had any pain he said, 'I have not energy enough to feel pain'—Another time he asked me to tell him the secret reason of his condition. 'Why am I lying in a dream in this room that used to be home?'—I said, 'because you are ill dear and it is home'—'No,' he said, 'there is some other reason underneath'. When I said I was afraid of his abandoning himself he said, 'No, I'll tell you what you are afraid of. You are afraid of the time when the doctor will say I may go out again'. God knows what he meant. I think some thought must have been in his mind that I would want him to leave home, to put himself under special care. When the nurse came he suggested that it was foolish to get a nurse when he was getting better—and about nine on Saturday night, this day fortnight, when the doctor came (I had been quite gay, laughing at the nurse and her professional way, thinking as the fever was gone all was well) he told me that he must give a stimulant, though much against his will in consequence of the other complaint. And then he had to perform a little operation to relieve him, which my dear boy was a little afraid of, but said he was much more comfortable after. I think it must have been about eleven or later when he suddenly got very ill, gasping and labouring for breath. The phlegm rattling in his throat. I cannot tell how long this lasted—it seemed dying—it was then that he spoke, muttering and low, of seeking God and God and, as they thought outside, Jesus. Then he became a little calmer and the nurse thought he would rally. Dr M. when I asked said no. He had thought for a time he was dying, but not now. Then I think it was while I was kneeling by his bedside that he put his arms round me, whether in one of his affectionate impulses or whether as a farewell I cannot tell—I think the first, and held out his hand to Cecco. And then he turned over on his side, threw his arms up in an easy attitude like a child going to sleep, and breathed away. It was about one o'clock when all was over. The spasm which lasted perhaps an hour, perhaps not so much, I don't think so much, was all the suffering there was.

Oh my son, my son—would God I had died for thee my son, my son*—but I know I ought not to say this, for what if I had died and left him to a desolate and miserable end.

I don't know if I have already put down the prayers that for some time past had been forced from me in the midst of my cries to God for my boys—I prayed that if recovery was not to be, I might have strength to nurse and care for my child to the end that nothing might be wanted, no indulgence, no kindness, no care. I used to feel myself forced to do this and it would burst from me with a sort of compulsion. It was not Tiddy I was thinking most of. It was when my whole soul was shaken quite from a lingering illness for his brother. God help us poor human creatures, I prayed for I know not what. It was put into my heart to do so, and the prayer was granted.

And he himself, my dear boy, had been singing every night Elaine's song—singing it so constantly that it got into my mind and I kept singing it too. 'O love, if death be sweeter let me die'*—thus he made this same prayer unconsciously as I did, unwillingly, not knowing what I meant.

I think that the little attack he was supposed to have had in the night while I was away was the last warning—And I think that in his confused mind during all the last words there was a fear that things could not go on in their previous footing—that I would want to take some other steps to save him from himself. And I feel as if in that last spasm there had suddenly come upon him a sense that all was passing—He said just before it came on 'I saw my name written full across——' across I know not what. He did not end the sentence. If he knew then what was coming that was the whole—the only bitterness.

Just a fortnight ago, just about now—and there he lay, his beautiful face quite calm, his hands lying so easily, turned on his side—towards the wall—

I am not so quiet now as I was—I can't follow him—I feel still that I am but a spectator, that I had so secondary a place, that God and he had to settle the question and there was no other way. And at first I felt a great calm, and almost as if I saw him arrived there, glad and wondering with his new life his better chance, anything but night—But I can't follow—I can almost realize that first step—but oh nothing beyond. He must be going on. He must have gone further from that point than [we / I] have done, but what to do?—Oh if I could but think, or even imagine what he is set to do—what intelligent life there is, what conditions at all. In the light of the Father's countenance all the foolish, foolish sins swept away, all the hampering weakness, the only indulgence gone—restored to full pure life, the life of his boyhood, all the interval blotted out—I felt all that so strongly at first—oh for but a step now across to imagine what he is beginning to do and how to live. He must be familiar with everything now, no longer a stranger—having seen the Lord. Will there not be some special understanding because of his age, our Lord's own age—a young man. Perhaps it is fantastic to think so, but why? My Tiddy sinned, but never, never was false to his Master's name, or not moved by it, or denied Him. God bless you, my dear, God bless you my dear, if I could but follow you one step, or think what you are doing—Oh Lord Jesus help me, if but with an imagination—I can't think of punishment—but what would it matter if it were punishment—We should not care for that, Tiddy dear, all being well and things set sure and straight for ever.

December 9th.

I am getting very quiet again in all those changes and goings round of the mind. For a few days it was always darting upon me in the midst of all my endless thought of him of a sudden, in a moment, as if I had never known it before, that it was him, Tiddy, my boy, that was gone—not any one else but him—going through and through me like an arrow—as if some one had struck me with it—Now that is quieted down a little—I only keep seeing scenes of the life that is now past—so large a slice of my life, more than half of it—since I was twenty-eight till now that I am sixty-two, in all which time from the delightful baby he was up to the man he has had so great a place—I can see him at all ages in his sweet childhood—in his beautiful youth, I see him walking with me just big enough for me to put my hand on his shoulder in a posture of supporting myself, a tiny, tiny Eton boy, only nine—one of the youngest there. And then the beautiful youth coming to join me as we came out of 'Speeches', bareheaded in the speaking dress* which became him so well—I can see the sun touching the side of his hair which was lighter then and curly, and oh, my pride and joy. Mr H—— has written me a little about their schooldays for which I will always bless his name. And then my mind will jump to the drawing-room at home and see him singing at the piano, in my study, coming forward that I might say something about his song, more pleased if I did not, and that, oh my God, but five or six weeks ago—always childlike in spite of all!—desiring praise and love however far he might wander. And now it is all past, all over—the wandering and the erring for him, thank God, but for me all the better part of my life—it is only the dregs that now remain. And I feel more and more strongly as if I never again could enter into the competition and strain of life. I ought not to require it at my age, but I do. It seems to me that if I can but do what I have in hand, which is a very great deal, I will be able to leave Cecco in what will not be so bad a position—better than if I lived longer. A quiet elation came into my mind the other day when I thought that I might do that in about eighteen months, and then if I might go it would be better for everybody. If my dearest Cecco is well, as God grant and as I hope, I can fancy him in a little house near the Castle which I might bargain for him—and I think that nobody would object to the girls, my good dear girls,* who are my children too in every sense of the words and brought up as his sisters and never a thought of anything else—going on with him till they marry, or if they don't marry, they would be able to provide for themselves by that time and he might have I hope about £200 a year from me safe, besides what he could make—and they might all go on together without suffering so much from my loss. I take pleasure in thinking of this and I fancy I can see a little cheerful house and they would study all his wants and wishes as they do now, as much as I myself do—until brighter prospects come for all of them. I hope they will all marry, but if not it would be something to have this safe little brother and sister home.

Cecco said to me the other day when I could not forego breaking down a little and speaking to him of that dreadful darting sense of reality, of which I have spoken, that what he felt was 'discouraged'. For the moment I was slow to see what he meant, but now I do—and feel it to the bottom of my heart. How ready one was to grasp at all the promises in what one read. Ask and it shall be given to you. If two or three agree to ask anything it will be done for them,* and all the cases both in the Gospels and the Psalms which seemed to come so appropriately, to be like personal communications. And now there seems a veil, a cloud over them all and all hopes, and all life is discouraged—the nearer the unseen comes to us, the farther off it seems. There is a sort of gleam of glory for the first step, when the soul goes, we can imagine its arrival there, I think I feel that—but after, nothing—a blank and we cannot see a step beyond, nor even imagine what he is doing, who was doing so many familiar trivial things by our side only the other day.

And it is as if it had been useless to pray—the one thing has been done that never can be undone. Even my prayers for my dearest Cecco seem to fall languid instead of being redoubled as they might be. There seems a sort of dreary sense of 'no use' in one's mind—one's thoughts stray off in the midst—to that endless thinking and thinking over those last days—wondering if something else had been done, or if anything was neglected or what he was thinking of when he said this or that—or now dwelling upon his name, my boy, my boy—Oh how I have cried and prayed for him since ever he was born—and that which has been heard was from the last dreadful prayers which must have been put into my heart—which I made against my will.

This is the moment in my life that often comes before me now—a very black moment when he had come back from Ceylon—and when my Cecco, though turning back to the right way was not assured and my heart torn within me—We were in St Andrews in Mrs Murray's house, I alone with them—And they had both gone out to the Club at night and I went out wandering across the links in the late twilight, almost dark, towards the sea. How clearly I can see the scene now. I went up round the Club to see if I could get a glimpse of them through the lighted windows, but could not, and then I sat down on the seat by the path before you come to the beach. There was a dull sky, hanging low, but away towards the East a hint of clearness, a band of soft yellow light falling into the grey clouds and there came out by moments on the other side the light on the Bell rocks, and another I think at Arbroath. I was very miserable, crying to God for them, both, feeling more miserable almost than I had ever done before—when suddenly there came upon me a great quiet and calm, and I seemed stilled and a kind of heavenly peace came over me—I thought after it must have been the peace that passeth all understanding.* It felt like that and came to me in a moment, stilling every thought. Sometimes now I ask for it—but it occurred to me the other day that it came that blessed moment when I was not asking for it, not thinking of any consolation for myself, only help and deliverance for them. And now, Cecco has come back out of all his wanderings which were short. And Tiddy has been taken from his, and his dear name covered over with love and grief so that nobody will ever reproach or say a word. Thou hast delivered his soul in perfect peace from the battle that was against him.* Yet oh that there should have been no other way.

I cut out of a newspaper and put in here a little poem of Swinburne* whom I never loved. It is dated three years ago, yet was published only the other day—for whom, for us? I have read it over and over again, scarcely able to see the words for tears.

Threnody

Watching here alone by the fire whereat last year
Sat with me the friend that a week since yet was near,
That a week has borne so far and hid so deep,
Woe am I that I may not weep,
May not yearn to behold him here.

Shame were mine, and little the love I bore him were,
Now to mourn that better he fares than love may fare
Which desires and would not have indeed its will,
Would not love him so worse than ill,
Would not clothe him again with care.

Yet can love not choose but remember, hearts but ache,
Eyes but darken, only for one vain thought's poor sake,
For the thought that by this hearth's now lonely side
Two fast friends, on the day he died,
Looked once more for his hand to take.

Let thy soul forgive them, and pardon heal the sin,
Though their hearts be heavy to think what then had been,
The delight that never while they live may be—

Love's communion of speech with thee,
Soul and speech with the soul therein.

Oh my friend, O brother, a glory veiled and marred!
Never love made moan for a life more evil-starred.
Was it envy, chance, or chance-compelling fate,
Whence thy spirit was bruised so late,
Bowed so heavily, bound so hard?

Now released, it may be,—if only love might know—
Filled and fired with sight, it beholds us blind and low
With a pity keener yet, if that may be,
Even than ever was this that we
Felt, when love of thee wrought us woe.

None may tell the depths and the heights of life and death.
What we may we give thee: a word that sorrow saith,
And that none will heed save sorrow: scarce a song,
All we may, who have loved thee long,
Take: the best we can give is breath.

A. C. Swinburne—Feb. 20, 1887

1st Jan. 1891

We have kept together the three of us, Cecco, Denny and I to see the New Year in and Cecco, my dearest, says to me, 'If someone whom you could properly trust had said "I will take Tiddy away from you, and you will have no communication with him, know nothing of my methods, nor where he is, not even how long the parting is to be, but at the end I will restore him as you have restored him as you have ever desired to see him, as he was before evil came"—would you have refused?' Oh no, no I would not have refused, nor have I refused him to God his Father whose perfect will is being performed in him now.* Oh no, I make no complaint. It is only nature that cries out. I wished my dear children as of old, many, many happy years. And my dear Madge who is away from us and longing so for her home.* God bless her and all of them—and my boys above, my own Tiddy, my darling and my dear Frank, who seems to have come nearer and my little Maggie, who is the eldest of them all—three above and three below. Cecco fully feels with me that he does not wish to think of them as knowing about us, as some people do. I should like to think that my Tiddy thought of us now and then as he might do were he away in India or America, an affectionate thought of what we would be doing in the old house—but oh I hope he has better things to think of, his work, whatever it may be, and the part he may be permitted to take in the great song that came into my mind the other day when I was importuning God to give me even in my imagination some glimpse of how he might be engaged. A minute or two after I got up from my knees. This came into my mind suddenly, 'The Lord God omnipotent reigneth'—I could not think how it came for a moment. And then it occurred to me that it is part of the Hallelujah chorus—and my mind leaped to the thought of my Tiddy in the heavenly choir in some humble place with his clear beautiful voice as clear as in his boyhood when I used to distinguish it among all the rest in Eton chapel—or think I did—Oh this was fantastic I know—and yet how can I tell that some tender messenger of God did not suggest the words to me that brought all that to my mind. I will try after this not to dwell so much on this subject which at present fills my mind every moment of my time and every thought—but resume the thread of my poor life—in this book I mean.

As for that life and that work for my daily bread which runs through everything with me, I dare not say how uninterrupted that has been. I have carried it on all this time steadily, a chapter a day, I suppose about twenty pages of an octavo book. Sir Walter when he was labouring to pay off his debts, speaks of writing a volume in twelve days* I think. I have done it steadily in sixteen. He says no man can keep it up for long—but I have kept it up in spite of everything now for months and months. The product is very different indeed—and the object so small beside his grand big magnificent struggle—this is for butter upon the daily bread—and little debts which I hoped to have cleared, but which all the dreadful expenses—and this move to Davos, which is so much dearer than living at home—will hinder me from doing. And I can't keep this up only because in all probability it will not be wanted, and I shall not have the work to do. In addition to this work I wrote a short story (worth thirty pounds) two or three nights after C and D had gone to bed. And I am perfectly well—quite well—I get through the day thus—and take a walk with Cecco in the afternoon in the snow and sunshine which he likes to take with me and sit through the evening with Denny alone generally, often reading a little Italian. And then when they are gone I write letters and cry (unless when I have proofs to do or some other work) cry often till I exhaust myself, thinking and thinking, sometimes pouring out my heart to the few people who care for it, who will bear with me, till I feel my head had been beaten and my heart thumps and throbs in my ears. And then I go to bed and sleep brokenly with many wakings, yet I sleep and next morning wake with still the beaten feeling in my head which goes off when I get up and I am quite well. And I am sixty-two, older than Sir Walter was when he died. I am a wonder to myself, a sort of machine, so little out of order, able to endure all things, always fit for work whatever has happened to me. And I take back what I said one of these evenings when I have written in this book, that I thought with elation of the fact that my press of work might be done in a certain time, and that I might hope to set far from this world. God will do to his servant as He thinks fit in this matter, but I will not desire to shorten my life by a day. *Non recuso laborem.** I said it when I had my boys to bring up. I say it again with tears. I *must* not desire to break up the house of the children who remain. My Tiddy has no need of me—and my longing for news of him is far less reasonable now when I know he is safe in His Father's hands, and that nothing can harm him, than when he was in Ceylon, when he was in the way of every harm.* But Cecco does need me and my poor girls to whom I mean home. Madge's painful sense of having to go on one visit after another with nobody of her very own to cling to shows me this very plainly. When it is God's will He will temper the wind to them, but I must not anticipate His time by a moment.

What a wonderful record is that journal of Sir Walter's which dear Annie Ritchie* has sent me—and with what love one watches everything he does. I have read over and over again what he says of his wife's death. It is so sober, so chastened, so true: 'I wonder how I shall do with the thoughts which were hers for thirty years.' And what shall I do with the thoughts that have been *his*, the endless anxieties, watching fears, hopes, questions, endeavours to understand, prayers for ever and ever, that have occupied so much of my life? I don't know how many prayers I have written out, to read out when my broken cries were all exhausted and incoherent. I have two in my purse now that I used to take out and repeat at odd moments. Oh vain repetitions,* but I cannot think that our dear Lord would think them so. And He has heard me for one if not for the other. God bless my Cecco and oh that he may give me his dear arm to support me, till he lays me in my grave. God grant this for Christ's sake that my son may lay me in my grave.

So one comes back again the weary round to one's self and to the prevailing thought which is not to be silenced. Sir Walter had no grief but that. His great struggle and the loneliness of which he complains so pathetically, the broken life, the endless courage were never brought to such an awful crisis as this of mine. No child died before him. It occurs to me that anything in the world could be lightly borne with that exception. And yet in the depths of my own sorrow I could weep for his and feel the choking in my throat, of which he speaks, for him. There never was a record so entirely of a man's own doings and thoughts which was so little egoistical, or entirely free of that self-regard which revolts even when it interests. He is so real in all, so sober, without exaggeration. Some fool in the newspaper speaks of him with the old foolish reproach about Abbotsford, that he cared nothing for his books, except as a way of making money, and so forth. It would be vain to try to explain him to such a mind, which is of a different species and knows not even the language which Scott speaks. It is the nationality perhaps, the national brotherhood that makes me feel as if it were a bigger me that was speaking sometimes, as if I could enter into anything, almost forgetting that these were not my own affairs. I feel I know him almost as I know myself.

[On 18 January 1891, Mrs Oliphant took up the thread of her chronological narrative. This portion of her story, which breaks at Frank's death in 1859, was written as a continuous manuscript, although the evidence suggests that it was in fact written at periods over the next three years and only given a formal conclusion after the next major event, Cecco's death on 1 October 1894.

Inserted at this point in the manuscript are two further pieces of writing from this period, the first (dated 13 February 1891), on a separate sheet, taken from the same loose-leaved volume in which the narrative is written, and the second (dated August 1892), written on her black-edged Windsor notepaper. She must have found the latter piece when she resumed her chronological narrative on 4 September 1892. Since the two fragments (February 1891 and August 1892) relate to her inner dialogue on the subject of Tids, I have placed them here before rejoining the chronological account of her past life.]

February 13, 1891

I came off my regular work just now, writing an article chiefly upon Newman* and it makes a difference to me having the support of that machinery, that framework, withdrawn. When I am left alone at night I feel as if I am left to meet the shadow that has been waiting for me all the day. The thought of all that is, and is not. The half of my life that is torn away. The keen consciousness coming upon me as it does periodically, like a new discovery, that it is the very Tiddy that is gone—not any other trouble, not any of the things that I am used to, but that he is gone, gone out of my life. Which is worst I ask myself. The dreadful care that used to fill my days, especially that evening time before dinner, when I remember saying so often that I was perfectly miserable, that I felt as if I could kill myself. Oh the habitual misery of that hour—the growing suspense and terror and expectation—more active misery perhaps than anything will cause me now—instead of it there is now this awful blank not to be relieved, the cloud that none lifts, the dull dark pressure, the empti-ness—which is worst? Oh how can I tell? I would not have that struggle removed for his dear sake who has got far from it. I would not have it removed. I would not return to the awful thoughts which used to seize upon me when I woke and which I so often compared to the vultures coming down upon Prometheus, the 'what would he do if I died?', 'who would care for him?', 'what would happen to him?' and all the terrible suggestions that used to come. I would not desire all that again, and yet,—Oh the blessed relief that would come by mo-ments when all was well, the unreasonable hopes, the lifting of my foolish heart always ready to rise whenever there was a possibility. The anguish was great, but it was life—now this is death—no hope any more, no lifting, the blank deepening down, the immoveable darkness, the silence; which is worst I know not. I know not: this because this is present, this is what I now have to bear.

And yet there are moments. The other morning before I got up there suddenly came into my mind a consciousness—as if he had come behind me and put his arm around me as he used to do and said with his head over my shoulder, 'And yet sometimes after all you were unjust to me, mother'—He has said these very words to me with this very look, not reproachful though it seems a reproach, smiling and tender as sometimes when there had been cause to blame and we had been reconciled. He was by nature only rarely resentful after the moment—was always sweet again directly. And so he was that morning, smiling in the affectionate, wistful way he had. It occurred to me that it was my own imagination that added the words, 'that is all over now'—I did not seem so sure of this—but I was of the others. It was no voice, nothing audible, only the look, the words in my heart. Was it he?, or was it only some trick of the mind? I cannot but think it was some momentary contact, permitted to give me a little strength—I do not wish to think that he lingers about us, that would be unnatural. I hope he has something better to do, some real work, something that occupies all his faculties. I keep praying and wondering if it is not presumptuous to pray for one whom his Father has taken into his own hands, praying that he may understand God's ways with him now and see more and more clearly what they are. I know nothing that I can ask for him but that, not any longer the endless prayer that he may be kept from temptation—but that he may see all the meaning of his Father's way and more and more clearly understand.

In one way it has set me free that he should have gone before me and I sometimes think it means that I am meant soon to be released. But my heart fails me when I think how entirely I represent home to the others—Oh if I could but see myself growing less necessary to them—if only they could learn to need me less. Perhaps I would not like it if they were all established in lives of their own. I might feel my loneliness as people say they do, but I think now it would be nothing but blessedness, that one of the girls at least, and my Cecco, should each find some one who would be the partner of their lives—and so be weaned from me—and not feel it so much, feel nothing but the natural regret, the few tears, wiped so soon: that is all that parents should have. Oh God grant me this great blessing. Grant that they may know that still close love of husband and of wife and homes and children. And that I may be made joyfully free, as thou has made me mournfully free, to think of my own dismissal.

I had forgotten this altogether, forgotten that I had ever written it down when I wrote this morning, Sept 4th. 92, the slip which I put in here with its mood so similar. Must there not be some meaning in the individuality, the distinct character of these two dreams?

August 1892

I want to put on record a dream which I do not pretend was any-thing more than a dream, but in which for the moment there was great comfort to me. I have very seldom dreamt of my boy, which is wonderful, seeing that my mind has always been full of him and that my last thought at night and my first in the morning is always of him, of both of them, mingled together, my two first and last prayers and thoughts as always—I dreamt that he came to me, behind me, which is always how I seem to be conscious of him and according to a habit he had in life, surprising me, putting an arm round me, then showing me his face. I recognized him however with joy and I think we walked a little together (in my dreams) in this positive in all happiness of a real meeting. I said to him 'are you forgiven' and he said, 'Yes'. Then I asked him 'what kind of life are you living?' and felt in my dream that I could not be sure whether he answered or whether I myself anticipated his answer by saying that it was not permitted to tell this. I remember clearly in my dreams my doubt whether he said it or whether it was suggested by my own mind. I woke in the morning with a strange sense of reality in this dream, but one knows how evanescent these impressions are and how soon the darkness comes back. Next night or soon after, before I went to bed, being very heavy and sorrowful, I entreated in my prayers that if there was anything true in the dream, if it was not delusion or imagination merely, there might be some repetition of it, but I felt in doing so that though the Father of us all would pardon the fond folly it was only a cry of trouble and longing and did not deserve to be called a prayer. But that night in my first deep sleep, I suddenly felt a great thrill of sensa-tion, a rush behind me (I seemed to be standing as before) as if it was the sudden rush of something coming quickly downward through the air; arriving almost with violence, with always that same feeling of an arm round me, and his head on my shoulder. I can remember nothing said, only the great rush of sensation, of touch, and certainty, and I woke saying aloud, 'Oh, my delightful boy, my delightful boy'.

January 18, 1891.

I forget where I left off in this pitiful little record of my life. It was with an attempt to remember somebody worth telling about in the old life in London. We began our housekeeping in Harrington

Square, a little place on the way to Camden Town, I think, whereabouts a number of artists had established themselves; though I remember at this moment only the Pickersgills,* and not even them very well. Then my Maggie was born, and my dear mother, then still living, had the joy and delight of her grandchild, the third Margaret,—one pleasure at least in that dreary ending of her life. I remember saying that there had been always something wanting to my mother, which I had felt without knowing what it was, till I saw her with my baby in her dear arms. Maggie was always a beautiful child. My dear little Marjorie was always pale and delicate, but with glorious eyes—to think of an eight months' old baby having these! But I remember that as she died she opened them widely and seemed to fix them on me as she lay on my knee, giving up her little soul in that look of consciousness, as it appeared to me. That was in 1855, thirty-six years ago, but I have never forgot the look with which that baby died.

After this we removed to Ulster Place, a larger house, which is the house in London upon which my mind dwells. I pass it sometimes going to King's Cross, when we have gone to Scotland, and a strange fantastic thought crossed my mind the first time I did so in these latter years, as if I might go up to the door and go in and find the old life going on, and see my husband coming down the road, and my little children returning from their walk. There was a kind of feeling of increasing prosperity when we went to that house, more feeling than reality; and I tried to make it pretty, though I fear it would have looked rather dreadful to the ideas of this changed time. It is at the corner of Ulster Place, looking down Harley Street, and next to a large square house with gardens, in which the Oudh princesses or begums lived when they came to England to plead their cause. Some of our windows looked over this garden, and we had glimpses of the strange eastern figures flitting about—the white robes and shawls, and gleaming ornaments and dusky faces.* Later Frank took a small house farther up the road near Baker Street, I think, to make a studio, and began to have his painted windows executed there under his own superintendence, partly because he was not satisfied with the way in which his designs were carried out, partly with the hope that he might then get into a substantial business, instead of precarious artistwork. There was a brightness and hopefulness about the beginning. We were both sanguine, and he dreamed of work that might go on under his eye and keep our household going, while he might return to his painting, which was the work he loved best. So things went on very brightly for a time. He painted his King Richard picture, which was sold for a tolerable price; and then that of the Prodigal, which I have still, and which I think a very touching picture. And orders came in for windows. And, best of all, our delightful boy was born. Ah, me! If I had continued this narrative at the time when I broke it off in 1888, I should have told of this event and all its pleasantness, if not with a light heart, yet without the sudden tears that blind me now, so that I cannot see the page. My beautiful delightful child, with all the little jests, that he had come too late for church, and so was unpunctual all his life after; my Sunday child, 'blythe and bonny and happy and gay,' as the old rhyme says. I was very anxious at his birth because of the two babies I had lost, and had implored the doctor, my old, kind, cranky Dr Allison, to examine him and tell me honestly if all was well with him. 'That fellow!' he said; 'he has lungs like a sponge.' How well I remember the room, the doctor's look, the baby that had brought joy with him, the flood of ease and happiness that came into my heart. The child was health itself, and vigour and sweetness and life. He was born on Sunday, November 16, 1856. And that winter was a happy and cheerful one. Sebastian Evans, then a fine young fellow fresh from Cambridge, turned aside from the current of his life because of the 'doubts,' then becoming a fashionable malady, which would not let him go into the Church, and drifting a little, not knowing what to do, came about a window, a memorial to his father; and he and Frank taking to each other, remained as an assistant to help with the cartoons, and by-and-by with the idea of being a partner and sharing the business. He is mixed in all this cheerful time for me. He cheered up my husband so; his great honest laugh recurs to me; his cheerful company, which drew Frank out of the worries and troubles with his workmen, and restored him to the buoyancy of youth and good fellowship. (I saw him, S. E., a few years ago with such a curious sense of the downfall that time makes—a limited rather petty person, instead of the genial young man to whom I had always been so grateful for the good cheer he brought into the studio, and the laugh that was so pleasant to hear.) When the idea of a partnership took shape, his brother, Mr John Evans, the well-known antiquary, who was also a business man—paper-maker, one of the

'Times' people—came to go through Frank's books (if he had any books), and see whether it was worth his brother's while. He came afterwards to dine, and it was not till he had gone, after all the long evening, that I heard what the decision was. After Mr Evans had seen and heard all there was to see and hear, he congratulated my husband that his circumstances permitted him to be so indifferent to profit. And there was an end of the partnership, to which I had looked forward for the sake of the companionship to Frank, I fear not with much thought of profit. We neither of us, I suppose, knew anything about business—so long as we could get on and live, that seemed all one cared for; but it was a little dash as of cold water when the businessman paid this satirical compliment, and showed us our true position. I was, of course, writing steadily all the time, getting about £400 for a novel, and already, of course, being told that I was working too fast, and producing too much. I linger upon this brief, and, as it feels to me now, halcyon time. I used the little back drawing-room, which was at first dining-room, for my work, the real dining-room of the house being Frank's painting-room, where I used to write all the morning, getting up now and then in the middle of a sentence to run down-stairs and have a few words with him, or to play with the children when they came in from their walk—my dear little Maggie, my baby-boy, two beautiful children, fresh and sweet, well and strong, reviving my heart, that had been so heavy and sore with the loss of my two infants, by the sight of their beautiful shining faces.

When I look back on my life, among the happy moments which I can recollect is one which is so curiously common and homely, with nothing in it, that it is strange even to record such a recollection, and yet it embodied more happiness to me than almost any real occasion as might be supposed for happiness. It was the moment after dinner when I used to run up-stairs to see that all was well in the nursery, and then to turn into my room on my way down again to wash my hands, as I had a way of doing before I took up my evening work, which was generally needlework, something to make for the children. My bedroom had three windows in it, one looking out upon the gardens I have mentioned, the other two into the road. It was light enough with the lamplight outside for all I wanted. I can see it now, the glimmer of the outside lights, the room dark, the faint reflection in the glasses, and my heart full of joy and peace—for what?—for nothing—that there was no harm anywhere, the children well above stairs and their father below. I had few of the pleasures of society, no gaiety at all. I was eight-and-twenty, going down-stairs as light as a feather, to the little frock I was making. My husband also gone back for an hour or two after dinner to his work, and well—and the bairns well. I can feel now the sensation of that sweet calm and ease and peace.

I have always said it is in these unconsidered moments that happiness is—not in things or events that may be supposed to caused it. How clear it is over these more than thirty years!

In the early summer one evening after dinner (we dined, I think, at half-past six in those days) I went out to buy some dessert-knives on which I had set my heart—they were only plated, but I had long wanted them, and by some chance was able to give myself that gratification. I had marked them in a shop not far off, and was pleased to get them, and specially happy. Some one had dined with us, either Sebastian Evans or my brother-in-law Tom,—some one familiar and intimate who was with Frank. When I came back again there was a little agitation, a slight commotion which I could not understand; and then I was told that it was nothing—the merest slight matter, nothing to be frightened at. Frank had, in coughing, brought up a little blood.

And so the happy time came to an end. I don't think I was much alarmed at first, I knew so little. I was quite ready to believe, after the first shock, that it might turn out to be nothing, and to have no consequences. I was much intent upon going to Scotland that year, I remember, to Mrs Moir at Musselburgh—and I did go, Frank promising to join me in a short time. After I was gone I took a great panic in my impulsive way and came in to Edinburgh on Sunday morning and telegraphed to him to know how he was, waiting about the railway station the whole of the Sunday to have an answer, but got none,—only a letter in due time scolding me for my foolishness. We had no habit of telegraphing in those days, it being still quite a new thing.

But he never was well after. I thought, and perhaps he too thought, that it was the worry of the work, which began to get too much for him, and the difficulty of managing the men, who were of the art-workmen class, and highly paid, and untrustworthy to the last degree. However important it might be to get the work done they were never to be relied upon, not even when they saw him—always most kind and friendly to them, incapable of treating them otherwise than if they had been gentlemen—ill, worn-out, dying by inches; not even when it became a matter of life and death for him to get free. They were well paid, educated in their way, thinking themselves a kind of artists—and I had always been brought up with a high idea of the honour and virtue of working men. I was very indignant at this behaviour, of course, and cruelly undeceived,—and I do not think I have ever got over the impression made upon me by their callousness and want of honour and feeling. I remember most wrathfully contrasting their behaviour with that of my maids, who stood by me to the last moment; knowing we were breaking up our home and going away, and that they would be in no respect advantaged by us, yet who were as loyal and true as the others were selfish and cruel. My husband did not like it to be said—but it was so. Before we decided definitely to give up everything and go abroad, Frank went to consult Dr Walsh, who was the great authority on the lungs at that time. He lived in Harley Street, I think. I went with my husband to the door, and leaving him there walked up and down the street till he came out again. I think he was to meet Mr Quain there, who was attending him at the time. And here again there is a moment that stands out clear over all these years. I was very anxious, walking up and down, praying and keeping myself from crying, sick with anxiety, starting at every sound of a door opening. He met me with a smile, telling me the report was excellent. There was very little the matter, chiefly over-work, and that all would be well when he got away. The relief was unspeakable: relief from pain is the highest good on earth, the most exquisite feeling,—I have always said so. It was in the upper part of Harley Street that he came up to me and told me this, and my heart leapt up with this delightful sense of anxiety stilled.

Afterwards, in Rome, Robert Macpherson* told me what he said was the true story of the consultation—that the doctors had told Frank his doom; that his case was hopeless, but that he had not the courage to tell me the truth. I was angry and wounded beyond measure, and would not believe that my Frank had deceived me, or told another what he did not tell to me. Neither do I think he would have gone away, to expose me with my little children to so awful a trial in a foreign place, had this been the case. And yet the blessed deliverance of that moment was not real either. The truth most likely lay between the two.

We left England in January 1859 to go to Italy. We neither of us knew anything about Italy, but that it was the sunny South—and of all places in the world it was Florence we chose to go to in the middle of winter,—Florence not as it is now, but cold and austere, without the comforts into which it has been trained since then. The journey was a dreadful one. Tom Oliphant went with us to Paris. I have no doubt that he felt he was taking leave of his brother for the last time. We were none of us experienced in Continental travelling, and in those days travellers were shut up in the waiting-rooms, not allowed to get into the train till the last moment. It was my first experience of having to take the management of things myself, and all was new to me, and my French of the most limited description. Thus it happened that what with my ignorance, and Tom's leave-taking, and the two children, and all the excitement and trouble together, our luggage was not registered, nobody thinking anything about it. We were to sleep at Lyons, and when we arrived there late at night the luggage was not forthcoming: we had no ticket,—I knew nothing about it. Nothing was to be done, accordingly, but to telegraph to Paris, and remain in Lyons till it came. We had travelled second-class, one of the few times we ever did so,—I have always had a stupid objection to this kind of economy, perhaps to all kinds of economy, though I have never been extravagant,—so I suppose our train was a slow one. I remember that there was a cheerful young fellow in our carriage who belonged to Beaucaire and who kept Frank amused, and, as it became cold in the afternoon, took off his own coat to add to the shawls and rugs that were piled upon him, and got out at one of the stations to bring a *chauffepied* or *chauffrette*—a thing filled with wood embers—for his feet: the hot-water stools which are such a nuisance now did not exist then, in second-class at least. How grateful I was to this young man, and how warmly I remember his kindness over all these years! The luggage episode made us very late. We were detained at the cold dark station at Lyons till all the other passengers were gone, and not a cab was to be found. At last we were allowed to share one that passed with a single passenger in it, and so got to our hotel—a helpless party as ever was. My poor Frank, ill and worn out, cold and miserable, myself so unaccustomed to manage, good Jane* who had never been in a foreign country before, and the two little ones, Maggie five, Cyril two—and nothing with us to make them comfortable, not even a hand-bag, not a nightgown for the chidren. These little miseries are very bad at the time, but I never was one to make much of them. I remember Lyons, however, as one of the coldest places I ever was in, and the great blank desolation of the immense Place Belcœur, I think. Next day Frank insisted that I should go out to see the place, though he would not leave the house himself, and I drove, taking Jane and the children with me, to Notre Dame de Fourvières, where there was a wonderful view over the town, and the strange little church full of ex-votos,* which I looked at with a bewildering ignorance, and with such an aching and miserable heart, realising for a moment all the misery of the journey, my inability to do anything for Frank, my utter solitude in this pretence at sight-seeing, which I was doing so against my will in obedience to his whim. I think that in some things I was younger than my years. I was thirty, but with very little experience of the world, and always shy and apt to keep behind backs. I forget if the luggage came that night, but I think it did, and there arose another difficulty. We were but very sparingly supplied with money, and had brought just enough for the journey to Marseilles and one night's rest at Lyons. Circular notes, I think, were scarcely used then,—at all events, what we had was a letter of credit. And next morning I found that we had not enough to pay our bill and journey, and that it was a *fête*, and the banks all closed. This sort of thing has never been a bugbear to me as to many people, and I went to the landlord of the hotel and told him exactly how things were, though with no small trembling. Nothing, however, could be more kind than he was. He would not even take from me what I could have paid him, but gave me the address of a hotel at Marseilles where he directed me to go, and pay his bill there. We went away, therefore, in much better spirits, having our boxes, and with that elated consciousness of having been kindly treated, which, I suppose, gives one a feeling somehow of having deserved it, of having been appreciated, for it certainly warms the heart and improves the aspect of everything. Frank must have been better, for I remember walking down to the harbour with him when we got to Marseilles, and discovering—with what thankfulness!—that the boat for Leghorn had sailed, and that we must either wait two days for another or go on by land. I hate the sea, and had always longed to do this, but had not, I suppose, liked to propose it, or else had been

overruled by my husband. We went on accordingly to Nice by diligence*, which was not very comfortable, for we were in the interior,
the five of us, with two other people,—a man and his son going to
Antibes, where the lad was to draw for the conscription. I forget
whether it was on this journey or when we were approaching Marseilles that the sunrise upon the new unaccustomed landscape struck
me so—'the awful rose of dawn'* coming over the wide sweep of the
country, the mulberry trees all stripped of their leaves, standing out
against the growing light. This seems rather a mingling of pictures;
but it is the impression that remains on my mind, and the great
silence and the sleeping faces of my companions grey in the rising of
the daylight. I remember, too, the delightful sweeps and folds of the
Maritime Alps, the green of the cork-trees, as I was told, and the
heavenly curves of the coast. Cannes, which I seem to see as little
more than a village, lying half on the hill and half on the beach, with
one great stout pine standing up against the extraordinary blue of the
sea. How familiar and commonplace later, how wonderful and novel
then, like Paradise, the gardens of oranges, the hedges of aloes! We
must have been about twenty-four hours in the diligence or more,
and got to Nice, I think, in the afternoon. By this time, I suppose, my
inclination to careless expenditure (such as it was, so little to anybody
that had any margin) must have got the better of Frank's wiser
instincts, for we stayed a day or two at Nice, and went the rest of the
way in a vettura.* So far as I recollect, we stopped only once—at
Alassio—between Nice and Genoa. I shall never forget that night: the
hotel was an old palace, and in those days comfort had scarcely
invaded even those coasts of the Riviera. We were taken into a huge
room with a shining marble floor, one or two rugs in front of the fire-
place and by the side of the bed, and no fire. The mere sight of the
place was enough to freeze the tired traveller, so ill and languid to
begin with. I feel still the chill that went into my heart at the sight of
this room, so unfit for him; but we soon got a blazing fire. I remember kneeling by it lighting it with the great pine cones, which blazed
up so quickly, and all the reflections, as if in water, in the dark
polished marble of the floor.

At Genoa we were somehow strangely fortunate. We went to what
I have always supposed to be the Hôtel de la Ville, but that must have
been a mistake, and I believe it was the Croce di Malta. It was one of
the hotels close to the bay, looking out over the terrace and promen-

ade that surrounds it. And here, again, the outlook being so lovely and rest so desirable, I wanted to stay. The landlady was English, and she offered me a beautiful suite of rooms, a great *salon*, commanding the view, with two large bedrooms attached to it. I was enchanted, but in terror for the price—when she said I might have it for eight francs a-day, the whole apartment. Why she was so good I never could tell. I think it was because of my bonnie little Maggie. Whether she had lost a child like her, or whether I only fancied so, I cannot tell. Perhaps the good woman was sorry for us all, and saw, as I did not see, how little chance there was that my husband would ever return. I recollect now the delight of the beautiful room—the walls all frescoed, not very finely perhaps, but yet the mere fact was something, the bay lying before the windows, and what was almost as beautiful at the moment—a great fire; not a few damp logs as we had been having, but a huge fire of coals and wood, which warmed my invalid through and through. I remember the glow of it and the children playing on the warm carpet, all so perfect a contrast to the last night's chill and misery, and the feeling of settling down in that comfort and warmth, though it was only for two or three days. My heart always contrived to rise whenever it had a chance, and I think Frank was pleased.

We got into Florence in a fog, and again very chill and tired. I remember thinking that it might have been Manchester for anything one saw or felt that was like the South, and as soon as that was possible left the hotel there for lodgings in Via Maggio. In all this our ignorance and want of experience did us great harm. The Via Maggio, a deep street of high houses on the other side of the Arno, was as unfavourable a spot as we could have chosen, and to make it worse we were on the shady side of the street. The recommendation it had was that the mistress of the house, Madame Gianini, was again an English, or rather I think, an Irish woman. We were on the second floor—a long straggling apartment with some rooms towards the Piazza Santo Spirito, I think; and these were sunny, and we ought to have hired them, but the *salon* was on the other side, and very cold. I had not sense to see how bad that must have been for Frank, but used the rooms as they were arranged in a helpless way. I think there was a dreadful time at first,—he suffering, unable for any exertion, sitting silent, without even books, till my soul was crushed, not knowing what to do or how to rouse him. I had to go on working all the time,

and not very successfully, our whole income, which was certain for
the time, being £20 a-month, which Mr Blackwood had engaged to
send me on the faith of articles. To think of the whole helpless family
going to Italy, children and maid and all, upon that alone!—but
things were very cheap in Florence then, and I don't think I was at
all afraid, nay, the reverse, always inclined to spend. Of course this
must have added to Frank's depression, for which I was sometimes
inclined to blame him, not knowing how ill he was. He got rheum-
atism in addition to other troubles; and I have the clearest vision of
him sitting close by the little stove in the corner of the room, wrapped
up, with a rug upon his knees, and saying nothing, while I sat near
the window, trying with less success than ever before to write, and
longing for a word, a cheerful look, to disperse a little the heavy atmosphere of trouble. I forget how we came to know a Mr Skottowe, a
lame man, who had been an artist, and who came to see us sometimes, to my great thankfulness, for he cheered Frank a little. There
was also the Scotch minister, Mr Macdougall, who is still in
Florence, and who sent several people to see me, a beautiful Miss
Macdonald among the rest, whose distinction was that she refused a
duke! and who had dedicated herself to her old father and mother,
then very old, and she no longer young,—a very attractive woman,
whose sacrifice I grudged dreadfully, though she did not. I might
have got into a little society, but had no desire to do so, nor any
pleasure in it. I remember Frank going to see the Pitti or Uffizi for
the first time, and coming back in a kind of despair: his feeling was
not the *anch' io pittore,* * but the other far less cheerful sense of what
wonders had been done, and how far he was from being able to come
within a hundred miles (as he thought) of what he saw. No doubt illness had much to do with this depression, which I, all sanguine and
sure that he could do what he would, were he but well, did not
sympathise in,—almost, I fear, felt to be a weakness. He recovered his
spirits a little after a time, when the winter began to pass away and
good weather came. I remember, however, with great and terrible
vividness one scene, one day. It was the funeral day of a young Arch-
duchess. I forget who she was: the wife of one of the Archduke's sons,
who had died away from Florence and was brought home for burial.
Frank, who was sometimes hard on me, as I on him, insisted that I
should go out to see the procession, which I did most unwillingly all
alone. It must have been very early in the year, for it was at his worst

time. I walked as far as the Porta Santa Trinità, I think, and I don't think I saw any procession. It was a grey day, the sky heavy, the Arno running grey under the bridge, the hills all grey, the air tingling with the tolling of the bells, and sombre streams of people flowing towards the gate where the funeral train was to come in; as sad as any could be, a young woman forlorn, with nobody to give me even a kind look, and nothing before or about me that was not as grey and tragic as the skies. I paused a little there, having been carried so far by the instinct of pleasing him who had sent me out to see; and then I could bear it no longer and went back again, to find him sitting silent as before by the fire.

But things brightened, as I have said, when the weather improved and it began to get warm. He thought of a picture to paint, a scene in which Macchiavelli should be the chief figure, and we began to visit the galleries, and to go out together. All sorts of strange things—not strange at all now, but wonderful then—went on in Via Maggio. Scarcely a night passed but we heard the chant of a passing funeral, and going to the window saw far below, as in a deep gorge, the torches glowing, the strange figures of the *confraternita** carrying the bier, and their tramp on the stony causeway. Sometimes it was the *misericordia*,* carrying not the dead but somebody hurt by an accident; and in the daytime the deep street underneath was always a diversion, and I used to look out for the dearest sight of all—two little figures at the feet of tall Jane, or rather the one dear figure at her feet, the other always with a song or shout, in her arm against her ample shoulder. She was always very big, at this time about four-and-twenty, a finely developed, strong, large, substantial tower of a woman—the ox-eyed Juno, as we used to call her. Ah me! would they come down from the Boboli gardens with their hands full of anemones if I were at the windows of the Casa Grassini now?

While we were there the revolution occurred*—which so much as we saw of it, was more like a popular *festa* than anything else. We had not known, being strangers and Frank so ill, going out little, what was going on; but a curious agitation and excitement made itself somehow felt in the air even up in our second floor. I don't know really except by a sort of sympathetic instinct what it was that took us to the windows to watch the unusual coming and going. And then suddenly opposite us, in the Casa Ridolfi, I think, there was unfurled a great Italian tricolour—the green, white, and red—and in a moment like fire the whole population seemed to blaze out in the national colours, man, woman, child, and horse, every living thing; and there began to be a shout of 'Viva l'Italia!' everywhere, wherever two people met in the deep streets, a shout that my dear baby boy took up in that little voice of his that was never silent. I was very eager too; but Frank was a little nervous, and unwilling to be in any way mixed up in the crowd, with whose doings we, as strangers, he thought, had nothing to do. I got him, however, at last to come out, and we went up to the front of the Pitti Palace, where a great many people were hanging about, and where at that moment the Grand Duke was in full colloquy with the representatives of the people. Notwithstanding the excitement of which I was full, it was a little forlorn to stand out there with our very faint knowledge of Italian, and nobody to tell us what was going on; and Frank had no desire to be in the heart of the revolution, if it was a revolution, as I had. Where all the cockades, the rosettes, the ribbons, the little bouquets, all the red, white and green came from, at a moment's notice, or without even a moment's notice, was an endless wonder to me; and the delight of the people, and the air of universal holiday, had none of the graver features that one expected. I am not sure that I was not a little disappointed at the entire peacefulness of the whole proceeding. We heard afterwards that the Grand Duke had given orders for the bombardment of the town, which would have had a fine effect indeed in Via Maggio had it taken place, but I don't know that the report was true.

Florence was at this time the very cheapest place to live in I have ever known. We had, like most other strangers, our dinner sent from the Trattoria every evening. It was the usual sort of meal, soup, two kinds of meat, one of them generally a chicken, a vegetable dish, and a *dolce*;* plenty for us all, with fragments left over, and the price was five pauls, not quite two francs fifty centimes. I wonder anywhere in Europe that could be had now?

We had brought an introduction to the Embassy, and the Embassy sent us huge cards in return, but took no more notice, which was just as well: what disappointed me more was, that the Brownings, to whom also we had letters, had left Florence for Rome, where we saw them subsequently. By this time I must have written, I suppose, some half-dozen books or more, and had a little bit of reputation, a very little bit in a small way, but was very anxious it should be kept to ourselves. Just before we left Florence, I remember Mr Skottowe came one day quite excited; he had heard this from Mr Macdougall, who had heard it accidentally from some one else. 'I thought,' he said, 'I had found out there was something out of the common for myself, and now it appears all the world knows.' I wonder if I should have remembered that, if it had not been a compliment. I did not get many sweetmeats of the kind, so I suppose it was a little pleasure to me. I do not know that Florence itself impressed me very much: how should it, with my mind so full of other things?—my sick husband, my little children, my work, and the precariousness of our means of living (though I don't think that troubled me much). I remember nature—as I always do—more than art, and the view from Bellosguardo above all the treasures of the galleries. Frank was profoundly, depressingly, as I have said, impressed by the pictures at first—and all the glory of them. I for my part used to stray into one small room in the Pitti, I think, where at that time the great picture of the Visitation—Albertinelli's—hung alone. By that time I knew that another baby was coming, and it seemed to do me good to go and look at these two women, the tender old Elizabeth, and Mary with all the awe of her coming motherhood upon her. I had little thought of all that was to happen to me before my child came, but I had no woman to go to, to be comforted—except these two.

Florence was just becoming warm and bright and good for an invalid to live in, when Frank was seized with a desire to go to Rome. I think he had heard from Robert Macpherson,* to whom he was ttached. I had only seen him once in London, and he was too noisy, o much unlike anything I knew, to please me. And I was very much aid for the children. It was just the time when people are leaving, going to, Rome; and one heard of malaria and fever and all sorts readful things. But Frank had set his heart upon it, and there was ing more to be said. I think it very likely that, feeling himself no er, and having the doctor's verdict, which he had not told me, in mind, he wanted me to be near the Macphersons, who would be a p and stand by. We went on accordingly to Rome in May. I had t been very successful in my work for 'Blackwood.' I sent a story of lorence called 'Felicita,'* I think (knowing nothing about Florence!), and other articles, not good, and I suppose I must have written something for Mr Blackett while in Florence, but I cannot recollect.* We could not certainly have struck our tents as we did and moved on to Rome, by steamboat from Leghorn to Civita Vecchia, on our twenty pounds a-month. I remember all about the journey strangely enough, from the green water, so translucent and profound under the boat, that took us out to the steamer at Leghorn, and the remarks of some Irish ladies, who were the companions of the voyage, and who made friends with the children, and suggested, perhaps guessing from some sad look in my face, that there had been some loss between the two,—there were but three years between them, but there had been two babies born to die: I don't remember their names nor anything about them except that, and that they were kind—and Irish. Half of the people I have met travelling have always been Irish. Maggie was five and a half, with her brown curls falling on her shoulders, and my little Cyril was two and a half; always the sweetest, most winning child. He had been called Cyril at first, then by himself when he began to talk Tiddy, which was always his family name all his life, though not a pretty one; sometimes Tids, which is almost too dear, too familiar and tender, the most caressing of all, to be thought of now. But I must not begin to write of my boy, or I will not be able to think of anything else—not five months yet since he has been taken from me!

The Macphersons had a curious position in Rome, and it is difficult to describe them. I believe he always had a curious position,—the son of a very poor man in Edinburgh with the humblest connections, yet not distantly related, I believe, to Cluny Macpherson, the chief of the clan; himself a poor painter—literally a poor painter, never good for very much, yet always, as I have been told, in society, and with friends quite beyond his apparent position. There was some romantic story about a lady in the Highlands, intercepted letters and so forth, which was told on one side as the reason for his leaving the country with something like a broken heart, but on the other was made to appear like the disappointment of a fortune-hunter. I don't know which was true. There was very little that was like a fortune-hunter in his careless, hot-headed, humorous, noisy Bohemian ways. He had given up his painting in Rome, and had taken to photographing; and his photographs of Rome were, I think, among the first that were executed. He had been a long time in Rome, had been there during the bombardment, and I suppose had rendered some services to the papal side, for he was always patronised more or less by the priests, and was *Nero** to the heart, standing by all the old institutions with the stout prejudices of an old

Tory quite inaccessible to reason. Indeed reason had nothing to do with him. He was full of generosities and kindness, full of humour and whim and fun—quarrelling hotly and making up again; a big, bearded, vehement, noisy man, a combination of Highlander and Lowlander, Scotsman and Italian, with the habits of Rome and Edinburgh all rubbed together, and a great knowledge of the world in general and a large acquaintance with individuals in particular to give force to the mixture, and to increase his own interest and largeness as a man. I could not bear him at first, poor Robert,—we used to quarrel upon almost every subject; but in the end I got to be almost fond of him, as he was, I believe, of me, though we were so absolutely unlike. Some years before I was married he had married Geraldine Bate,* a niece of Mrs Jameson, very much against the aunt's will, to whom the Roman photographer seemed a very poor match for her pretty Geddie at eighteen. And so he was, and it was not a very successful marriage, chiefly perhaps, notwithstanding my indignation with the popular fallacy about mothers-in-law, because of the constant presence in their house of Mrs Bate, who, though entirely maintained by his bounty, constantly encouraged Geddie in her little rebellions against her husband and her love of gaiety and admiration. But Robert was no meek victim, and never hesitated to tell Mamma his mind. There used to be a fierce row often in the house, from which he would stride forth plucking his red beard and sending forth fire and flame; but when he came back would have his hands full of offerings, even to the mother-in-law, and his face full of sunshine, as if it had never known a cloud. Geddie was of course full of faults, untidy, disorderly, fond of gaiety of every kind, incapable of the dull domestic life which seemed the right thing to me, ready to go off upon a merrymaking at a moment's notice, indifferent what duty she left behind, yet just as ready to give up night after night to nurse a sick friend, and to put herself to any inconvenience to help, or take entirely upon her shoulders, those who were in need. And though full of natural indolence, working like a slave—nay, as no slave ever worked—at the common trade, the photographing, at which she did quite as much, if not, people said, more than, he did. And a pretty creature, and full of vivacity and wit, a delightful companion. A strange house it was, a continual coming and going of artists and patrons of artists; of Scottish visitors, of Italian great personages and priests, and more or less of all the English in Rome. They were, I think, in one of their best times (for they had many vicissitudes) when we went to Rome first in 1859—and saw everybody.

My husband was much revived at first by the change and by the company of Robert, to whom he had a faithful and long attachment from his boyish days, and we went with them to their *villeggiatura** at Nettuno in May. It is now, I believe, a sea-bathing place, well enough known; but then it was the rudest Italian village, one of the most curious places I have ever seen. I described it in a little sketch I made for 'Blackwood,' calling it a seaside place in the Papal States, or some such title.* The rooms, the living, everything was inconceivably rough, the place like a great medieval fortress upon the rocks, with the natural agglomeration of houses hanging about its skirts. The women were handsome and wore a beautiful dress, red satin in long box-plaits, Greek jackets embroidered with gold, and beautiful embroidered white aprons and kerchiefs, with a very pretty half-eastern, half-houri head-dress. We had some very bad and some good days there. Very bad at first, and I very miserable; but later Frank took to working, and made one very pretty picture of a group of lads from the country, whom he saw and brought into the loggia to stand to him. It hangs in my drawing-room now. He also made two sketches of the place itself, which are in my own room, his last work. This must have meant that he was feeling better. But I remember some dreadful scenes in the middle of the night, when his nose-bleeding came on, and I stood by him for hours, holding the nostril till the blood dried, he going to sleep in the meantime, while I stood with the traces all about as if I were murdering him. I remember one time when they all went off along the coast to Astura, the Macphersons and Frank with them, leaving me alone with the children,—probably my own fault, as I always had a foolish proud way of holding back,—and how I got over my little disappointment, and did my very best to get a good dinner for them to come back to, and arranged everything as nicely as possible, yet when they did come, could not keep it up, and was sulky, and injured, and disagreeable, notwithstanding that I had really taken a great deal of trouble to have everything ready and pleasant for the party. What trifles remain in one's mind! I suppose it was because I contrived to be half sorry for myself, and half ashamed of myself, that I remember this so clearly.

When we left Nettuno we went to Frascati, where we lived for more than three months, I think, and which at first was very pleasant with its great prospect over the misty Campagna, where St Peter's was visible, the only sign of the existence of Rome. We used to go out and walk on the terrace from whence there was that view,—and sometimes had a little society, the Noccioli, and Monsignor Pentini, afterwards Cardinal—an old benign priest, who had been a soldier in Bernadotte's army, and then was supposed too liberal for promotion, having been kept back a long time from the Cardinal's hat he ought to have had. He was very kind, very benignant, the providence and at the same time the judge of all the poor people round, whom he kept from litigation, settling all their quarrels. I remember once or twice supping with him and good Ser Antonio, and his fat big Irish wife,—such good simple people, Monsignor not able to talk to me, nor I to him, though he gave me many a kind look. I understood pretty well what he said, but could not express myself either in French or Italian. The Noccioli lived in the upper floor of his big old square house, with a wonderful view from the windows, and partially frescoed walls, scarcely any furniture, and a supper-table gleaming under the three clear flames of the Roman lamp, and on the melons on the table, which Monsignor ate, I remember, with pepper and salt. But Frank grew very ill here. He became altogether unable to eat anything, not comparatively but absolutely; and the awful sensation of watching this, trying with every faculty to find something he could eat, and always failing, makes me shiver even now, though, God help me! I have had almost a repetition of it. We got an Italian doctor there, who was quite cheerful, as I believe is their way when nothing can be done, and spoke of our return next year, which gave me a little confidence. On the 1st of October we went back to Rome, to an apartment we had got in the Noccioli's house in the Babuino, where he got worse and worse. We had Dr Small, who brought a famous French doctor, and they told me there was no hope: it was better to tell me *franchement*, the Frenchman said, and that word *franchement* always, even now, gives me a thrill when I read it. They told me, or I imagined they told me in my confused state, that they had told him, and I went back to him not trying to command my tears; but found they had not told him, and that it was I in my misery who was taking him the news. I remember he said after a while, 'Well, if it is so, that is no reason why we should be miserable.' In my condition of health I was terrified that I might be disabled from attending my Frank to the last. Whether I took myself, or the doctor gave me, a dose of laudanum, to check incipient pains, I don't remember; but I recollect very well the sudden floating into ease of body and the dazed condition of mind,—a kind of exaltation, as if I were walking upon air, for I could not sleep in the circumstances nor try to sleep. I thought then that this was the saving of me. I nursed my husband night and day, neither resting nor eating, sometimes swallowing a sandwich when I came out of his room for a moment, sometimes dozing for a little when he slept—reading to him often in the middle of the night to try to get him to sleep. And when I came out of the room and sat down in the next and got the relief of crying a little, my bonnie boy came up and stood at my knee and pulled down my head to him, and smiled all over his beaming little face,—smiled though the child wanted to cry too, but would not—not quite three years old. When his father was dead I remember him sitting in his bed in the next room singing 'Oh that will be joyful, when we meet to part no more,' which was the favourite child's hymn of the moment. Frank died quite conscious, kissing me when his lips were already cold, and quite, quite free from anxiety, though he left me with two helpless children and one unborn, and very little money, and no friends but the Macphersons, who were as good to me as brother and sister; but had no power to help beyond that, if anything could be beyond that. Everybody was very kind. Mr Blackett wrote* offering to come out to me, to bring me home; and John Blackwood wrote bidding me draw upon him for whatever money I wanted. I had sent for Effie M., my husband's niece, to come out to me, sending money for her journey; but her mother arrived some time after Frank's death, his sister, Mrs Murdoch—a kind but useless woman, who was no good to me, and yet was a great deal of good as a sort of background and backbone to our helpless little party,—for I was young still, thirty-one, and never self-confident. And there we waited six weeks till my baby was born—he as fair and sweet and healthful as if everything had been well with us. My big Jane was my stand-by, and took the child from the funny Italian-Irish nurse, Madame Margherita, who attended and cheered me with her jolly ways, and brought me back, she and the baby together, to life. By degrees, so wonderful are human things, there came to be a degree of comfort, even cheerfulness; the children being always bright,—Maggie and Tiddy the sweetest pair, and my bonnie rosy baby. While I write, October 5, 1894, he, the last, is lying in his coffin in the room next to me—I have been trying to pray by the side of that last bed—and he looks more beautiful than ever he did in his life, in a sort of noble manhood, like, so very like, my infant of nearly thirty-five years ago. All gone, all gone, and no light to come to this sorrow any more! When my Cecco was two months old we came home—Mrs Murdoch and Jane and the three children and I—travelling expensively as was my way, though heaven knows our position was poor enough.

When I thus began the world anew I had for all my fortune about £1000 of debt, a small insurance of, I think, £200 on Frank's life, our furniture laid up in a warehouse, and my own faculties, such as they were, to make our living and pay off our burdens by.

2nd October 1894

Four years have not quite passed since the terrible event which rent as I have said my life in two. What can I say now? It is gone altogether, like a bladder that has burst. I have no life any longer, for Cecco has followed Tiddy. The younger after the elder and on this earth I have no son—I have no child. I am a mother childless. My dear Madge and Denny are as dear and as near as if they were my daughters, yet they are not in point of fact and my own children, my very own, born of me, have all been taken away from me. The little ones I have no occasion to think of, they are so far away, babies and no more. My Maggie was a deep rent in my life, but that too has gone into the distance. But my two boys were left, my two boys, the two boys always so spoken of though they were men, for which some people smiled at me. Cecco, my darling, has been his mother's boy all his dear life. He was born after his father died. He has known nobody but me, no protector, no provider, but his mother. They say I have been foolish in my treatment of them. One cruel man the other day told me I had ruined my family by my indulgence and extravagance.* I do not honestly before God think so. It is my comfort (a little, little comfort) to think now that nothing they wanted which was good and honest and which I could get for them was ever denied them, but these were not evil things, not wrong things for them to have. I meant, having no money to leave them, to endow them with the best education, and a happy youth. I could get them that. I could not make a fortune for them, alas, alas. This education has not come to much, in any case—my Tiddy, God forgive and bless him, partly by his own fault, my Cecco by the long burden of illness which has kept him back, have not achieved those high hopes which I seemed so fully justified in forming. They were well-equipped and beyond the average in ability, both, but did nothing to verify this to the world. We ourselves only know, and a few people here, what they were. When Tiddy was taken from us, Cecco did everything for me. He was in a hopeful way of health then. He came forward as my inspiration and the master of the house and was my steadfast support and help and even guide at that dark moment—so much so that now when this still darker——comes and he himself is taken, I keep watching and thinking that surely he is coming up the stairs, coming in to stand by me, though it is he who is lying in the next room where he has slept since he was a little boy, always next me with a door between us. He is lying there now on his own bed, looking so calm, so strong, as well as if he had never known what sickness was, his face rounded out, looking as he looked when we went to Pau. God bless him. He died not of the lungs, which we have been so unhappy about, but of exhaustion after inflammation of the throat and tongue which Dr Miller ascribes to the drains, which I had so carefully put in order last year. So are we mocked. He had been ill about ten days, getting better and then relapsing, but the disease was gone. But his strength went too, he had very little to begin with. He was very ill all Monday; it is only yesterday, but it seems to me so far away—only at the very last he made a rally, that the doctor and even I were deceived, but then suddenly fell back and in a few minutes breathed as peacefully away as ever an infant did. He had no pain. He knew nothing about it, had no apprehensions so far as I am aware, but just went in a moment from his mother holding his cold hands to God. And oh to see him lying there. What have I left now? No life, for all my days were filled out with him. No hope, for this world, no anxiety more, no prayers. I feel as if I had even quarrelled with my God who says so often whatever you ask believingly . . . My life for these some years past and still more for the last three months has been one long continued prayer and every day I have looked and watched for its fulfillment. It seems to me as if God had broken his word to me, leaving me here helpless with my hands stretched out, refusing me with an unreasonable silence. Everything has gone from me—my two sons who were my all, and all the stir of life, and all the occupations that were in them. Denny now will take care of me and I have no one henceforward to take care of. My work is over, my house is desolate. I am empty of all things. I don't feel as if I had anything even to pray about, or, if there was any hope, that my prayers would ever be granted. The heavens are to me as brass*—no answer comes, except about work and the means of living for which God has always opened the way to me, almost miraculously I have often thought. I would pray that he would take me with my boy, but I am as strong as an elephant. All this misery does not give me even a headache. I neither eat nor sleep for days together and I am as well at the end of them as at the beginning. What is to become of me, shall I never die?, but just linger on, making a little struggle for daily bread, like Lady Bell forever and ever. Lady Bell is ninety and has all her sons and daughters within reach, and thinks it the course of nature. So it is, but not for me. Self pity is a great temptation, but it is strange above reason how everything has failed with me. My three boys, for Frank was mine too—all now gone—and all the hopes that were involved in them. Madge married too and in an unfortunate way.* All failure, failure everything, and I am thought a successful woman, but everything I touch seems to go wrong.

Can I tell what my Cecco was—he was only my Cecco to me, more than half of myself, my dearest child, closest, most confidential companion, with sharpness sometimes and impatience and then outbursts of childlike confidence. I wait for his cry of 'Mamma'—for he never gave up the childish title—from the other room, a little impatient, knowing full well that everything would be thrown aside to answer it. Tiddy called 'Mother' in a different way, but I was always 'Mamma' to Cecco and I think, though he had all a man's experience, that save for one boyish inclination towards a pretty girl, he never put any woman near his mother in his heart. My boy, my own, my child, though he was a man, thirty four, and Tiddy four years ago was thirty three—in the fullness of their life. I used to think of both that they were the age our Lord is supposed to have been and would have a special fellowship with Him. Has he shown it by taking them away? Does he provide, as I sometimes think, some special work for those whose lives were unfulfilled here? Oh so many, so many, all unfulfilled—whom I used to pray for in the fullness of my heart. And now both of my own are among them—my sons born and bred and tended all their lives by me, no-one else doing anything for them. And now my trust is over, but in such a way. Once more has that prayer of mine which I think I recorded when writing about Tiddy,* which seemed to be forced from me against my will, that if it was indeed God's will to take them and they needed me I might have strength to guard them and save them to the end. This only of all my prayers has been granted. I have brought them all the way through many a trouble from their birth to their graves. Tiddy was only three when his father died—and no one ever helped me. I have done every-thing for my boys—I have been very faulty in their education, but what was wrong was done in love and not wrongly meant. And now my work is accomplished, my trust fulfilled however badly. Lord now lettest thou thy servant depart in peace.* Make me not to live and live and never die.

Everybody is very kind of course—people are always kind and I am like Job, such a monument of endless sorrow, always beginning and beginning once again. And it is so hard not to ask why—I made myself a theory long ago that when one dies it is a secret between God and them and that no one else, however their lives or happiness may be involved, has anything to do with it. And I think this is true. But no, asking is no good, nor discussing the terrible question. My son, my Cecco was so weak that he could not have lived much longer anyhow, but that is no reason, for it would have been as easy for God to make him completely well, or partially well—and there would have been no miracle wanted—only a turn of the balance for good—instead of for evil—it all hung on a thread, and if it had pleased God. How vain is all this for it has not pleased God, and all is vain, their very birth, their careful education, my endless struggle that they should have every training, every enjoyment, all vain, vain, and they as if they had never been born. All my life is vanity. What a struggle I have had, what endless work and striving, and all ending in these two graves. If I had broken down as many women might in that sad time in Rome after my husband died, before Cecco was born, how very, very little difference would it have made. The children would have sunk too, with nobody to take care of them, and it would all have ended so much sooner—whereas there has been between nearly thirty-five years of warfare and hard labour and this the end, but nobody thinks that the few books I will leave behind me count for anything. I have no such thought. The world would have been none the worse and the children little the worse if I had dropped by the side of their father's grave, they would only have got to the end a little earlier, or perhaps by hard training or adversity have lived and thriven as had not been granted to me. Cecco would have gone with me unborn had that been so—I am wrong to say it—his dear life, his spirit so fanciful, so sensitive, yet in its way so strong could not have been left out. It is only now it comes upon me in writing to Mr Hutton* that for all these years which the shadow of his illness has been upon him, he never repined. He did not complain of being unable to do what other young men did, never, never—but always looked forward to resuming his life—I think he never thought of death. He wrote to me now and then when he was away, wonderful letters, full of the deepest, sometimes of very sad thoughts—but never complained. His little impatiences and irritations and hasty temper were his only faults, except for one little awful moment in Oxford long past [sic] away and forgotten. And of the companion, the master, the object of every thought that he has been to me—my son—how I have said my son, quoting him for ever—and now nevermore can I quote him, or tell anybody 'Cecco says', words that were always in my mouth—But yes, I must resist that impulse that has made me hitherto bury any dear name in my heart and make me feel I could not bring it to ordinary talk.

6th October

Cecco's funeral day. I thought at first I could not go, but then bethought me that I could not let him be laid in his grave only by those who loved him in a secondary degree. They were all fond of him. God bless them for it, but only I and Denny were his very own. So I went and laid my boy in his last rest. I can feel at least that I have never left him until the moment when no one earthly would be with him any more. He was still as beautiful as ever this morning. I sat about an hour by him before the final moment came and covered his dear beautiful face with my handkerchief before I left him, never to be moved. His look was more even than I have already described. It was so fresh, even with those closed eyes seeming to meet everything, that solemn feeling, undaunted, with a manliness and fearlessness, as of one who had perfect dependence, yet independence—gazing straight before him with open face—those words 'with open face' come constantly into my mind. I don't remember where they come from, they seem to embody everything. 'With open face beholding the glory of God'*—I forget if that is right, and independent too, as if in utter confidence and frankness, keeping always an individuality of his own—all this was in his look. I feel as if we had never known and never done justice to his character, any more than to his face till now. Ah me these are fine things to say and in a way they comfort one and give a character above truth for the moment, but God knows I would give all the noble thoughts in the world for that one impatient quick cry of 'Mamma' from the next room, the empty room, whence he has been taken away for ever—God bless him. I can say nothing else. I said it over his grave before I left it—but what need is there of that —for God has blest him, and he wants none of my prayers now. But I must pray for him, for I have no habit of any other prayers, all was for him—when I stop that I must be silent altogether. My heart is warm to George——who says he was his best friend and to Dr Hornby who says he has an affectionate recollection of both of my boys and above all Mr Rose who writes I am sure out of a full heart saying 'my Cecco'—God bless them all for loving him—it is the only thing in which a little solace lies.

And now we have come back to the empty room and the empty home, but we cannot stay here, three forlorn women, for Fanny* has made herself one of us for ever by her certain share in our sorrow. We must go away, I think to London, though the London darkness rather frightens me. Something that will not be here and yet will be within reach of their graves. I have no worship of the graves myself. I have always felt with Tiddy that I would rather, if possible, forget it and remember him only as living not dead, but the two together breaks down that anti-superstition as if it were a superstition. This in Eton is another home, there is my place waiting, there are they both, the two men of the family, all our stay and comfort. We must keep within reach.

I have found a little, not comfort, but fellowship in reading about Archbishop Tait.* I did not like his book. I thought it too personal, too sacred for publication, but now brought down to the very dust, I turned to it with a sense of common suffering.* We are none of us pious like him and his wife, not praying together or talking as they do—too little, I know too little. Sometime Cecco has written to me, and I to him out of the depths of our hearts, but we have scarcely prayed together except that one night, before Tiddy was carried away to his grave. I think he would not have liked it from me, the two boys had that impression, got I don't know how, that a woman should not lead in that way—at least I think so. And then I am so slow of speech, and frightened, but we all know how we felt. They went seldom to Church, and I too have gone seldom of late—but never a shadow came over this faith, either one or the other. I was very very much touched tonight to read that Archbishop Tait used the very same words that I have been doing—that he was only three years and a half from 70 and therefore could not be long after his boy.* He was just four years, and his wife only six months. May that fate be mine, or if not hers, at least his. She was the strongest of the two. Oh, how thankfully I should take up my life again. How cheerfully I should finish my work if I could be sure of being like her.

Bishop B—came today and gave us Communion, very kind, full of feeling—and I was able to feel a little, to be moved out of this deadness for a few minutes, but always impressed by the ceremony, by the force of observation that wakes in me by my consciousness of every trivial incident, of the look of his figure against the light, of every detail, and with the sense of winding myself up to it and being wanting—of thinking of everything but the one thing, distracted by everything, only quite real when I am quite alone. God help me as from a trivial irritation with such a load to bear. Tait must have been exactly my age when his Crauford died, sixty six and a half—and to have taken precisely the same comfort—but oh much better than I.

Monday 8 October.

I am trying to wile away the dreadful afternoon, the day week of his death day. He was sleeping on unconscious but very naturally at this time—the nurse came at five o'clock. I said to the nurse 'I think my son is dying'. She said, 'Oh no, not to cry', that she had seen illness as bad, but very falteringly and then shortly after, she began to give his spoonful of brandy and he did come round a little, a faint flutter came back to his cold wrist—by the time the doctor came after hours of this the last rally had begun. Oh I have told it all before—why should I repeat it now? I am in a fever of endless misery I cannot keep still. Oh Cecco where are you? my trouble is more than I can bear. Can none of you come to me my boys to help me? Oh surely, surely, you must know how watchful and desolate I am. I am not the better for anybody else. I am best alone. I want my Cecco. Oh I want my God, my God to put his hand on me and either kill or calm—the first best—If I could be ill, not always in this horrible kind of bodily well-being, it might do me a little good—But what is the use? I must quiet myself, I cannot die. I must wait God's pleasure. It is not in me to take a dose and end it. Oh I wish it were, but my mind rejects the thought as unworthy. Lord, I can't kill myself, I can't move away, release me for Jesus sake. Oh Lord, Lord forgive me, but I would do for his sake what thou wilt not do. I would not refuse a poor woman's prayers for his sake. And He is thy son and there blest lives in ever-lasting communion, yet takest my sons from me and refusest to help me. Oh father, forgive me I know not what I say.*

Oh the cheerful light and the warm fire downstairs and the girls who would fain do anything for me. But nobody can do anything for me. I sat by his bedside holding one of his cold hands in mine trying to warm it with my cheek upon it and my lips, but never even when he rallied did any warmth come. The suggestion of horrible accident in it all—of those drains, drives me into a fever. Oh not that, not that. Let me feel it was the will of God that it was well for him, though cruel for me. Lord if thou hadst been cruel to me to save him how willingly I would have accepted it—make me to feel that it is thus now, that to deliver him, which had to be, thou wouldst not spare me—I could bear it if I could feel this. But what folly is all this, for bear it I must. I cannot escape. I must take up my cross. I must submit. Oh this body and soul so full of anguish, my head that I could dash against the wall, but I cannot, I cannot, I am not that kind. I am bound to bear till the very last and to live out every day and to hear every dreadful hour strike and to linger on. Oh good archbishop you are better than I, only three years and a half off 70 and surely one can't be made to live longer than that, but how much better was he than I. This morning I said I was dead and felt nothing, now I am all wildly alive, suffering and aching and hardened in my sins, but of my mind not my body, my body is well, well, the horrible thing. I could turn to and work or write a love story or draw or skate or walk a mile—anything, anything—but my burden is more than I can bear.

Christmas Night, 1894.

I feel that I must try to change the tone of this record. It was written for my boys, for Cecco in particular. Now they will never see it—unless, indeed, they are permitted, being in a better place, to know what is going on here. I used to feel that Cecco would use his discretion,—that most likely he would not print any of this at all, for he did not like publicity, and would have thought his mother's story of her life sacred; but now everything is changed, and I am now going to try to remember more trivial things, the incidents that sometimes amuse me when I look back upon them, not merely the thread of my life.

Robert Macpherson came down with us to Civita Vecchia to see us off, and, I remember, read to me all the way there a story he had written, one of the stories flying about Rome of one of the great families, which he wanted me to polish up and get published for him. It was very bad, poor dear fellow, and beyond doing anything with. I used another of these stories which he told me, in a little thing I did for 'Blackwood' some time later, the strange tale of the Cæsarini*—but that was bad too. Robert introduced me to Dr Kennedy of Shrewsbury* when we got on board the steamer,—a large, loose-lipped, loquacious man, full of talk, whom I liked well enough, and who talked to me pleasantly enough. He had two or three young men with him. I have always had a half-amused grudge against him, however. We were a very helpless party, the baby two months old and three other children, for I was bringing Willie Macpherson home to his aunt. In those days we had to land at Marseilles by small boats, which crowded round the steamer as soon as she came to anchor, and waited till the passengers had shown their passports and got through all the preliminaries. I saw that Dr Kennedy had engaged a large boat, and, though he said nothing to me, I was so foolish as to take it for granted that he meant me and my helpless party to go to the shore with him. It amuses me to think how astonished, how wounded and indignant I was, when, getting through before me, he and his young men stepped into their boat without a word, and left me to get ashore as I could—which, of course, I did all right, never having had any difficulty in that way of taking care of myself and my own belongings. I dare say he was quite right, and I had no claim upon him whatever,—and he was a good man, no doubt, and a great scholar. But it could not have hurt him to have helped a young woman and her children. I was so much astonished that I could scarcely believe my eyes. I remember that same night at the railway station, when we were all getting off by the *rapide*,* I haughtily desired one of the young men to stand by two of the children while I got them all into a compartment, which he did meekly and rather frightened. I did not know where to go in Paris, as I could not go back to the same hotel where we had been when my husband was with me; and in our innocence we went to the Bristol!—my sister-in-law having been advised to go there, at second or third hand, through Mr Pentland.* The rooms were delightful, but so were the prices, which I inquired, as we had been taught to do in Italy, before taking possession. I faltered, and said we had been sent there by Mr Pentland—but——The name acted like magic. Mr Pentland, ah! that was another thing,—the rooms were just half the price to a friend of Mr Pentland. He was the editor of Murray's Handbooks—but of that important fact I was not aware.

We arrived late at night in London, having been detained at Calais by a storm, and got in with the greatest difficulty to the Paddington hotel, where my dear old friend, Mr Laing,* of whom I can't remember more than that he was a clergyman, the founder of the Governesses' institutions and homes, and one of the people I had been used to meet when I lived in London. He had always been very kind to me, singling me out, saying he did not like literary ladies, which was a joke all my friends were fond of making with me—I never was much of a literary lady and certainly my pretensions were very small then.

After this we passed some time with my brother's family at Birkenhead, which was not very successful. I think it was rather more than I could bear to see his children rushing to the door to meet him when he came home, and my fatherless little ones ready to rush too, though it was so short a time since their father had been taken from them. I was always fantastical—and there were other things. It is a perilous business when one is very sorry for oneself, and the sight of happy people is apt, when one's wounds are fresh, to make the consciousness keener—alas for Frank and Jeanie, there was sorrow enough and to spare awaiting them.

In the summer of '60 we went to Fife to Elie, where I had a quaint little house, a drawing room with a deeply bowed window in which I worked, and where I remember people spoke of seeing my white cap always bending over the table—I was working at a translation of Montalembert's Monks of the West* which was blessed work for me at that agitated and troubled time. It soothed me and brought me back to the full use of my strength. Mr Blackwood, who was almost always liberal, gave me sixty pounds for each volume and it was a godsend. I was not even very strong in my French. However, Count Montalembert was pleased with the translation. I do not for a moment suppose that it paid the publisher, but I hope that it has been accounted to him that he did this good turn to a friendless young woman. I was very friendless, but totally undismayed, and afraid of nothing, so long as my babies were well—why Maggie, the eldest, was only seven.

[As the opening lines suggest the second volume of the manuscript begins here. The date 1860 appears at the top of the first page, presumably to remind Mrs Oliphant of the point she had reached in her story.]

December 30, 1894.

I resume this from the old book which contains my recollections up to 1859, when I came home from Rome with my three children, Cecco a baby of two months old. I stayed for some months, as I have said, with my brother in Birkenhead, and then went to Scotland—to Fife—for the summer, taking a small house in Elie. The Milligans (Mrs Milligan was Anne Mary Moir, a daughter of Delta, one of the girl friends whom I liked to have to stay with me in the early days of my married life in London) were at Kilconquhar, where Mr Milligan was minister, a man afterwards distinguished in his way, a well-known Biblical scholar and professor at Aberdeen, but a personage of the old school so much too old for my pretty Anne Mary, and too solemn and heavy, but especially too old and rather irritating to me as being apt, while in reality older than I was, to assume the air of a kind of son-in-law in consequence of my affection for his wife. I was still only thirty-one, and in full convalescence of sorrow, and feeling myself unaccountably young notwithstanding my burdened life and my widow's cap, which, by the way, I put off a year or two afterwards for the curious reason that I found it too becoming! That did not seem to me at all suitable for the spirit of my mourning: it certainly was, as my excellent London dressmaker made it for me, a very pretty head-dress, and an expensive luxury withal.

The Blackwoods were at Gibleston for the summer, a place quite near, so that I had friends within reach. I had not seen very much of

John Blackwood, but he was already a friend, with that curious kind of intimacy which is created by a publisher's knowledge of all one's affairs, especially when these affairs mean struggles to keep afloat and a constant need of money. Though we had seen so very little of each other, he had bidden me draw upon him when my husband died, and I was very grateful and apt to boast of it, as I have or had a way of doing; so that people who have served me in this way, even when, as sometimes happened, the balance changed a little, have always conceived themselves to be my benefactors. But he was a genial bene-factor, and he and his wife used to come to see me; so that, though lonely and a stranger, I was not entirely out of a kind of society. I must, however, have been very lonely, except for the sweet company of my three little children and my good Jane, my factotum, who had gone with me to Rome as their nurse, and helped me in my trouble, and stood faithfully by me through all. I always remember, immedi-ately after we came home, one dreadful night when my dear baby was very ill, and was laid upon her capacious shoulder as on a feather-bed, while I watched in anguish, thinking the night would never be done or that he would not live through it, when suddenly, with one of those rapid turns peculiar to infants, he got almost well in a moment! And this picture got itself hung up upon the walls of my mind, full of a roseate glow of happiness and deliverance instead of the black despair which had seemed to be closing round me. She was a very large woman, very good-looking with beautiful soft brown eyes, the ox-eyed Juno, my husband used to call her.

That winter we went to Edinburgh, where I got a droll little house in Fettes Row, down at the bottom of the hill, the lower floor and the basement with a front door, in truly Edinburgh style—for 'flats' were not known in England in those days. It was a very severe winter, 1860–61, and it was severe on me too. I have told the story of one incident in it in my other book, but I may repeat it here. I had not been doing very well with my writing. I had sent several articles, though of what nature I don't remember, to 'Blackwood,' and they had been rejected. Why, this being the case, I should have gone to them (John Blackwood and the Major were the firm at that moment) to offer them, or rather to suggest to them that they should take a novel from me for serial publication, I can't tell,—they so jealous of the Magazine, and inclined to think nothing was good enough for it, and I just then so little successful. But I was in their debt, and had very little to go on with. They shook their heads of course, and thought it would not be possible to take such a story,—both very kind and truly sorry for me, I have no doubt. I think I see their figures now against the light, standing up, John with his shoulders hunched up, the Major with his soldierly air, and myself all blackness and whiteness in my widow's dress, taking leave of them as if it didn't matter, and oh! so much afraid that they would see the tears in my eyes. I went home to my little ones, running to the door to meet me with 'flichterin' noise and glee';* and that night, as soon as I had got them all to bed, I sat down and wrote a story which I think was something about a lawyer, John Brownlow, and which formed the first of the Carlingford series,*—a series pretty well forgotten now, which made a considerable stir at the time, and *almost* made me one of the popularities of literature. *Almost*, never quite, though 'Salem Chapel' really went very near it, I believe. I sat up nearly all night in a passion of composition, stirred to the very bottom of my mind. The story was successful, and my fortune, comparatively speaking, was made. It has never been very much, never anything like what many of my contemporaries attained, and yet I have done very well for a woman, and a friendless woman with no one to make the best of me, and quite unable to do that for myself. I never could fight for a higher price or do anything but trust to the honour of those I had to deal with. Whether this was the reason why, though I did very well on the whole, I never did anything like so well as others, I can't tell, or whether it was really inferiority on my part. Anthony Trollope must have made at least three times as much as ever I did, and even Miss Mulock. As for such fabulous successes as that of Mrs Humphry Ward,* which we poorer writers are all so whimsically and so ruefully unable to explain, nobody thought of them in these days.

I did not see many people in Edinburgh. I was still in deep mourning, and shy, and not clever about society—constantly forgetting to return calls, and avoiding invitations. I met a few people at the Blackwoods', and I remember in the dearth of incidents an amusing evening (which I think, however, came a few years later) when Professor Aytoun* dined at Miss Blackwood's, he and I being the only guests. Miss Blackwood was one of the elders of the Blackwood family, and at this period a comely, black-haired, dark-complexioned person, large, and much occupied with her dress, and full of amusing peculiarities, with a genuine drollery and sense of fun, in which all the family were strong. She was sometimes the most intolerable person that could be conceived, and insulted her friends without compunction; but the effect upon me at least was always this—that before the end of one of her tirades she would strike, half consciously, a comical note, and my exasperation would explode into laughter. She was full of recollections of all sorts of people, and of her own youthful successes, which, though stout and elderly, she never outgrew,—still remembering the days when she was called a sylph, and never quite sure that she was not making a triumphant impression even in these changed circumstances. She was very fond of conversation, and truly exceedingly queer in the remarks she would make, sometimes so totally out of all sequence that the absurdity had as good an effect as wit, and often truly droll and amusing, after the fashion of her family. I remember when some people were discussing the respective merits of Rome and Florence, Miss Blackwood gave her vote for Rome. 'Ah,' she said with an ecstatic look, 'when you have read the "Iliad" in your youth, it all comes back!' Another favourite story of her was, that when one of her brothers asked her, on mischief bent, no doubt, 'Isabella, what are filbert nails?' she held out her hand towards him, where he was sitting a little behind her, without a word. She had a beautiful hand, and was proud of it.

But I have not told my story of Aytoun. Miss Blackwood had asked him to dine with us alone, and he came, and we flattered him to the top of his bent, she half sincerely, with that quaint mixture of enthusiasm and ridicule which I used to say was the Blackwood attitude towards that droll, partly absurd, yet more or less effective thing called an author; and I, I fear, backing her up in pure fun, for I was no particular admirer of Aytoun, who was then an ugly man in middle age, with the air of being one of the old lights, but without either warmth or radiancy. We got him between us to the pitch of flattered fatuity which all women recognise, when a man looks like the famous scene painter, 'I am so sick, I am so clevare'; his eyes bemused and his features blunted with a sort of bewildered beatitude, till suddenly he burst forth without any warning with 'Come hither, Evan Cameron'*—and repeated the poem to us, Miss Blackwood, ecstatic, keeping a sort of time with flourishes of her hand, and I, I am afraid, overwhelmed with secret laughter. I am not sure that he did not come to himself with a horrified sense of imbecility before he reached the end.

I got rather intimate with old Mrs Wilson,* a very dear old lady, the mother of my sister-in-law, Jeanie, and of Dr George Wilson and Sir Daniel Wilson—who lived at quite a great distance from me, a very long walk which I used to take every Sunday afternoon, with a complacent sense that it was a fine thing to do. She had a lonely day on Sunday, being very deaf, and unable to go to church, and her daughter much occupied by Sunday classes, &c. She was very deaf, but an amusing and good talker, and used to give me all sorts of good advice, and tell me stories of her life. Her advice was chiefly about my children, whom she wished me to bring up on Museums and the broken bread of Science, which I loathed, pointing out to me with triumph how this system had succeeded with her own sons, while I sat and listened and laughed within myself at the thought that my beautiful little boys could ever grow into men like them. What mother of little children, children full of every hope and delight would not feel the same: as if any man could have attained what they had it in them to be! It was a very long walk to Elm Cottage. I don't know Edinburgh well enough to say exactly where it was, but I had to mount the hill to Princes Street, and then go somehow by Bruntsfield Links, I think, past a Roman Catholic Convent (St Margaret's?), and a long solitary way beyond that. I was rather proud of myself for resisting all temptations to take a cab, though the dark road by the Nunnery, which was very lonely, used to frighten me considerably.

It was then I first became acquainted with the Storys,* Mr, afterwards Dr, Story coming to see me in respect to my proposed Memoir of Edward Irving, which he had by some means heard about. My article in 'Blackwood' on Irving must have been published that winter: no, no, it was published much before we went to Italy,* and I had been to Albury to see Mr Drummond,[1] my husband accom-

---

[1] Mr Drummond* wrote to me when the article on Irving, which was in a manner the germ of the book, was published. It must have been in the end of 1858. He and all his community were much pleased with it, and had a notion, which my Roman Catholic friends always share, that since I went so far with them I must go the whole way. They gave me great encouragement accordingly, and I was supposed to be going to do just what they wanted to have done. We went to Albury on Mr Drummond's invitation, where we stayed three days, I think; and I remember the sensation with which I sat and listened while Mr Drummond, the caustic wit and man of the world, explained to me how they were guided in setting up their church, and in building their quasi-cathedral in Gordon Square, and of the pillars called Jachin and Boaz, and

panying me, which was the first beginning of that project. Mr Story
told me of his father's long intimacy with Irving,* and promised me
many letters if I would go to the manse of Roseneath to see them. I
went accordingly, rather unwillingly in cold February weather,
grudging the absence from my children for a few days very much. I
did not know anything about the West of Scotland, and, winter as it
was, the lovely little loch was a revelation to me, with the wonderful
line of hills called the Duke's Bowling Green, which I afterwards
came to know so well. The family at the manse was a very interesting
one. The handsome young minister, quite young, though already
beginning to grow grey—a very piquant combination (I was so
myself, though older by several years than he)—and his mother, a
handsome old lady full of strong character, and then a handsome
sister with her baby, the most interesting of all, with a shade of
mystery about her. They were, as people say, like a household in a
novel, and attracted my curiosity very much. But when I was sent to
my room with a huge packet of letters, and the family all retired for
the night, and the deep darkness and silence of a winter night in the
country closed down upon me, things were less delightful. The bed
in my room was a gloomy erection, with dark-red moreen curtains,
afterwards, as I found, called by Mr Story—witty and profane—'a
field to bury strangers in.'* I had a pair of candles, which burned out,
and a fire, which got low, while I agonised over the letters, not one of
which I could make out. The despairing puzzle of that diabolical
handwriting, which was not Irving's after all (who wrote a beautiful
hand), but only letters addressed to him, and the chill that grew upon
me, and the gradual sense of utter stupidity that came over me, I can't
attempt to describe. I sat up half the night, but in vain. Next day Mr
Campbell of Row* came specially to see me, a little shocked, I am

a great deal more, while Lord Lovaine, his son-in-law, now Duke of Northumberland,
a grave man, whose aspect impressed me much, listened gravely, as if to an oracle, and
I looked on and wondered, amazed, as I sometimes used to be with Montalembert, at
the combination of what seems to my hard head so much nonsense with so much keen
sense and power; though I had much more sympathy with Montalembert, even with
his medieval miracles, than with Jachin and Boaz. These good people thought, partly
because of their deep sense of their own importance, and partly by a trick of sympathy
which I had, and most genuine it was, that I was interested beyond measure in them
and their ways, whereas it was in Irving I was interested, and listening with all my ears
to hear about him, and much less concerned about the Holy Apostolic Church. They
were disappointed accordingly, and not pleased with the book.

afraid, to find the future biographer of Irving a young person, rather apt to be led astray and laugh with the young people in the midst of his serious talk. Mr Campbell had been a very notable character in these parts, and was at that time reverenced and admired as an apostle, though perhaps to me a little too much disposed, like everybody else, to tell me of himself instead of telling me of Irving, on whom my soul was bent. I never have had, I fear, a strong theological turn, and his exposition at family prayers, though I did my best to think it very interesting, confounded me, especially next morning when I had to catch the boat at a certain hour in order to catch the train and get home to my babies. All these details, however, gave a whimsical mixture of fun, to which, a sort of convalescent as I was from such trouble and sorrow, and long deprived of cheerful society, my mind yielded, in spite of a little resistance on the part of my graver side, which had honestly expected never to laugh again. This visit laid the foundation of a long friendship and much and generally very lively intercourse.

How strange it is to me to write all this, with the effort of making light reading of it, and putting in anecdotes that will do to quote in the papers and make the book sell! It is a sober narrative enough, heaven knows! and when I wrote it for my Cecco to read it was all very different, but now that I am doing it consciously for the public, with the aim (no evil aim) of leaving a little more money for Denny, I feel all this to be so vulgar, so common, so unnecessary, as if I were making pennyworths of myself. Well, but if it does make poor Denny more comfortable and independent, what does it matter? Will my boys ever see it? Do they ever see me? Have they the power, as some one says, of being present when they desire to be by a mere process of thought? I would rather it were not so. I should not like to fix them to earth, to an old mother, an old woman, when they are both young men in the very height of life. But why should I turn back here to this continual strain of my thoughts? There is too much of this already. I got a letter from Dr Story the other day, from Taymouth, about which we had wandered once together in a little holiday expedition full of talk and frolic, more than thirty years ago. It was a very kind letter. I could see that his heart swelled with pity for the lonely woman, bereaved of all things, whom he had known so different. Good fellow, good friend, though we have drifted so far apart since then. But I must try to begin again.

I saw various other people besides Mr Campbell and the Storys, in pursuit of information about Irving, and came across some amusing scenes, though they have passed out of my recollection for the most part. I remember making the discovery already noted—which, of course, I promulgated to all my friends—that every one I saw on this subject displayed the utmost willingness to tell me all about themselves, with quite a secondary interest in Irving. One gentleman in Edinburgh told me the whole story of his own wife's illness and death, and that he had reflected on the evening of her death that his children were almost more to be pitied than himself, since it was possible that he might get a new wife, while they could never have a new mother. Not an original thought, perhaps, but curious as occurring at such a moment. This was told me *apropos* of the fact that Irving, I think, had once dined in the house during the reign of that poor lady. She had more than one successor, if I remember rightly.

One of my people whom I went to see on this subject was Dr Carlyle,* whom I found surrounded with huge books,—books of a kind with which I was afterwards well acquainted—the 'Acta Sanctorum' and the like. He was writing a life of Adamnan, the successor of Columba. My recollection of him is of a small, rather spruce man, not at all like his great brother. (Mrs Carlyle used to say of Dr John that he was one of the people who seemed to have been born in creaking shoes.) It must have been he who told me to go and see Carlyle himself, who could tell me a great deal more than he could about Irving. I fancy that I must have made a run up to London from Edinburgh in the summer of 1861, and stayed with Mrs Powell in Palace Gardens—a sister of Mr Maurice, who had been very kind and friendly to me for a year or two before my husband's death. This must have been my first visit to her after, for I remember that she questioned me as to how I was 'left,' and that I answered her cheerfully, 'With my head and my hands to provide for my children,' and was truly surprised by her strange look and dumb amazement at my cheerfulness. I suppose now, but never thought then, that it was something to be amazed at. I don't remember that I ever thought it anything the least out of the way, or was either discouraged or frightened, provided only that the children were all well.

It was on this occasion that, shy as I always was, yet with the courage that comes to one when one is about one's lawful work, and not seeking acquaintance or social favour, I bearded the lion in his den, and went to see Mr Carlyle in the old house in Cheyne Row, which people are now trying, I think very unwisely, to make a shrine or museum of, which I should myself hate to see. He received me (I suppose I must have had an introduction from his brother) with that perfect courtesy and kindness which I always found in him, telling me, I remember, that he could tell me little himself,* but that 'the wife' could tell me a great deal, if I saw her. I forget whether he took any steps to acquaint me with 'the wife,' for I remember that I left Cheyne Row with a flutter of disappointment, feeling that though I had seen the great man, which was no small matter, I was not much the wiser. I remember his tall, thin, stooping figure between the two rooms of the library on the ground floor, in the pleasant shadow of the books, and subdued light and quiet in the place which seemed to supply a very appropriate atmosphere. I did not even know, and certainly never should have learned from any look or tone of his, that I had run the risk of being devoured alive by thus intruding on him. But though I was fluttered by the pride of having seen him, and that people might say 'Il vous a parlé, grand'mère,' I felt that my hopes were ended and that this was to be all. However, I was mistaken. A day or two after I was told (being still at Mrs Powell's) that a lady whose carriage was at the door begged me to go out and speak to her, Mrs Carlyle. I went, wondering, and found in a homely little brougham a lady with bright eyes and very hollow cheeks, who told me she had to be out in the open air for certain hours every day, and asked me to come and drive with her that we might talk about Irving, whom her husband had told her I wanted to hear about. She must have been over sixty at this time, but she was one of those women whom one never thinks of calling old; her hair was black without a grey hair in it (mine at half the age was already quite grey), her features and her aspect very keen, perhaps a little alarming. When we set off together she began by asking me if I did not come from East Lothian; she had recognised many things in my books which could only come from that district. I had to answer, as I have done on various occasions, that my mother had lived for years in East Lothian, and that I had been so constantly with her that I could never tell whether it was I myself who remembered things or she. This made us friends on the moment; for she too had had a mother, whom, however, she did not regard with all the respect I had for mine. What

warmed my heart to her was that she was in many things like my
mother; not outwardly, for my mother was a fair radiant woman with
a beautiful complexion, and Mrs Carlyle was very dark, with a darkness which was, however, more her meagreness and the wearing of
her eager spirit than from nature, or, at least, so I thought,—but in
her wonderful talk, the power of narration which I never heard
equalled except in my mother, the flashes of keen wit and sarcasm,
occasionally even a little sharpness, and always the modifying sense
of humour under all. She told me that day, while we drove round and
round the Park, the story of her childhood and of her tutor, the big
young Annandale student who set her up on a table and taught her
Latin, she six years old and he twenty ('perhaps the prettiest little
fairy that ever was born,' her old, old husband said to me, describing
this same childhood in his deep broken-hearted voice the first time I
saw him after she was gone). I felt a little as I had felt with my
mother's stories, that I myself remembered the little girl seated on
the table to be on his level, repeating her Latin verbs to young
Edward Irving, and all the wonderful life and hope that were about
them,—the childhood and the youth and aspiration never to be
measured. We jogged along with the old horse in the old fly and the
steady old coachman going at his habitual jog, and we might have
been going on so until now for anything either of us cared,—she had
so much to say and I was so eager to hear.

I have one gift that I know of, and I am a little proud of it. It is that
of making people talk—at least, of making *some* people talk. My dear
Lady Cloncurry* says that it is like the art of driving a hoop,—that I
give a little touch now and then, and my victim rolls on and on. But
my people who pour forth to me are not my victims, for I love to hear
them talk and they take pleasure in it, for the dear talk's sake on both
sides, not for anything else; for I have never, I am glad to say, been 'a
student of human nature' or any such odious thing, nor practised the
art of observation, nor spied upon my friends in any way. My own
opinion has always been that I was very unobservant,—whatever I
have marked or noted has been done quite unaware; and also, that to
study human nature was the greatest impertinence, to be resented
whenever encountered.

My friendship with Mrs Carlyle was never broken from this
time—it must have been the summer either of 1860 or 1861—till her
death. She came to see me frequently, and I spent some (but few)

memorable evenings in her house, but at that time did not see her
husband again.

January 22

I have been reading the life of Mr Symonds,* and it makes me
almost laugh (though little laughing is in my heart) to think of the
strange difference between this prosaic little narrative, all about the
facts of a life so simple as mine, and his elaborate self-discussions. I
suppose that to many people the other will be the more interesting
way, just as the movements of the mind are more interesting than
those of the body, or rather of the external life. I might well give
myself up to introspection at this sad postscript of my life, when all is
over for me but the one event to come, which will, I hope and believe,
do away with all the suffering past and carry me back, a happy
woman, to my family, to a home; though whether it will be like the
home on earth who can tell? Nothing can be more sad than the home
on earth in which I am now,—the once happy home that rang with
my boys' voices and their steps, where everything is full of them, and
everything empty, empty, cold, and silent! I don't know whether it is
more hard for me to be here with all these associations, or to be in
some other place which might not be so overwhelming in its connection with what is past. But it is not a question I need discuss here.
Indeed I must not discuss here any question of the kind at all, for any
attempt at discussing myself like Mr Symonds, if I were likely to
make it, only would end in outlines of trouble, in the deep, deep
sorrow that covers me like a mantle. I feel myself like the sufferers in
Dante, those of whom we have been reading, who are bent under the
weight of stones, though I think I may say with them that *invidiosa
non fui*;* but this is not to put myself under a microscope and watch
what goes on in so paltry a thing, but only the continual appeal I am
always making to heaven and earth, consciously or unconsciously,
saying often, I know, as I have no right to say, 'Is this fair,—is it right
that I should be so bowed down to the earth and everything taken
from me?' This makes of itself so curious a change even in this quite
innocent little narrative of my life. It is so strange to think that when I
go it will be touched and arranged by strange hands,—no child of
mine to read with tenderness, to hide some things, to cast perhaps an
interpretation of love upon others, and to turn over all my papers

with the consciousness of a full right to do so, and that theirs is by nature all that was mine. Good Mr Symonds, a pleasant, frank, hearty man, as one saw him from outside! God bless him! for he was kindly to Cecco, who in his tender kindliness made a little pilgrimage to Davos the year after Mr S. died to see his family and offer his sympathy—one of the many unrevealed impulses of kindness he had which they never probably guessed at all. But it is vain for me to go on in this strain. I have fallen back into my own way of self-comment,—and that is such a different thing.

In the beginning of the winter of 1861 I went to Ealing, and settled down there in a tiny house on the Uxbridge Road. It had a small drawing-room opening on a rather nice garden, a long strip of ground truly suburban, with a pretty plot of grass, a hedge of lilacs and syringas, and vegetables beyond that,—very humble, but I had no pretensions. I think by moments I must have been quite happy here. I remember the cluster of us on the grass, my little Maggie, a little mother in her way, and the two boys. We kept pigeons for the first and only time, and the pretty creatures were fluttering about, and the house standing all open doors and windows, and the sunshine and peace over all. I wrote a few verses, I remember, called 'In the Eaves,' and had a pang of conscious happiness, always touched with foreboding.

I had gone to Ealing to be near the Blacketts, who, much better off than I and in a much bigger house as became a publisher, lived also in the village, which was not half the size it is now. I had got very intimate with them somehow, I can scarcely tell how. Mrs Blackett was about my age, and a fine creature, very much more clever than her husband, though treated by him in any serious matter as if she had been a little girl,—a thing quite new to me, and which I could not understand. I remember later by some years, at a time when she had got to be very anxious about the education of her boys and he had been somehow moved—a little, perhaps, by myself, impelled in secret by her—to think of sending Arthur to Eton, that while talking it over with me, he suddenly turned to her and said, 'Come, Nell, tell me what you think—let us hear your opinion.' I remember the frightened look that came on her face, the same look which came over it when she flew before the cow for which she was frightened, and she cried, 'Oh, Henry, whatever you think best,' and morally ran away, though it was indeed her movement through another which was in reality setting him agoing. Now, why was she afraid of him? He was as good to her as a rather goodhumoured but self-important man could be, very fond of her and very proud of her. She was a pretty woman, bright and full of spirit, and much his superior, knowing nothing about books, indeed, but neither did he,—why was she frightened to express an opinion while privately moved very strongly, much more strongly than he was, with the desire to get that important matter decided, and secretly working upon him by all the means at her command? What a curious light it throws upon the relations of husband and wife, and the nature of the bourgeois English. They were eminently Philistine both, and he a little apt to blow himself out and assume importance and through their costly house—planned like so many houses of the same kind, on the system of having everything as expensive as could be got, and making as little show as possible for the money, the latter not, perhaps, intentional, but from preference for the humdrum—there fluttered a confused drift from time to time of literary persons, somewhat small beer like myself, novel-writers and suchlike. These were all very literary: our hosts were not literary at all, but with a business interest in us, along with a certain kindly contempt, such as publishers generally entertain for the queer genus writer. It was kindly at least on the part of the good Blacketts, who were the kindest folk, he always very brotherly to me, and she most affectionate. I was very fond of Ellen Blackett, admired her and thought much of her. Their house was full of big noisy boys, some of them just the same ages as mine—a great bond between young mothers; handsome boys, wild and troublesome in later life, but with that stout commercial thread in them which brings men back to a life which is practicable when they have sown their wild oats,—not the highest motive, perhaps, but a recuperative force, such as it was.

I had introduced Mr Blackett by his desire to Miss Mulock in London,—he, apparently with some business gift or instinct imperceptible to me, having made out that there were elements of special success in her. Probably, however, this instinct was no more than an appreciation in himself of the sentimentalism in which she was so strong. He had at once made an arrangement with her, of which 'John Halifax' was the result, the most popular of all her books, and one which raised her at once to a high position, I will not say in literature, but among the novel-writers of our species. She made a spring thus quite over my head with the helping hand of my particular friend, leaving me a little rueful,—I did not at all understand the means nor think very highly of the work, which is a thing that has happened several times, I fear, in my experience. Success as measured by money never came to my share. Miss Mulock in this way attained more with a few books, and that of very thin quality, than I with my many. I don't know why. I don't pretend to think that it was because of their superior quality. I had, however, my little success too, while I lived in Ealing. I began in 'Blackwood' the Carlingford series, beginning with a story called 'The Doctor's Family,' which I myself liked, and then 'Salem Chapel.' This last made a kind of commotion, the utmost I have ever attained to. John Blackwood wrote to me pointing out how I had just missed doing something that would have been made worth the while; and I believe he was right, but the chapel atmosphere was new and pleased people. As a matter of fact I knew nothing about chapels, but took the sentiment and a few details from our old church in Liverpool, which was Free Church of Scotland, and where there were a few grocers and other such good folk whose ways with the minister were wonderful to behold. The saving grace of their Scotchness being withdrawn, they became still more wonderful as Dissenting deacons, and the truth of the picture was applauded to all the echoes. I don't know that I cared for it much myself, though Tozer and the rest amused me well enough. Then came 'The Perpetual Curate' and 'Miss Marjoribanks.' I never got so much praise, and a not unfair share of pudding too. I was amused lately to hear the comments of Mr David Stott of Oxford Street, the bookseller, on this. He told me that he had been in the Blackwoods' establishment at the time, and of the awe and horror of Mr Simpson* at the prodigal extravagance of John Blackwood in giving me the price he did, £1500, for 'The Perpetual Curate.' One could see old Simpson, pale, with the hair of his wig standing up on his head, remonstrating, and John Blackwood, magnanimous, head of the house of Blackwood, and feeling rather like a feudal suzerain, as he always did, declaring that the labourer was worthy of his hire. Stott had the air too of thinking it was sinful extravagance on the editor's part. As for me, I took what was given me and was very grateful, and no doubt sang praises to John. On the other side, it was Henry Blackett who turned pale at Miss Mulock's sturdy business-like stand for her money. He used to talk of his encounters with her with affright, very grave, not able to laugh.

This was also the time when I wrote the 'Edward Irving.' It must have been my good time, the little boat going very smoothly and all promising well, and, always my burden of happiness, the children all well. They had the measles, I remember, and were all a little ill the day of the Prince of Wales's marriage, Tiddy least ill of all, but feverish one day, when, as I stood over him, putting back his hair from his little hot forehead, he said to me with a pretty mixture of baby metaphor, which I was very proud of and never forgot, 'Oh, mamma, your hand is as soft as snow.' How like him that was, the poetry and the perception and the tenderness! Cecco too had a momentary illness,—a little convulsive fit which frightened me terribly, one of the few times when I quite lost my head. I remember holding him in his hot bath, and all the while going on calling for hot water and hearing myself do so, and unable to stop it. It was a day on which Mrs Carlyle was coming for the afternoon. When she arrived I was sitting before the fire (though it was summer), with my baby wrapped in a blanket, just out of his bath, and humming softly to him, and he had just startled me out of my misery and made my heart leap for joy, by pulling my face to him with a way he had and saying, all himself again, 'Why you singing hum-hum? Sing "Froggy he would a-wooing go."' He was only two and a-half. Mrs Carlyle sat by me, so kind and tender and full of encouragement, as if she had known all about babies, but did not stay very long. I think I can see her by the side of the fire, telling me all kinds of comforting things; and by the first post possible that same evening, I got a letter from her telling me that Mr Carlyle had made her sit down at once and write to tell me that a sister of his had once had just such an attack, which never was repeated. God bless them, that much maligned, much misunderstood pair! That was not much like the old ogre his false friends have made him out to be.

Here is a pretty thing. I should like if I could to write what people like about my books, being just then, as I have said, at my high tide, and instead of that all I have to say is a couple of baby stories. I am afraid I can't take the books *au grand sérieux*. Occasionally they pleased me, very often they did not. I always took pleasure in a little bit of fine writing (afterwards called in the family language a 'trot'), which, to do myself justice, was only done when I got moved by my subject, and began to feel my heart beat, and perhaps a little water in my eyes, and ever more really satisfied by some little conscious felicity of words than by anything else. I have always had my sing-song, guided by no sort of law, but by my ear, which was in its way fastidious to the cadence and measure that pleased me; but it is bewildering to me in my perfectly artless art, if I may use the word at all, to hear of the elaborate ways of forming and enhancing style, and all the studies for that end.

A good deal went on during that short time at Ealing. I had visitors, Miss Blackwood for two months, and much driving up and down to London to the Exhibition of 1862, which I loathed; but she enjoyed and dragged me, if not at her chariot wheels yet in the 'smart fly,' which added very much to my expenses and wasted my time, with the result of being set down by her as very extravagant,—a reproach which has come up against me at various periods of my life. Mr Story came with her, or at least at the same time, and afterwards Principal Tulloch and his wife, whose acquaintance I had made at Edinburgh, St Andrews, and Roseneath in the intervening summer of these two years, which I spent at Roseneath, for which I had taken a great fancy—the beautiful little loch and the hills. I must have gone then to Willowburn, a small house on a high bank, with a lovely view of the loch and the opposite shore, all scattered with houses among the trees, with the steamboat bustling up and down, and a good deal of boating and singing and Highland expeditions,—all very amusing, almost gay, as I had seldom been in my life before. There was always a youthful party in the manse, and the Tullochs generally for a time, and various visitors coming and going,—from the high respectability of Mr Edward Caird, now Master of Balliol, and Mr Moir, to all sorts of jocular and light-minded people. I remember coming home from some wildish expedition, sunburnt and laden with flowers,—a small group full of fun and laughter sitting together on deck,—when suddenly the handsome serious form of Mrs M., always *tirée à quatre épingles*,* always looking propriety itself, was seen slowly ascending up the cabin stairs, to the confusion and sudden pallor of myself in particular, to whom she was coming on a visit. I doubt if I had ever been so gay. I was still young, and all was well with the children. My heart had come up with a great bound from all the strain of previous trouble and hard labour and the valley of the shadow of death. There was some wit, or at least a good deal of humour, in the party, and plenty of excellent talk. The Principal talked very well in those days—indeed he always did, but never so well as at that time; and Mr Story, too, was an excellent talker, and his sister very clever and bright; and my dear *padrona*,[1] if she never said very much, always quick to see everything, and never able to resist a laugh. We got to have a crowd of allusions and mutual recollections after all our boatings and drivings and ludicrous little adventures on the loch and the hills, which produced a great deal of laughter even when they were not witty—Jack Tulloch's appetite, for instance, when he was taken with us on one occasion, and looked on with exquisite contempt at our admiring raptures over the scenery, but came to life whenever lunch was going, and was devotedly attended by the Highland waiters, who entered into the joke and plied him with dish after dish. He was only about eleven, poor boy. We were like Farmer Flamborough and his daughters,* just as much amused by all these small matters as if they had been the most amusing things in the world. Miss Blackwood continued to make part occasionally of our expeditions, and always an amusing part. She was full of the humour and drollery of her family, gifts in which they were all strong, with many little eccentricities of her own, fits of temper almost always redeemed at the end by a flash of fun which made the incipient quarrel end in a burst of laughter.

I worked very hard all the time, I scarcely know how, for I was always subject to an irruption of merry neighbours bent on some ramble, whom, when they came in the evening, my big Jane, now more cook than nurse and general factotum, fed with great dishes of maccaroni, which she had learned to make in Italy, and which was our social distinction: everything was extremely primitive at Willowburn. We had one cab in the place, which took me solemnly now and then to dinner at the manse and other places, and which was driven by a certain Andie Chalmers who was our delight, who spoke in a soft, half-articulate murmur, all vowels, very tolerant of the pouring rain through which he drove us occasionally through many a wet mile of road, allowing with a smile that it was a 'wee saft' when there was a deluge, and who used to come to the cab door at the foot of a hill with mild insistence, inaccessible to remonstrance, till we one by one unwillingly, yet with merry jests, got out to ease the horse.

[1] Mrs Tulloch.

I suppose after all that I only went for two summers to Rose-neath, but it seems to have bulked very largely in my life: there was a third later, but that was in another age, as will be seen, and I was not quite three years in Ealing. Here I had often with me, as I had a fancy for having, a young lady on a long visit. It would be cruel to name by name the dear good girl, who was brought by her mother, the immaculate friend of whom I have spoken, to join us one time where we were living, the whole party of us,—myself, big Jane, and the three children. The girl was very tearful and pale, and her mother whispered to me to take no notice, that she had been *praying for strength* to pay me this visit, in which, however, she enjoyed herself very much, I believe. This was, I fear, too good a joke to be kept from my friends.

It was in the summer of 1863 that Geraldine Macpherson came to spend some time with me at Ealing. She was much shattered with Roman fever, and she had a very bad illness of another kind, almost fatal, in my house. The high-spirited creature never gave in, kept her courage and composure through everything, but was as near as possible gone. How one wonders vainly whether, if some one thing like this had not happened, the tenor of one's entire life might have been changed. It was she who persuaded me to go back to Rome when she returned. She persuaded the Tullochs also, to my great surprise, and I daresay their own. The Principal had been ill. It was the first of those mysterious illnesses of his when he fell under the terrible influence of a depression for which there was no apparent cause. He was in the depths of this when he and his wife were with me in 1862, and he told me the whole story of it. It originated (or he thought it did) in (of all things in the world) a false quantity he had made in some Latin passage he had quoted in a speech at some Pres-bytery or Assembly meeting. He told it with such impassioned seriousness, with his countenance so full of sorrow and trouble, his big blue eyes full of moisture, that I was much impressed, and, I remember, gave him out of my sympathy and emotion the equally inconceivable advice to call the men together to whom that speech had been made, and make a clean breast of it to them. I remember he was staggered in the semi-insanity of his talk by this queer insane suggestion, and perhaps a touch more would have awakened the man's wholesome humour and driven the strange delusion away in a shout of laughter; but I was deadly serious, as was he. He was beginning to mend, and had been ordered a sea-voyage, and somebody offered him a passage in a Levant steamboat to Greece. And now, what with Geddie's persuasions and a spring of eager planning on my part how and when to go, Mrs Tulloch made up her mind to come to Rome to meet her husband, then on his way back, bringing her two eldest girls while he took his eldest boy. There was a crowd of little children left at home, and I have no doubt if I heard of such a proceeding now I should think it the wildest plan. But we carried it out notwithstanding, with a delightful indifference to ways and means which makes me shudder when I look back upon it. We set out the merriest party, ready to enjoy everything, the *padrona*, as I soon began to call her, with her daughters Sara and Fanny, Geddie, myself, my Jane, and the children, all so small, so happy, so bright, my three little things—Maggie approaching eleven. We took out a French governess with us for the sake of the children, a Mdlle. Coquelin, I think, who soon dropped out of my life after the great calamity came. But in the meantime we were all gay, fearing nothing. I remember very distinctly our journey from Paris to Marseilles, because it was a cheap journey, second class, and monstrous in length, twenty-seven hours, I think; but we were all very economical to start with. The endless journey it was! We were all dead tired when we arrived, but when we reached our hotel and got round a table, and well warmed and refreshed with an innocent champagne, St Peray, which I made them all drink, our spirits recovered. I was always great in the way of feeding my party,—would not hear of teas or coffee meals, but insisted upon meat and wine, to the horror but comfort of my companions. That, I believe, was one reason why there were never any breakdowns among us while travelling. I think with pleasure of the pleasant tumult of that arrival,—the delight of rest, the happy sleepy children all got to bed, the little party of women, all of us about the same age, all with the sense of holiday, a little outburst of freedom, no man interfering, keeping us to rule or formality. I don't know why it should present itself to me under so pleasant a light, for I never liked second-class journeys, nor discomforts of that kind. How often have I travelled that road since, but never so free or light of heart! Heavy and sad are its recollections now, but it is a blessing of God that a happy moment (which is so much rarer) is more conspicuous in life, lighting up the long dreary lane like a lamp, than the sad ones. Oh, the bonnie little dear faces! the rapture of their wellbeing and their happiness, all clinging round mamma with innumerable appeals,—the 'bundle of boys,' as my Maggie said with sweet scorn, who left no room for her arms to get round me, but only mine round her. I am old and desolate and alone, but I seem to see myself a young mother, the two little fellows in the big fauteuil* behind me, clinging round my neck, and their sister at my knee. God bless them, and God bless them,—are they all together now?

We went next day, I think, in the great Messageries steamboat, by Genoa and Leghorn, to Civita Vecchia, and got to Rome in three days, with time enough in Genoa to get a glimpse of the town, and in Pisa next day, making a run from Leghorn. All was well when we got to Rome, where my poor brother William was with Robert Macpherson, helping him to sell his photographs, and pouring out his stores of knowledge upon all the visitors, to good Robert's great admiration. The Tullochs and I got a joint-house in Capo le Case. We had two servants—a delightful *donna da faccenda,** called Leonilda, and the only detestable Italian servant I ever saw, Antonio; but the two did everything for us somehow. We had our dinner, I think, from the Trattoria. And we had a month, or a little more, of pleasant life together. The Principal arrived from Greece—or was it Constantinople?—and all was well.

Ah me, alas! pain ever, for ever. This has been the ower-word of my life. And now it burst into the murmur of pain again.

1894.

On the 27th of January 1864 my dear little Maggie died of gastric fever. I have written about it all elsewhere. I had escaped, I thought, from the valley of the shadow of death, and had been happy, in sheer force of youth and health and the children: now I was plunged again under the salt and bitter waves. I laid her by her father, and it seemed to me that all light and hope were gone from me for ever. Up to five years ago I could not say her dear name without the old pang coming back; since then, when there came to be another to bury in my heart, my little girl seemed all at once to become a tranquil sweet recollection; and now that all are gone she is but a dear shadow, far in the background, while my boys take up in death as in life the whole of the darkened scene. All three gone, and only I left behind! I must try not to dwell on that here. There is enough of distracted thoughts and fancies elsewhere. I have never ventured to go back to Rome. I dared not while I had still the boys to think of. Twice fatal to us, I did not venture to face it a third time. I used to say that if I knew I had a fatal disease, or was sure that they needed me no longer, I would go by myself, and would be happy to die there, but never that they should go. I feel as if I should like to go now, but not to die there, for I must, if it is possible, lie beside my Cyril and Cecco at Eton and it would be such a trouble for Denny and expense to have to bring me home. But this belongs to a later time.

We left Rome in May, the party still together, the Tullochs and I. I felt that if I left them then I could never bear to see them again; and thus it was that Sara and Fanny Tulloch were left with me for a year, their parents returning home. I remember very little in Rome. The people I met there, the things I saw, seemed all wiped out of my mind, except some strange broken scenes. The first week after that calamity Geddie took me out to Frascati, to their house there, for a little change; and I never can forget the aspect of that summer place, where we had once lived through the hot July and August, in the desolation of the winter and of my misery. We were on the upper storey of a great cold Italian house, the cold penetrating to the heart, cold such as never was seen or felt surely in the North,—no servants, no comforts, sitting crying over the fire through a dismal day or two in a great, gaunt, half-empty room, my heart breaking for the children. It did not last long, but I have never forgotten these dismal days. There is another day in my memory like a dream. It was then March, and we had gone to Albano and were living there. The Macphersons came out to visit us, and, as they could never be without company, asked some of their friends out from Rome on the Sunday to go to Nemi. Then, finding how I shrank from the strangers, Robert took me through the woods,—a wonderful, wild, beautiful way,—leading my donkey to the place where we were to dine. I recollect a kind of soothing in the sensation of the spring, the wild freshness of the wood; a party of charcoal-burners, whose encampment we passed, appear to me like a picture,—wild men, not safe to meet, but my kind old Robert knew them all and their dialect and their ways. Nemi, the wonderful blue lake, bound within the circle of its deep banks, and an old Palazzo with frescoed rooms looking sheer down into the wonderful metallic water, which looked something like molten sapphires, but of a warmer colour. I had half a mind, I remember, to take an *appartemento* in that house, and throw myself into the rut of artist life, though my instincts were not of that kind,—a life not exactly disorderly, but a little wild and wandering and gregarious. I have curious superstitions about localities. I used to have a dizzy feeling sometimes in later years when I passed our old house in Ulster Place that if I had the courage to knock at the door and go on asking no questions I might find, who could tell that all the rest was a dream and that the babies were safe in their nursery and Frank in the studio, wondering what had kept me so long. I wonder, if I had stayed at Nemi and brought the boys up so—how bewildering the thought is of things one might have done.

After that we went to Naples and Capri, where we stayed a long time and got to know all the guides and people, riding about every day over all the lower island and up to Anacapri—all like a dream. And Santella, the good hunchback maid whose face the Principal said was so full of moral beauty, and Feliciello, who was not by any means so good, but whom we liked and petted. I wrote, I think, a little sketch of it afterwards, called 'Life on an Island,'* or some such name, in the Magazine.

In May we left Rome finally and moved northward to the Lake of Como, where we stayed at Bellaggio; then into Switzerland, where we spent the summer, chiefly on the Lake of Geneva; then to Paris, where we passed the winter. The Principal and the *padrona* had gone home long before, and my party in Paris consisted of my two little boys, the two girls, Sara and Fanny, Jane, and a Swiss-French governess, Mademoiselle Pricam, whom we had picked up at Montreux. In Paris we got a cheerful apartment on the Champs Elysées, the sunny side. It was at the height of the gaiety and prosperity of the Empire, and I used to say that the sight of all the gay stream of life from the windows, all the fine people coming and going, the brightness and the movement, were a kind of salvation to me in that dark and clouded time. I remember going off to St Germain to spend the first anniversary of my Maggie's death, taking my delightful boy with me; and the dark gloomy evening after I had put him to bed in the inn, once more sitting desolate and crying over the fire; but next morning the terrace in the wintry sunshine, and all the thoughts that came to one then, and still more the going back to the cheerful rooms in Paris, which were a kind of home, and my other dear little fellow rushing with his shout of welcome to mamma, brought a little sunshine back; though it was not till the 4th of April after that, when I found the rooms crowded with flowers which they had all gone out to get for me on my birthday before I was up, that I began to feel as if I had passed again from death into life. I took them all out to St Cloud in reward for their flowers, and they were all so gay, and the morning and the drive so bright.

In Paris I saw a good deal of the Montalemberts. I have described how I translated the Count's book when I first went to Scotland after my widowhood. He had been pleased with it, I don't know why, for it was badly done; and by John Blackwood's desire and introduction came to see me in Paris, and I dined there once or twice, though under protest, for I had never gone anywhere or cared to see anybody. There was one party I remember which was interesting, where were Prévost-Paradol* and some other literary people. I was too shy and out of my element to make much of them, and have never been proud of my French; so I did not get the good I ought out of this glimpse of society. On one occasion Miss Blackwood, who came to Paris and paid me a long visit, was with me,—a little alarming in her large bare shoulders in the small party with the other ladies all decorously covered. There was, I remember, a pretty graceful Madame L'Abbadie, whose husband came up to me, a man with a dreadful brogue, and said, 'I speak English better than Montalembert; the reason is I am born in Dublin, and he is born in London.' Montalembert's English was delightful, perfect in accent and idiom; I don't remember any mistake of his except the amusing and flattering one with which he expressed his surprise when we first met to find me 'not so respectable' as he had supposed. I daresay it was a mistake made on purpose; for to be sure I was still young, and perhaps, in the still lingering exaltation of my sorrow and the tears that were never far off from my eyes, looked younger than I was. It was then 1865, and I must have been thirty-seven, and had grey hair. Montalembert himself was, I think, one of the most interesting men I ever met. He had that curious mixture of the—shall I say?—supernaturalist and man of the world (not mystic, he was no mystic, but yet miraculous, if there is any meaning in that) which has always had so great an attraction for me,—keen and sharp as a sword, and yet open to every belief and to every superstition, far more than I ever could have been, who looked at him and up to him with a sort of admiring wonder and yet sympathy, not without a smile in it. He was a little like Laurence

Oliphant in this, but Laurence was not a highly educated man like Montalembert. M. de Montalembert struck me as the most delightful, benign, and genial of men when I saw him first; but afterwards I used to say that he was one of the few men I was afraid of, and that he had a fine way of picking one up as on some polished pair of tongs, and holding one up to the admiration of the world around, in all the bloom of one's powerful foolishness. I remember on one occasion, when there was great talk of vacant fanteuils in the Académie, and of the candidates, two of whom in particular were being discussed, I asked him, rather sillily, whether there were two vacancies or two candidates for one vacancy—something of that sort,—when he turned to the company and called their attention to the orderly, temperate, English mind, in which there was no rush at a prize, but a well-balanced competition of two, as I had suggested. There was a great deal of laughter, in which, of course, any shy explanation of mine was completely drowned. I doubt whether an Englishman of equally fine manners would have held up a French stranger to the gentle ridicule of the company in this way. And yet I always liked him in the midst of my alarm, and he was very kind. I gave him the 'Life of Irving,' with a little protest, which was quite true, that it was not because I had written it, but because of the man Irving that I wished him to read it, which protest he received with a little banter and look of seeing through me; but afterwards avowed that he was touched by the character of Irving and its truth, mightily apart as it was from all his own prepossessions, which were so strong, however, that he could not bear Scotland,—could not even persuade himself to permit the glamour of Sir Walter to excuse the black anti-Catholic desolation of that dreadful country, all but Iona.* Happening to speak of Carlyle, he expressed great dislike for him. I had mentioned that unfortunately Carlyle had no children. 'Why unfortunately?' said Montalembert; 'happily, rather, for he was not a man to have the bringing up of children.' I made some sort of indignant reply, but added, 'I don't believe in education.' He paused a moment, laughed, and said, 'Neither do I.' Carlyle had an equal dislike of him, and shot forth a thunder-bolt at him on one occasion when I mentioned him; but spoke of Lamennais* in a half tender tone,—'There is no hairm in him, no hairm in him,' he said. Lamennais was tragic from the Montalembert point of view,—a name to be spoken of with bated breath.

It was Count de Montalembert who gave me tickets for one of the side chapels in Notre Dame, where Père Félix* was preaching to men during Lent,—a scene I have described somewhere, and which I read a description of lately in the life of Mrs Craven. The nave was packed closely with men, a dark mass, their immovable faces whitening the whole surface of that great area under the not abundant lights, and the spare figure of the monk in the pulpit, his face whiter still, like ivory. It was very dark in the side chapels, and we did not hear very well; but the sight was very impressive, and specially so on, I think, the Thursday of Holy Week, when this immense crowd of men sang the Stabat Mater in unison,—the most wonderful volume of sound, which was quite overwhelming in the depth and strength of it, rolling like a kind of regulated and tempered thunder, or like the sound of many waters,*—a perfectly new and extraordinary effect. (I remember finding out afterwards, to my great confusion, that these tickets had been given to me only for one night, and that I had kept other people out of them—the sort of horrible ridiculous want of sense which makes one hot all over when one discovers it.)

On the Easter morning we went very early to Notre Dame to see the communion of these men, which was also a very touching sight. There was an old lady in the gallery where we were who looked down all the time, crying and talking to herself, 'Dix soldats—et un petit bon homme en blouse.'* I, more profane, smiled a little, and was a little ashamed of myself for doing so, at the air of conscious solemnity with which most of the men came up to the altar, very devout, but yet with a certain sense of forming part of a very great and ennobling spectacle.

I made little of the ladies of the Montalembert household on this occasion, my attention being chiefly attracted to him. The girls were quite young, and I did not see enough of them to make friends as afterwards with Madame de Montalembert,—a person to whom it is difficult to do justice in words, the fine, ample, noble Flamande, *grande dame au bout des ongles*,* ready and capable to do anything in the world of which there might be need, to defend a castle, or light a fire, or nurse the sick, but helplessly unable to 'do' her own hair,—a characteristic failure which amused me much when I found it out, which was not, however, till much later. As usual I did not make half the use of my opportunities which I ought to have done, was shy of going to see them, and held back generally after my fashion, which I

always regret afterwards. I am not sure that I ever saw Montalembert
again.

   At the other end of the social scale we picked up a curious pair in
Paris,—a man who was an Oxford man, far from a refined specimen,
indeed, who advertised in 'Galignani' for pupils, and whom I
engaged to begin my boy with Latin. He came, I think, every morning, and Cyril, aged eight, began his serious education under him. He
was of a species of which I saw various specimens later,—the half
rustic, half vulgar son of a country clergyman, gone all wrong at the
University, but not a bad scholar, and, above all, not a bad man—
coarse, red-faced, perhaps a little vicious, certainly addicted to drink.
He had a wife, a kind of falsely pretty creature, or with a false air of
being pretty, very pink and white, with one leg a little shorter than
the other in consequence of some illness, who had come to Paris to be
under Nêlotan, the great doctor and was periodically 'fired'* by him
as is done to horses. There was a baby and an English, or rather
Welsh, nurse, who stood by them through thick and thin, strongly
disapproving of both, but faithful all the same. It was she, I think,
probably through Jane, from whom we heard how the man—D.—had
been engaged to his wife before her illness, and had helped to nurse
her through it and made light of the defect it left, which he would not
permit to interfere with their marriage. This prepossessed me much
in his favour. Then came the report that she had a dreadful temper,
and threw plates and cups at him in her fury, which made his good-
humour and apparent devotion to her more touching still. Afterwards it appeared that she had a tolerable income and he not a penny,
besides being in innumerable scrapes, which discouraged us a little.
They used to come and spend one evening in the week with us, and I
think D. did his preliminary teaching very well. Fanny was his pupil
too, as well as Cyril; they were both, it is true, exceptional scholars.

   We had another regular evening visitor once a-week—a man whom,
though I never saw more of him than those regular weekly visits, I
got to think of as a dear friend, and I think he had the same sort of
feeling for me—Giovanni (or, as he wrote himself, John) Ruffini,*
the author of 'Dr Antonio,' an Italian refugee of the 1848 times, and
for years a resident in London, where he had written that delightful
book in English. His written English was beautiful, but he spoke it
badly and with difficulty. He was a large mild man, with blue eyes,
heavy-lidded and large—large externally, and specially remarkable

when they were cast down, which sounds odd but was true. He lived with an English family, with whom he had been for years—partly brother, partly lover, partly guest. I did not know them, and I don't know the rights of the story. The father had died some time before, but he still kept his place among them, and went about with the mother of the house, both of them growing old with what seemed to me a delightful innocence and naturalness. They made their *villeggiatura*, these two together, sometimes in a couple of chalets on a Swiss mountain, as if there had not been such a thing as an evil tongue in the world, which interested me exceedingly; and indeed his weekly visit, his pensive Italian mildness, the look of the traditional exile, though in so perfectly natural a man, was very interesting: that exile look with the faint air of fiction in it, and its absolute sincerity all the same, has gone out of mortal ken nowadays.

Another queer pair that I used to see were old Father Prout (Mahony, or O'Mahony, as he called himself)* and the old lady about whom he circled, and who was a very quaint old lady indeed, with the air of having been somebody,—a very dauntless, plain-spoken old person in old shiny black satin and lace, and looking as if everything was put on as well as the satin—hair, teeth, and everything else. I don't know if there had been anything wrong in their connection. It was certainly patriarchal then, they were so old and such born commanders and so entirely at ease with each other. It was wicked of me I fear, but it amused me to think that these old people had perhaps indulged in a *grande passion* and defied the world for each other. I thought no worse of them somehow! which I am aware is a most immoral sentiment. But perhaps there had never been anything in the least wrong. Peace to their ancient ashes!—they were a strange pair. She—I have forgotten her name—came to see me, and I went to her house once in the evening, somewhere in the heart of Paris, up a great many stairs, where she had an apartment exactly like herself, with much dingy decoration and a great many curious things, and the air somehow of being dressed like its mistress, and scented and done up with an artificialness which, as in the lady's case, by dint of long continuance had grown to be perfectly sincere. She bade her old gentleman sing me his great song, 'The Bells of Shandon,' which he did, standing up against the mantelpiece, with his pale head, like carved ivory, relieved against the regular *garniture de cheminée*,* the big clock and candelabra. He had a fine face with delicate features, almost an ascetic face, though his life had been not exactly of that description I fear. He was an unfrocked priest and I think was one of the Fraser group, which was, more or less, an imitation of the Blackwood group, with much real or pretended rivalry, and had knocked about a great deal in his life, and was poor. I think I heard that the old lady died, and that he became poorer still. There were thus two elderly romances, in old fidelity and friendship, under my eyes, made innocent, almost infantile, especially in the latter case, as of old babies, independent of sex and superior to it, amid all the obliterations of old age. I had several curious visitors of this kind, chiefly sent to me, I think, by Robert Macpherson,—one of them Miss Cushman, the actress, whom I had met in London and had not liked, but who touched my heart with her evident deep knowledge of trouble and sorrow. I think I have described her and others in some other places, though I can't tell where. I had visitors too from home,—Mrs Fitzgerald, the inevitable Miss Blackwood, and the Principal, who came to take the girls home, and in his turn brought some odd Scotch-cosmopolitan people. Not cosmopolitan, however, was the Scotch minister, who held his little conventicle in the Oratoire, and who said sturdily, and with the courage of his opinion, that he had not learned French, and did not mean to do so, as he disapproved of it altogether.

We were about six months in Paris, in the little bright apartment which I remember cost over a thousand francs for wood and coal during that time, and was as warm as a nest. The party consisted of the two girls, my two dear little boys,—Tiddy so full of wit and fun, Cecco always so original even in his babyhood, learning to read in Mademoiselle's wonderful way in a fortnight without a tear,—Mademoiselle herself, Jane, and a servant and a half—the *bonne à tout faire** and her child. The Champs Elysées, full of sun and brightness and fine carriages, and all the fine people passing in a stream every afternoon, did me much good, and it all bears a radiant aspect now as I look back, heavy though my heart often was. I heard then for the first time of our afterwards so familiar and beloved cousin Annie,* in reality a second cousin, whom I had never seen, but who wrote introducing herself to me, with some literary aspirations, taking at that time the shape of poetry, against which I remember I advised her, suggesting a novel instead. I cannot remember what I was then doing, nor how I was in the matter of money, but I presume I must have been going on with a flowing sail, working a great deal and not requiring to take much thought of my expenses, which, alas! was my way. I ought to have been saving, of course, but I didn't, with a miraculous ease of mind which some people have thought criminal. I sometimes think, too, that it was so, and also have sometimes lately (1895) pondered upon a sadder[1] theory still, as if that had something to do with the great sorrows that have clouded the end of my life. I never had any expensive tastes, but loved the easy swing of life, without taking much thought for the morrow, with a faith in my own power to go on working, which up to this time has been wonderfully justified, but which has been a great temptation and danger to me all through in the way of economies. I had always a conviction that I could make up by a little exertion for any extra expense. Sickness, incapacity, want of health or ability to work, never occurred to me, I suppose. At the same time, I never was very highly paid for my work, and perhaps this had its effect too on my carelessness in pecuniary matters. I made enough to carry me on easily, almost lavishly but not enough to save, never a large sum which could be partly put away at once and give one a taste of the sweetness of possessing something. I could not do this, and I fear it was not in me to practise that honourable pinching and sparing by which some women do so much. I had not the time for it, nor, indeed, I am ashamed to say, the wish. I am ashamed too to make the confession that I do not in the least remember what I was working at at this time. It is not that I have ever been indifferent to my work. I have always been most grateful to God that it was work I

---

[1] This is what I thought—that I had so accustomed them to the easy going on of all things, never letting them see my anxieties or know that there was a difficulty about anything, that their minds were formed to that habit, that it took all thought of necessity out of my Tiddy's mind, who had always, I am sure, the feeling that a little exertion (always so easy *to-morrow*) would at any time set everything right, and that nothing was like ever to go far wrong so long as I was there. The sentiment was not ungenerous, it was in a way forced upon him, partly by my own *insouciance* and partly by the fact that he was always saved from any practical effect of foolishness, so that at the last, what with the growth of habit, there was no other way for it but that,—'There is no way but this,' words I used to say over to myself. And my Cecco, who had not these follies, but who was stricken by the hand of God, until that too rendered further going on impossible, by the drying up of my sources and means of getting anything for him—so that I seem sometimes to feel as if it were all my doing, and that I had brought by my heedlessness both to an impasse from which there was no issue but one. It was a kind of forlorn pleasure to me that they had never wanted anything, but this turns it into a remorse. Who can tell? God alone over all knows, and works by our follies as well as our better ways. Must it not be at last to the good of all?

liked and that interested me in the doing of it, and it has often carried me away from myself and quenched, or at least calmed, the troubles of life. But perhaps my life has been too full of personal interests to leave me at leisure to talk of the creatures of my imagination, as some people do, or to make believe that they were more to me in writing than they might have been in reading—that is, my own stories in the making of them were very much what other people's stories (but these the best) were in the reading. I am no more interested in my own characters than I am in Jeanie Deans,* and do not remember them half so well, nor do they come back to me with the same steady interest and friendship. Perhaps people will say this is why they never laid any special hold upon the minds of others, though they might be agreeable reading enough. But this does not mean that I was indifferent to the work as work, or did not beat it out with interest and pleasure. It pleases me at this present moment, I may confess, that I seem to have found unawares an image that quite expresses what I mean—*i.e.*, that I wrote as I read, with much the same sort of feeling. It seems to me that this is rather an original way of putting it (to disclose the privatest thought in my mind), and this gives me an absurd little sense of pleasure.

We left Paris in the summer—my little boys, the governess, Jane, and I. I did not want to go back to England till the end of the year, and we strayed about a little. The tutor aforesaid and his wife had taken a house in Normandy with the intention of having boarders, and there it occurred to me to go for a short time—especially while Jane went home for her holiday. The house called itself the Château de Montilly, which sounded well. It was, however, a new square house in a garden, without any attractions whatever; and the unfortunate pair were rather insufferable at such close quarters, and I was very thankful to get away in about a fortnight—staying that time merely for decency's sake. Mr Story, who was in Paris, came down to visit me, I remember; and we went to see Bayeux and the tapestry, jogging along in a country shandrydan* with a huge red umbrella. That fact and a wonderful thunderstorm there was—which he and I sat at an open window to watch, much to the annoyance and terror of our hosts, who would have liked to shut it out with bolted shutters —are about all I recollect, except the discomfort of the forced stay with people totally out of my way and kind, and the little meannesses of the household, and the annoyed interest we began to take in what there would be for dinner as soon as we discovered that the fare was sure to be scanty and bad. We escaped as soon as we could, having taken in a few views of French village life, and made the discovery that to take out an ill-tempered Mrs—D.—for a little diversion—even if it were no more exciting than a Norman fair, and the drive thereto in a carriole* was good for her soul's health, poor thing, and cleared the skies. I am a little hazy about what followed. We went to Avranches, to the little country town hotel, where the good people of the place came in to dine, and tied their dinner napkins round their half-finished bottles of wine; and we went to Mont St Michel, which delighted me, and where I had half a mind to take one of the many empty houses left by the prison officials when it ceased to be a prison. One imposing white house dominating the village I was told I could have for a hundred francs a-year! There would have been economy, and a certain amount of interest and picturesque surroundings, but the sea and the vast sands were very grey. We bivouacked in an almost empty house, containing little but what are called box-beds in Scotland, and a table and chair or two, which belonged to an old priest, very snuffy and shabby, who was called M. L'Aumonier, and had, I suppose, filled that office in the economy of the great prison, though I don't quite know what office it is. He took me to window after window to show me little shelves of garden which he had on the slopes of the rock—one here and another there, but each provided with certain conveniences, on which the good man insisted much. The first night there I was seized by a sudden panic to find that I had lodged myself and my helpless little party in the midst of a strange, unknown, and rather rough community—in a house which had not a key even to its outer door,—and sat up till daylight to watch over them. The light reassured me, and the thought of my big and dauntless Jane, who was worth two men, and who would have faced an army for her two little boys. Oh, my little boys! and the happiness of watching over them and all their ways and sayings, though I was sad enough then, thinking there was no sadder mother, longing for my Maggie wherever I went.

We spent a long time at St Adresse, near Havre, in a house which belonged to Queen Christina of Spain, where there was capital sea-bathing; and the children, or at least Cyril, began to learn to swim, and enjoyed themselves in all the amusements of the sea-side. One half tragic experience we had. Setting out to row, I and my little man, only eight, with a recklessness which I shiver now to think of, we were caught by the current, and had not our plight been seen from the shore and a man sent after us, I don't know what might have happened. The current was well known, only not to me, newly arrived and, as it appeared, very imprudent. We had rowed a great deal on the Gairloch, and we were close inshore, and the shining sunlit water looked like burnished glass or gold, or both. Mademoiselle was with us, and as bold as a little stout Swiss lion. I had luck in that way at least. How much would have been spared if that boat had drifted out to sea! many years' toil coming to so little, many years' misery and sorrow, though many happy too—and this long tragedy at the end! To have ended all together under that rippled sheet of gold, what an escape from all that came after! But it would have been hard on Mademoiselle and her old mother at Lausanne. It makes one's head go round, however, to think how little difference it would have made had such a little catastrophe taken place, and made a paragraph in the papers,—an innocent, not undesirable, not unlovely catastrophe, all over sweetly and suddenly that has taken so many years to get over, and yet is over or soon will be: how little important to any one else! probably so much better for ourselves! I feel a kind of envy now of the situation and of the possibility—but this is all so vain.

I suppose it must have been after St Adresse that we went to St Malo, where the delightful bay, crowded with rocky islets and downy white sails, delighted me. We found a small cabin of a house on the very edge of the cliff at Dinard, which was then a little village, very primitive and quiet, whence we crossed to St Malo in a small boat with a big sail,—always a little alarming to me, notwithstanding my rash boating. It was called the *bateau de poissage*,* I remember, in the Norman-French that always sounded to me like Scotch. We had a noble Marie for our *bonne*, a woman with the finest thoughtful face, whom I had photographed in her beautiful cap, in spite of her protestations that it would have been much better to take her niece, a commonplace, pretty little girl. Probably they do not wear those caps now, in which they looked like medieval princesses, wandering after the procession of the *Fête Dieu*,* which took place while we were there. But these are all very trivial recollections. I remember being extremely touched by the playing of the local band in the Dinard church, I suppose on this occasion. They played where the anthem would come in in the English service, and what they played was *Ah* *che la morte,* and other airs from the 'Trovatore,' which shocked me at first into the usual English sense of superiority, and then affected me greatly with the thought that it was absolutely the best thing they could do which they were offering to God, whether very worldly or not, and what could the finest genius do more? My other best recollection is of the country doctor, whom I called to see my dear little Cecco in some illness, just enough to make an anxious woman more anxious, and who laughed and prescribed the *galette* of the place, a kind of cracknel, and *confiture* and cider, the drink of the place. I could have hugged him for his laugh, which proved how little was the matter, and administered the cracknel and the jam, but not the cider, which was sour. So little a thing dwells on one's mind, but it was not little at that moment, when these infantile vicissitudes were the most important matters in life.

We had rather a wild, rather a wearisome, but in some ways an amusing, journey from St Malo to Boulogne. There was a boat direct from St Malo, which, if I had been a wise woman, I should have taken, and so got home quite cheaply. But I had a great dislike to the sea; and with some compunction for the expense and more pleasure in the adventure,—though adventure there was really none, except that the manner of the journey was by that time a little out of the way,—we set off by land. So far as I remember, we went sixty miles the first day, if that is possible, but I don't recollect where we halted or how many days we took to the journey altogether. We started with that perfect ignorance of where we were going, and perfect confidence that everything would go well, which, I suppose, is peculiar to women (when they are not nervous and timorous). The carriage was packed with toys and books and all kinds of things for the children, and the progress through the air, the little exhilaration of the start, the glimpse of village interiors as we rattled past, the arrivals and departures, were quite enough amusement for me. I suppose Mademoiselle must have liked it too, for she threw herself completely into the frolic. And as for Jane, it was all in the day's work to her. I think we passed one night at Granville. I remember distinctly that we all lunched in the middle of the day at an unknown and nameless village, upon potatoes *en robe de chambre,** which Mademoiselle sagely advised as a thing we could be quite sure of, whereas other dishes might be doubtful, and the fragrant tray of fresh sponge biscuits, taken warm and sweet out of the oven while we were there and added to our meal as desert, which made me feel that the capabilities of the place were greater than we thought. The rush across a broad level of country without many features was monotonous in the end; but the quiet and fresh air, and long silences and sense of progress, were all soothing and pleasant. I have a kind of shadowy recollection of the journey, like a dream, that is refreshing still. We spent a day or two in Dieppe, intending at first to take the boat there, but having got into the habit of driving, with the old delightful connections of the *vetturino** coming back, we finally decided to continue our drive along the coast to Boulogne, and, though we did not deserve it, were rewarded at last by the smoothest of passages across the Channel—a thing which in those days I always dreaded. We found rooms in London in the Bayswater Road, opposite Kensington Gardens—a place I have always liked; and then I set to work to find a home for us, where there should be means of education for the boys. My mind was at first inclined for Harrow, but something, I forget what, induced me to come to Windsor, which captivated me at once. Either then or later I wrote a letter to Mr Warre, now the Head Master, then young and 'rising,' whom I found very agreeable, and who decided, but with some reluctance, that it might be possible to educate my sons at Eton in all respects like the other boys there, but sleeping at home; which possibility, combined with the beauty of the river and the castle, and the air of cheerful life about, decided me very quickly to settle here. And a house was found very quickly; not this in which I now sit, and where almost all the events of my later life have taken place, but one in the same Crescent, within two doors of me, smaller than this. We came into it in November, I think, 1865. I have been here ever since. The house was very bright, the sun on it almost from its rising to its setting, a pleasant little garden behind, and the Crescent garden—a piece of ground of considerable extent, which we called, I don't know why, the plantation, beautifully planted, and, considering its position, a wonderful little piece of landscape gardening,—of which we took possession by acclamation. Very few people used it in these days: the day of lawn-tennis was not yet, and I suppose most of the people were elderly, for we had it almost altogether to ourselves. I never knew till a long time after of how much importance it was in the first chapter of my boys' life, this bit of town garden with its fine trees and wild nooks and corners. Lately my Cecco has told me of so many things

that were done there, 'when we were small,' as he always said. It lies
under my windows now, but I can't trust myself to go into it.

Here we got to know gradually various people about. The
Hawtreys, a family of old brothers and sisters, relatives of the old
Provost Hawtrey of Eton, and in themselves a very characteristic
household. They lived in a large red-brick house near the church, the
centre of an enormous connection, married brothers and sisters,
nephews and nieces innumerable. The Windsor portion of the family
were known universally by their Christian names, Stephen and
Anna, Henry and Florence. They have all lived in my ken to be very
old people,—the two first having both died over eighty, while the
younger pair still survive, still ascending towards the snows. It
was a house full of entertainment, of family gatherings, Christmas
festivities, in which the overwhelming atmosphere of Hawtreyism
pervaded everything. They were all kind, much so naturally, a good
deal more so fictitiously. But anything so bland as John Hawtrey,
who was an Eton master, or so effusively benignant as old Stephen, I
never saw. There was a little perhaps of Pecksniff* in the last, who
was full of schemes, almost always benevolent, always more or less as
people thought, profitable, as exemplified in certain transactions
which are not worth telling, which were mere gossip, though if I had
time or was sure to give pain to nobody, they were not without
amusing points. A wicked wag at Eton declared that Stephen got up
in the morning to build the walls of his new mathematical school out
of the materials which were lying ready for more slothful workmen to
build Mr Somebody's house hard by,—a story everybody laughed at
as *ben trovato*,* though I cannot say I ever knew these good people to
do anything to the disadvantage of their neighbours. They were good
people, whether or no. They had all kinds of parties continually
going on,—dinner-parties, garden-parties, musical-parties. In one of
the latter a family quartette played what was rather new and terrible
to me, long sonatas and concerted pieces, which filled my soul with
dismay. It is a dreadful confession to make, and proceeds from want
of education and instruction, but I fear any appreciation of music I
have is purely literary. I love a song and a 'tune'; the humblest fiddler
has sometimes given me the greatest pleasure, and sometimes gone to
my heart; but music properly so called, the only music that many of
my friends would listen to, is to me a wonder and a mystery. My
mind wanders through andantes and adagios, gaping, longing to

understand. Will no one tell me what it means? I want to find the old unhappy far-off things or battles long ago, which Wordsworth imagined in the Gaelic song.* I feel out of it, uneasy, thinking all the time what a poor creature I must be. I remember the mother of the sonata players approaching me with beaming countenance on the occasion of one of those performances, expecting the compliment which I faltered forth, doing my best not to look insincere. 'And I have that every evening of my life!' cried the triumphant woman. 'Good heavens! and you have survived it all this time,' was my internal comment. I can see the kind glow on her face and the mother's pride, and thought myself, I am glad to say, a very poor creature to be left so helplessly behind, though not without a rueful amusement too.

I had a little neighbour in one of the smaller Crescent houses, whom the children soon got to call Aunt Nelly,* and I 'Little Nelly,'—I hardly know why, unless for the too perfect reason that she was Nelly and very little, which of course was much too simple to be the true meaning of the name. She it was who, dying in her sleep without so much as the movement of a finger—little happy woman, always of the angel kind—put the story, if story it can be called, of 'The Little Pilgrim' into my mind. Many simple people here had a sort of grotesque notion that there was something of her in it more than the suggestion, as if, alas! it were possible to follow and describe the ways of those who are gone. She was far from being wise or clever, generally reputed rather a silly little woman; but with a heart of gold, and a straightforward, simple, right judgment, which was always to me like the clear shining of a tiny light. She was, perhaps, a silly little woman, in fact, in some ways. There are kinds of foolishness I like for my own part, as there is also a kind of benignant gentle dulness which always soothes me, and which I constantly recommend to Miss Lawless* as so good a relief from the intellectualism she loves; but then she does love the intellectual, and I don't—much. My little Nelly had been trained to be unselfish, which, being far better than unselfish without training, was the only little fictitious trait in her—but so superficial and innocent. I often point the moral to the girls of that kind of technical unselfishness, by telling how little Nelly on a muddy road exhausted herself in finding a dry part for me, while she hobbled through the mud, as if I was to be outdone in that cheap generosity! But the woman was of the angel kind, and breathed goodness round her. She was the guardian, when I first knew her, of an old, old mother, whose head and memory were gone, and of a brother with a nervous disease—a poor man cast out of life in the middle of his days, and feeling himself to the bottom of his heart a cumberer of the soil. Her life was spent in amusing and caring for these two invalids, playing cards for hours with them. My little Cecco used to go in the evening, rather proud of being wanted, seven or eight years old, in his little velvet suit, to make the fourth at whist, and when he was a man would speak of the long whist 'which was Aunt Nelly's way.' The invalid brother was rarely visible, but sometimes I found a bouquet of flowers laid on my balcony, which was low enough to be reached from outside, which he laid there, stealing unnoticed into the garden.

Both these poor people died after long years, and left my little Nelly free—to take other burdens on her shoulders, and save other wounded creatures of God. Once when I was in great straits, and very anxious and unhappy, I asked her to help me in praying for the great boon I desired. I am not of the kind who do that usually, and perhaps when the trouble had been softened away I forgot even that I had done it; but thinking of it all years after, in the great and deep joy of knowing that the change I desired had come to pass, though without knowing what had led to it, I suddenly remembered how in my trouble I had sought her help, and it seemed to me like a flash of light upon the road by which we had come, not knowing. I have never asked any one else to do that for me.

Notwithstanding, she was the object of perpetual banter in the house. There was almost always some current joke about what little Nelly had done or said, at which she herself was the first to laugh. How many of those foolish, dear, affectionate mockeries I remember! Not mockeries—the word is too harsh: the ring of the laughter, the shining of the young eyes, and the light in her own, as beautiful as the youngest eyes among them, worn and faded as she was, are as fresh as ever. I wonder sometimes if what has been ever dies! Should not I find them all round the old whist-table, and my Cecco, with his bright face and the great blue vein that showed on his temple, proud to be helping to amuse the old people, if I were but bold enough to push into the deserted house and look for them now? I have so often felt, with a bewildered dizziness, as if that might be.

Then there was another near neighbour, one whom I have seen

to-day, who lives on as I do, lonely and forlorn, with all the elements
in her then of a brilliant life,—clever, witty, pretty, a woman not to be
passed over, and who, had her lot fallen otherwise, might have filled
any position almost, and perhaps been a leader of society, had life
been more auspicious to her. When I knew her first she lived in one
of the most important houses in the place, with a delightful old
mother, in a delightful house and much apparent comfort. She had a
handsome son in London, a beautiful daughter who had made a distinguished marriage abroad. She herself had read a great deal, was an
accomplished musician, spoke the purest French, knew foreign
society tolerably well, and had been one of the 'county' people more
or less, but when I knew her first was very lonely, not in perfect intelligence either with son or daughter, and either negligent or frettingly,
insufferably kind and anxious over her mother. I don't know, and
have never desired to know, notwithstanding the eagerness of many
people to inform me, what her past had been. It was not the least a
past such as is now meant when a woman with a past is spoken of, but
there had been some foolish rash attempt to secure a very brilliant
marriage at home for the beautiful daughter, which had prejudiced
the little society about against her, and she was very solitary, her
mother old and an invalid, and nobody who was the least her equal at
all in her way. There are some people who never get any credit for
what is good in them, and some who get too much credit. My friend
was one of those who are never done justice to, and indeed, if one may
say it, did not deserve to be done justice to, if such a contradiction
were ever true. She thought or said that she had been more than done
justice to in the former part of her life,—that she had been admired,
followed, and adored with more than her share of devotion; and
indeed this might have been quite true, for she must have been beautiful when she was young, and full of a sparkle of wit and cleverness
and accomplishments. But certainly there was very little of this in the
latter part of her life, though she was still a pretty woman at forty-
five, and infinitely superior to many of those who had no good word
for her. It might be because she was abandoned by her fine friends, or
it might be that she found something sympathetic in me, who have
always been a very good listener, and apt to admire and be interested
in attractive people, but she fell into a great intimacy with me, and
used to spend at least half of her time in my house. I believed at first,
of course, all she told me of the unkindness of others: some of

it was true; some of it, it became apparent in the course of years, was not true, or at least not all true, though probably she was not aware of this, and took her own part always with a zeal and vehemence which made her feel everybody else more completely in the wrong than it is safe to believe everybody who is against one can be. She had not the merry heart which goes all the way,* the happy blood that Mrs Craven speaks of;* and yet she had a certain version of the merry heart, and threw herself into all the little entertainments and pleasures which I gradually began to be drawn into, by reason of the household of girls I soon had. Cousin Annie, whom I did not know before, drifted towards me almost as soon as I came to Windsor, and as she was an orphan without a home, stayed with me for a number of years; and Sara and Fanny Tulloch paid me long visits; and my boys began to spring up and carried me along on the stream of their rising life. My neighbour threw herself into all we did, and we soon began to do a great deal. It makes me wonder, looking back, how, after the despair of my grief, which found so much utterance, I should have risen again into absolute gaiety thus, twice over. But so it was. I thought it was for the young people round me, and no doubt it was so, but equally without doubt my own life burst forth again with an obstinate elasticity which I could not keep down. The merry heart goes all the way. I worked very hard all the time, but could always spare a day or any amount of evenings to please the girls, still more to please the boys. For the children, after my Cyril went to Eton, we began to have theatricals, which grew into more and more importance, till we used to play Shakespeare and Molière in my little drawing-room, alternating with innocent versions of 'Barbe Bleue,' &c., but that in the earlier days. I never attempted any performance myself* but once, that of Mrs Hardcastle in 'She Stoops to Conquer.' Of course the great inspiration of these performances was Mr Frank Tarver, an Eton master, an excellent amateur actor, who, as he very soon fell in love with Sara, made himself prime minister, or, at least, master of the revels, with great energy, and helped to keep up the circle of amusement. There were others, too, full of character, and as interesting in their way as if they had been great lights in the literary or any other world, whom I might describe, and who made up a very intelligent and light-hearted society; but as not one of them turned out remarkable in any way, I need not insist upon them. One, who was one of the first to break the circle, my young friend Captain Gun, an engineer officer stationed here, I may mention. He was the Tony to my Mrs Hardcastle,—a large plain young man, full of ability and force. Had he lived he would, no doubt, have come to something. He had the readiness and resource of a soldier, seeing in a moment in a way that seemed magic to me where there was any kind of danger. I remember in Romney lock, in the dusk of a summer night, a sudden incomprehensible movement of his which filled me with alarm for a moment, as he suddenly made a step out of our boat, which shivered with the motion, into another close by and dimly seen. He had perceived that it was in unskilful hands, and that the bow had caught in the side of the lock,—a dangerous position, which his sudden additional weight at once remedied. This to my ignorance was wonderful, though, of course, it was the simplest thing in the world; but the quick sight and the quick action were delightful to witness, as soon as one understood them. He would fain have married F. and Mr Tarver did marry S., my two young and frequent guests, and these threads of interest added to the full life. Captain Gun married a few years later a lady wonderfully like Fanny, who died soon, and he died shortly after, on which last occasion there were some very curious incidents took place with the table-rapping, to which we had given ourselves, with much levity, for the moment,—the only serious experience we ever had.

Into the midst of this half-childish gaiety there came a very sudden and alarming interruption. My brother Frank had married at the same time as I myself did, and had lived a very humdrum but happyish life with a wife who suited him, and had now four children —a boy and three girls. He had been in rather delicate health for a year or two, and had fallen into rather a nervous condition, his hand shaking very much so that it was difficult for him to write, though he still could do his work. For this reason I heard from them rarely, as Jeanie, his wife, was a bad correspondent too. One morning very suddenly, and in the most painful and disagreeable way, I heard that he had got into great trouble about money, and was, in fact, a ruined man. It was the thunderbolt out of the clear sky, which is always so tremendous. I spent a day of misery, expecting him to come to me, not knowing what to expect, and fearing all sorts of things. A day or two after I went to look for him, and found him absent and his wife in great trouble. His health, from what I now heard, was altogether shattered; and it was that as much as anything else which had brought his affairs into the most hopeless muddle, from which there seemed no escape. They had not very much money at any time, but what they had had somehow slipped through his fingers. His wife and I did everything we could, but that was very little. He was a man without an expensive taste, the most innocent, the most domestic of men, but what he had had always slipped through his fingers, as I well knew. Poor dear Frank! how well I remembered the use he made of one of my mother's Scotch proverbs to justify some new small expense following a bigger one which he would allow to be imprudent. 'Well,' he would say, half-coaxing, half-apologetic, 'what's the use of eating the coo and worrying [choking] on her tail?' Alas! he had choked on the tail this time without remedy, and the only thing to be done was to wind up the affairs as well as was possible, and to further the little family, whom he could not live without, after him, which was what we did accordingly, with a prompt action which was some relief to our heavy hearts. We neither of us had a word of blame on our lips or a thought of anger in our hearts. Frank and Nelly, the two elder children, came to me, and Jeanie with her two little girls (my two girls this many a year, and now the only comfort of my life) joined her husband in France. It was a terrible break in life, and affected me in many ways permanently; but after the shock of seeing that chasm opening at our feet, and all their life shattered to pieces, everything quieted down again. The children were well. Oh, magic of life that made everything go smooth! they had taken no harm. They had their lives before them, and unbounded possibilities of making everything right. I am not sure that I had not a sort of secret satisfaction in getting Frank, my nephew, into my hands, thinking, with that complacency with which we always look at our own doings, that I could now train him for something better than they had thought of. This was in 1868. My Cyril was twelve and at Eton, having his room at his tutor's, and living precisely like other Eton boys, though coming home to sleep, which was one of the greatest happinesses in my life. Frank was fourteen, a big strong boy. I planned to send him to Eton too, but coming home for his meals, which was much less expensive, as I could not afford the other for him, and it answered very well. He was always the best of boys, manful, and a steady worker. Cyril had begun to be by this time noted as one of the cleverest boys, far on for his age, and promising everything, besides the brightest, wittiest, most sparkling little fellow, as he always was. I used to make it my boast that both my boys received Frank as a true brother, and never would have allowed me, had I wished it, to give them any pleasure or advantage which he did not share. Nelly after a while went to her mother's sister, Mrs Sime, and so we all settled down. If Denny publishes this, or any part of it, she will, of course, or any one else who may have the charge of it, cut out any of these details she pleases. It is not likely that such family details would be of interest to the public.

And yet, as a matter of fact, it is exactly those family details that are interesting,—the human story in all its chapters. I have often said, however, that none of us with any of the strong sense of family credit which used to be so general, but is not so, I think, now, could ever really tell what were perhaps the best and most creditable things in our own life, since by the strange fate which attends us human creatures, what is most creditable to one is often least creditable to another. These things steal out; they are divined in most cases, and then forgotten. Therefore all can never be told of any family story, except at the cost of family honour, and that pride which is the most pardonable of all pride, the determination to keep unsullied a family name. This catastrophe was tremendous in appearance, and yet was more or less a good thing for the children, whose prospects seemed to be utterly ruined,—not for the parents. Poor Jeanie—not strong enough, I suppose, to bear what fell upon her, as she had not been strong enough to do anything to prevent it—died most unexpectedly in her sleep, in a mild attack of fever which excited no alarm. My brother had been glad to get an appointment among the employees of a railway that was being made by the Walkers, of all places in the world, in Hungary, and went there with his wife and the little girls. I forget how long they were there,—only a very short time. The shock of their downfall was over, they were more or less happy to be together, and Frank and Nelly were happy enough here. We had returned to all our little gaieties again, our theatricals,—our boating, and the rest,—without much thought on my part, I fear, of the additional responsibility I had upon me of another boy to educate and set out in the world. We were all assembled, a merry party enough, one summer evening, after an afternoon on the river, at a late meal,—a sort of supper,—when a telegram was put into my hand. I remember the look of the long table and all the bright faces round it, the pretty summer dishes, salad, and pink salmon, and ornamented sweet things, and many flowers, the men and boys in their flannels, the girls in their light summer dresses,—everything light and bright. I have often said that it was the only telegram I ever received without a certain tremor of anxiety. Captain Gun, who was there, had been uncertain of his coming on this particular day, and a good many telegrams on that subject had been passing between us. I held the thing in my hand and looked across at him, and said, 'This time it cannot be from you.' Then I opened it with the laugh in my mouth, and this is what I read: 'Jeanie is dead, and I am in despair.' It was like a scene in a tragedy. They all saw the change in my face, but I dreaded to say anything, for there was her son sitting by, my good Frank, as gay as possible. He was only about fifteen, or perhaps sixteen. We managed to keep it from him till next morning, not to give him that shock in the midst of his pleasure; and somehow the supper got completed without any one knowing what had happened.

A very short time after my poor brother came home with the two little white-faced, forlorn children, with their big eyes. I never thought but that it must kill him, but it did not; though, when I met them at Victoria, I thought I never should have got him safely back, even to Windsor. He was completely shattered, like a man in a palsy, for a time scarcely able to stand or to speak, but not so overwhelmed with grief as I expected. Grief is the strangest thing, or rather it is very wonderful in how many different ways people take those blows, which from outside seem as if they must be final. Especially is it so in the closest of human connections, that between man and wife. People who have seemed to be all the world to each other are parted so, and the survivor, who is for the moment as my poor brother said 'in despair,' shows the most robust power of bearing it, and is so soon himself or herself again, that one, confounded and half-ashamed, feels that one is half-ridiculous to have expected anything different. Frank, poor fellow, had got over his sorrow on the long journey. He came to me like a child glad to get home, not much disturbed about anything that could happen. He lived for about six years after, for a great part of the time in tolerable comfort, but, so far as work was concerned, was capable of no more. The shaking of his hand was never cured, nor even sufficiently improved to make writing of any kind possible. He settled down to a kind of quiet life, read his newspaper, took his walk, sat in his easy-chair in the dining-room or in his own room for the rest of the day, was pleased with Frank's progress and with Nelly's love for reading, and with his little girls, and so got through his life, I think, not unhappily. But he and I, who had been so much to each other once, were nothing to each other now. I sometimes thought he looked at me as a kind of stepmother to his children, and we no longer thought alike on almost any subject: he had drifted one way and I another. He did not even take very much interest in me, and I fear he often irritated me. Poor Frank! it was sometimes a great trial, and I often wonder how the life went on, on the whole, so well as it did. He entertained delusive hopes for a time of going back and of being able to do something; but they were evidently from the first delusions and nothing more, and it did not hurt him so much as might have been thought when they vanished, —he had too little strength to feel it, I suppose.

Of course I had to face a prospect considerably changed by this great addition to my family. I had been obliged to work pretty hard before to meet all the too great expenses of the house. Now four people were added to it, very small two of them, but the others not inexpensive members of the house. I remember making a kind of pretence to myself that I had to think it over, to make a great decision, to give up what hopes I might have had of doing now my very best, and to set myself steadily to make as much money as I could, and do the best I could for the three boys. I think that in some pages of my old book I have put this down with a little half-sincere attempt at a heroical attitude. I don't think, however, that there was any reality in it. I never did nor could, of course, hesitate for a moment as to what had to be done. It had to be done, and that was enough, and there is no doubt that it was much more congenial to me to drive on and keep everything going, with a certain scorn of the increased work, and metaphorical toss of my head, as if it mattered! than it ever would have been to labour with an artist's fervour and concentration to produce a masterpiece. One can't be two things or serve two masters. Which was God and which was mammon in that individual case it would be hard to say, perhaps; for once in a way mammon, meaning the money which fed my flock, was in a kind of a poor way God, so far as the necessities of that crisis went. And the wonder was that we did it, I can't tell how, economising, I fear, very little, never knowing quite at the beginning of the year how the ends would come together at Christmas, always with troublesome debts and forestalling of money earned, so that I had generally eaten up the price of a book before it was printed, but always—thank God for it!—so far successfully that, though always owing somebody, I never owed anybody to any unreasonable amount or for any unreasonable extent of time, but managed to pay everything and do everything, to stint nothing, to give them all that was happy and pleasant and of good report* through all those dear and blessed boyish years. I confess that it was not done in the noblest way, with those strong efforts of self-control and economy which some people can exercise. I could not do that, or at least did not, but I could work. And I did work, joyfully, with pleasure in it and in my life, sometimes with awful moments when I did not know how I should ever pass some dreadful corner, where the way seemed to end and the rocks to close in: but the corner was always rounded, the road opened up again.

I recollect one of these moments especially, I forget the date: I always do forget dates, but the circumstances were these. We were a family of eight, children included, two boys at Eton, almost always guests in the house,—every kind of thing (in our modest way) going on, small dinner-parties, and a number of mild amusements, when it so happened that I came to a pause and found that every channel was closed and no place for any important work. I had always a lightly flowing stream of magazine articles, &c., and refused no work that was offered to me; but the course of life could not have been carried on on these, and a large sum was wanted at brief intervals to clear the way. I had, I think, a novel written, but did not know where I should find a place for it. Literary business arrangements were not organised then as now—there was no such thing as a literary agent. Serials in magazines were published in much less number, magazines themselves being not half so many (and a good thing too!). The consequence was that I seemed to be at a dead standstill. It was like nothing but what I have already said,—a mountainous road making a sharp turn round a corner, when it seems to disappear altogether, as if it ended there in the closing in of the cliffs. I was miserably anxious, not knowing where to turn or what to do, hoping every morning would bring me some proposal, waiting upon God, if I may use the word (I did the thing with the most complete faith,—what could I else?), for the opening up of that closed way. One evening I got a letter from a man whose name I did not know, asking if he could come to see me about a business matter. I forget whether he mentioned the name of the 'Graphic,' then just established,—I think not; at all events there was nothing in the letter to make me think it of any importance. I replied, however (I didn't always reply so quickly), appointing the second day after to receive him. I had decided to go to London next day to see if I could persuade some one to take my novel and give a good price for it. I think it was to Mr George Smith* I went, who was very kind and gracious, as was his wont, but would have nothing to say to me. I fancy I went somewhere else, but I had no success. I recollect coming home in a kind of despair, and being met at the door when it was opened to me by the murmur of the merry house, the cheerful voices, the overflowing home,—every corner full and warm as if it had a steady income and secure revenue at its back. My brother, I remember, who I suppose had seen some cloud on my face before I left, came forward to meet me with some trivial question, hoping I had not felt cold or taken cold or something, which in the state of despair in which I was had a sort of exasperating effect upon me; but they were all dispersing over the house to get ready for dinner, and I escaped further notice. No one thought anything more than that I was dull or cross for the rest of the evening. I used to work very late then, always till two in the morning (it is past three at this moment, 18th, nay, 19th April 1895, but this is no longer usual with me). I can't remember whether I worked that night, but I think it was one of the darkest nights (oh, no, no, that I should say so! they were all safe and well), at least a very dreadful moment, and I could not think what I should do.

Next morning came my visitor. He came from the 'Graphic': he wanted a story, I think the first they had had. He wanted it very soon, the first instalments within a week or two; and after a little talk and negotiation, he came to the conclusion that they would give me £1300. The road did run round that corner after all. Our Father in heaven had settled it all the time for the children; there had never been any doubt. I was absolutely without hope or help. I did not know where to turn, and here, in a moment, all was clear again—the road free in the sunshine, the cloud in a moment rolled away.

It was not, however, the story which I had finished at the time which I gave them (which did not seem suitable). I began another instantly, and went on with it in instalments, I think. It was the novel called 'Innocent,'* and was not very good, so far as I can remember, though the idea was one that had pleased me,—the development by

successive shocks of feeling of a girl of dormant intelligence. I believe
the trial scene in it was very badly managed—not unnatural, for I
never was present at a trial, though that, of course, was no excuse. It
was seldom that an incident so dramatic as this little episode I have
described took place in my life; but it was checkered with similar, if
lesser, crises. It was always a struggle to get safely through every year
and make my ends meet. Indeed I fear they never did quite meet;
there was always a tugging together, which cost me a great deal of
work and much anxiety. The wonder was that the much was never
too much. I always managed it somehow, thank God! very happy
(and presuming a little on my privilege) when I saw the way tolerably
clear before me, and knew at the beginning of the year where the
year's income was to come from, but driving, ploughing on, when I
was not at all sure of that all the same, and in some miraculous way
getting through. If I had not had unbroken health, and a spirit almost
criminally elastic, I could not have done it. I ought to have been worn
out by work, and crushed by care, half a hundred times by all rules,
but I never was so. Good day and ill day, they balanced each other,
and I got on through year after year. This, I am afraid, sounds very
much like a boast. (I was going to add, 'but I don't mean it as such.') I
am not very sure, however, that I don't mean it, or that my head
might not be a little turned sometimes by a sense of the rashness and
dare-devilness, if I may use such a word, of my own proceedings; and
it was in its way an immoral, or at least an un-moral, mode of life,
dashing forward in the face of all obstacles and taking up all burdens
with a kind of levity, as if my strength and resource could never fail.
If they had failed, I should have been left in the direst bankruptcy;
and I had no right to reckon upon being always delivered at the
critical moment. I should think any one who did so blamable now. I
persuaded myself then that I could not help it, that no better way was
practicable, and indeed did live by faith, whether it was or was not
exercised in a legitimate way. I might say now that another woman
doing the same thing was tempting Providence. To tempt Providence or to trust God, which was it? In my own case, naturally, I said
the last, and did not in the least deserve, in my temerity, to be led
and constantly rescued as I was. I must add that I never had any help
from outside.* I never received so much as a legacy in my life. My
publishers were good and kind in the way of making me advances,
without which I could not have got on; but they were never

—probably because of these advances, and of my constant need and inability, both by circumstances and nature, of struggling over prices—very lavish in payment. Still, I made on the whole a large income—and spent it, taking no great thought of the morrow. Yes, taking a great deal of thought of the morrow in the way of constant work and constant undertaking of whatever kind of work came to my hand. Perhaps I say all this because I have been assailed from a very unlikely quarter with furious upbraidings as to my extravagance which made me very wroth and very sore—and so feel the need of defending myself. But, indeed, I do not defend myself. It would have been better if I could have added the grace of thrift, which is said to be the inheritance of the Scot, to the faculty of work. I feel that I leave a very bad lesson behind me; but I am afraid that the immense relief of getting over a crisis gave a kind of reflected enjoyment to the trouble between, and that these alternations of anxiety and deliverance were more congenial than the steady monotony of self-denial, not to say that the still better kind of self-denial which should have made a truer artist than myself pursue the higher objects of art, instead of the mere necessities of living, was wanting too. I pay the penalty in that I shall not leave anything behind me that will live. What does it matter? Nothing at all now—never anything to speak of. At my most ambitious of times I would rather my children had remembered me as their mother than in any other way, and my friends as their friend. I never cared for anything else. And now that there are no children to whom to leave any memory; and the friends drop day by day, what is the reputation of a circulating library to me? Nothing, and less than nothing—a thing the thought of which no makes me angry, that any one should for a moment imagine I car for that, or that it made up for any loss. I am perhaps angry, le reasonably, when well-intentioned people tell me I have done goc or pious ones console me for being left behind by thoughts of th good I must yet be intended to do. God help us all! what is the good done by any such work as mine, or even better than mine? 'If any man build upon this foundation . . . wood, hay, stubble; . . . if the work shall be burned, he shall suffer loss: but he himself shall be saved; yet so as by fire.'* An infinitude of pains and labour, and all to disappear like the stubble and the hay. Yet who knows? The little faculty may grow a bigger one in the more genial land to come, where one will have no need to think of the boiling of the daily pot. In the meantime

it was good to have kept the pot boiling and maintained the cheerful household fire so long, though it is smouldering out in darkness now.
. There is one thing, however, I have always whimsically resented, and that is the contemptuous compliments that for many years were the right thing to address to me and to say of me, as to my 'industry.' Now that I am old the world is a little more respectful, and I have not heard so much about my industry for some time. The delightful superiority of it in the mouth of people who had neither industry nor anything else to boast of used to make me very wroth, I avow,—wroth with a laugh and rueful half sense of the justice of it in the abstract, though not from those who spoke. The same kind of feeling made me angry the other day even, comically, not seriously angry, at a bit of a young person who complimented me on my 'Beleaguered City.'* Now, I am quite willing that people like Mr Hutton should speak of the 'Beleaguered City' as of the one little thing among my productions that is worth remembering (no, Mr Hutton does nothing of the kind—he is not that kind of person), but I felt inclined to say to the other, 'The "Beleaguered City," indeed, my young woman! I should think something a good deal less than that might be good enough for you.' By which it may perhaps be suspected that I don't always think such small beer of myself as I say, but this is a pure matter of comparison.

I need scarcely say that there was not much of what one might call a literary life in all this. I was very seldom in town, Windsor being near enough to permit of almost all that one wanted to do in town, except society, being done in a day, between two trains so to speak, which was the most convenient thing in the world, and the most impossible for any sort of social intercourse. Even a dinner-party, which could only be done at the cost of a visit, thus became much more out of the question than if I had lived at a greater distance, and thus been compelled to pass a week or two occasionally in London. Now and then I went to a luncheon-party or an afternoon gathering, both of which things I detested. Curiously enough, being fond on the whole of my fellow-creatures, I always disliked paying visits, and felt myself a fish out of water when I was not in my own house,—not to say that I was constantly wanted at home, and proud to feel that I was so. The work answered very well for a pretence to get me off engagements, but I could always have managed the work if I had liked the pleasure, or suppposed pleasure. I need not speak, however, as if I had been a person in much request, which would be giving an entirely false view of myself. I never was so in the least. From the days when my Jewish friend complained that I did not do myself justice, with the aggrieved tone of a woman to whom I had thus done a great injustice by not doing anything to make myself agreeable or remarkable, being asked to her house for that purpose, I have always been a disappointment to my friends. I have no gift of talk, not much to say; and though I have always been an excellent listener, that only succeeds under auspicious circumstances.

I think I never met so many people as in the days of Mrs Duncan Stewart,* that dear and bright old lady who used to fill her little rooms in Sloane Street with the most curious jumble of entertaining people and people who came to be entertained, the smartest (odious word!) of society, and all the luminaries of the moment, many writers, artists, &c., and a few mountebanks to make up. She herself was very worthy of a place in any picture-gallery. There is a very dull sketch of her by Mr Augustus Hare, which does no justice to the subject. She was an English and nineteenth-century shadow of the French ladies who take up so much space in the records of the eighteenth, and who were, indeed, I suppose, of no more personal consequence than she, were it not for the mention they have secured in so many records of a memoir-writing time, and the numbers of great people who circled round them. Mrs Stewart had known almost everybody in her day, which of itself is a wonderful attraction. She had at one time seen much of Disraeli—almost at one time run the risk of having her head turned by him. The loves (but this never came to be a love—on her side at least; 'For, my dear,' she used to say, 'I had the great preservation of being in love with my husband') of a lady of eighty are always amusing and pathetic. Age takes all the doubtfulness out of them, and gives them a piquancy as of the loves of children. She had ancient suitors, worshippers of her old age, always about her. I believe she refused a proposal of marriage after she was seventy. She was at the time I knew her of the most picturesque appearance, with a delicate small face of the colour of ivory, fine features, except that always troublesome mouth, which is imperfect in almost every face that is good for anything, and those dim blue eyes which have a charm of their own—half veiled and mystic. She was one of those people who do not grow grey, and she wore a peculiar head-dress—a kerchief of fine muslin and lace falling upon her shoulders, and softly veiling her small erect head. In the middle of the flutter of general company about her, she had always (as indeed every one has) a constant circle of intimates always the same, and sometimes not quite worthy of the idol they surrounded. It seems a law of nature that this should be so, and that every remarkable person should have a little ring of commonplace satellites, who are apt to make the object of their adoration a little absurd, out of pure love and desire to do her or him honour, with perhaps the leaven of a little hope to do themselves honour too, by being known as her or his friends. This delightful old lady was very fond of seeing and knowing everything. She went to every entertainment, grave or gay, and was all agog to go to the Greek play at Eton, where it came to entrance us from Oxford, with a chorus *pour rire** of a dozen dreadfully recognisable young Dons and scholars *affublés** in inconvenient robes and beards; as well as to see Sarah Bernhardt, or any and every novelty that turned up. 'La pièce m'intéresse,'* she said, looking out upon her parties with her dim eyes that saw everything, and never so pleased as when the crowd fluttered about her, and a little special court gathered round her sofa. Some vile young journalist, I remember, made a cruel sketch of her, which was published in a cruel and wicked series then giving great piquancy to the 'Saturday Review' (I think it was in the Girl of the Period and Mature Siren time, which are all so forgotten nowadays), for which I hope he has had his deserts somewhere. Of course, nothing could be easier than to travesty this sweet and bright old lady into a spectre of society, clinging on to the last to social dissipations, and incapable of being alone—and nothing more absolutely untrue. Her grandchild said of her after she was dead, in the hush of that pause in which the longing to know what they are doing, what they are thinking who have left us, is overwhelming, 'Oh, she will have no time to think of us, she will be so much interested in seeing everything.' Even in the shock of loss it was impossible not to be consoled by the thought of that vivid curiosity and interest and enjoyment with which she would find a new sphere before her, with everything to be found out.

(Of Mrs Stewart's daughter, my dear friend Christina Rogerson,* it is difficult to speak. She is more original, more attractive in some points of view than her mother. She too has known everybody in the half of the time her mother had for that purpose, but she will live to be eighty like Mrs Stewart. She has had all manner of adventures and gone through all sorts of phases. She is the most varied, complex, bewildering character, yet the most simple and transparent, full of wiles, intrigues, plots and conspiracies which take in the ignorant I suppose at first but are like a child's tricks when one knows her better, always pitifully easy to fathom and foresee. She is often very wrong and I entertain no illusions on the subject, but think never the worse of her and like her never the less whatever she does—an odd effect which I think grows on me. I am in her house now and there has been a little plot about our coming here which I have found out and have been for an hour or two very angry about, yet it makes absolutely no difference to my rich affection for her and liking—are the two the same? Or is there a difference? I think there must be a difference for I have a feeling of affection for people whom I should not in the least welcome with pleasure as I am about to welcome Chrissie. Notwithstanding my yesterday's displeasure and sense that she meant to deceive me and has partially succeeded in doing so. It is highly immoral and very cynical I fear to laugh and not to mind after the little demonstration she has made of 'smartness' in the American sense of the word, and indifference to my comfort while making me serve her purpose. I am perfectly aware of it all, and yet like her just the same. It is pretty Chrissie's way. She is the kindest soul in the world all the same. She would do anything in the world for me, but yet take the credit of her intention as if she had done all she meant to do. How delightful she is with those children, how loving and mother like—and how they adore her—gutter children, with nothing but the mud of London natural to them, but now made into the healthiest children, of the fields, breathing love and care, not knowing what it is to be neglected, thought of and cared for in everything as if they were in the nursery of a duke, yet all judiciously, no absurd petting, but good honest care and love. Nothing can be too much to say for her in this respect. And among her dependents she is the most imperious mistress and the kindest familiar friend, far too imperious for me, far kinder than I am capable of being, always a paradox and a delightful one, always extravagant, always poor, pursuing rather oblique ways of getting that wretched money sometimes, and then flinging it away in generosity and help. There is no end to the amusement to be got out of her. I am afraid this present project of coming here to occupy the house which seemed such a famous project, so secretly what she wanted while also convenient to

THE AUTOBIOGRAPHY 141
us, will come to harm, chiefly by her aim to exploit the house all the
same, and do with it as if we were not here—however perhaps it will
all come all right and things go better than appears. She has married a
newspaper now, and my glimpse through her at the young men who
make newspapers is not agreeable, that is another story as Rudyard
Kipling says. They are by way of being literary society too—but the
queerest aspect of it—they don't seem so far as I can see to read
anything, even their brother (or sister) newspapers. They talk the
ugliest slang, they write slapdash.)—All this was a mere utterance of
the moment and not worth pursuing.

Whom did I meet at Mrs Stewart's? I forget; nobody, I suppose, of
any great consequence. She had little boxes of rooms over a tailor's
shop in Sloane Street, and there gave the most elaborate luncheons,
all sorts of delicacies, to which a number of very fine people would
crowd in, sitting at all the uneasy angles of a table with adjuncts to it,
which completely filled the room. Her income, I believe, was as small
as her rooms; and her pleasant way was to tell her daughter or some
intimate friend she had so many people coming to lunch, and then to
prepare her pretty head-dress and her careful little *mise en scène* to
receive them, with no further thought of more substantial prepara-
tions. But the table groaned all the same, and there was every costly
and delicate viand on it that was to be had, and heaps of flowers,
thanks always to Chrissie, who would grumble a little and triumph in
it, being always in such matters a person of genius and proud of her
mother's successes, though the cost in all ways was her own. There
used to be Lady Martin often, in a large Rubens hat and long
sweeping feather, though long past the age of such vanities, seventy
or thereabouts, with all the old world graces, and the consciousness
of having been more admired than any woman of her day, which
gives an ineffable air to an old beauty, though she had never been a
beauty. Her husband, the excellent Sir Theodore,* was so evidently
and so constantly the first of all her admirers, leading the band,
that the group was always interesting and touching in its bygone-
ness yet perfect sincerity and good faith. She wrote her book after
this about the Shakespeare parts she had played,—that strange,
elegant, antiquated expression of the graceful feminine enthusiast
accustomed to applause in every pose she assumed or word she
uttered which, at least in the case of a good woman, at her age is so
touching as to make one ashamed of the horrid laugh which quavers

away almost into sentiment while we look on and are ashamed of our-selves. There was the twinkle of Bon Gaultier in Sir Theodore's eye on other matters, but never where his wife was concerned. And a very frequent visitor was the kind, the gentle, the sympathetic Censor of Plays, dead only this year, Mr Pigott, a man to whom everybody's heart went out, I don't know exactly why or how, except from an intuition of friendship, a sort of instinct. He was always interested, always kind,—a sort of atmosphere of humanity and warm feeling and sympathy about him, his little round form and round head radiating warmth and kindliness. He is the only man I have ever met, I think, from whom I never heard an unkind word of any one. This, to tell the sad truth, is apt to make conversation a little insipid; but he had the most extensive acquaintance both with people and things, and had many a happy turn of expression and *mot* of social wisdom which preserved him from that worst of faults: he was never dull, though always kind, which is almost a paradox. I have my own way of dividing people, as I suppose most of us have. There are those whom I can talk to, and those whom I can't. With the first no subject is needed, the conversation goes on of itself; with the other all the finest subjects in the world produce no result. (I remember as I write one story of Mr Pigott which slightly, but very slightly, contradicts this statement that he never said an unkind word. We were talking once of the son-in-law of a friend of ours,* who had most gratuitously and unnecessarily appeared against her in a trial in which she was unhappily involved, to prove (as if any one could prove such a thing) that certain anonymous letters were written by her. We were discuss-ing his conduct with indignation, when Mr Pigott looked up with a smile,—'Look in his face and you'll forgive him all,' he said. It was true that the man was a fool, and bore it on his face.)

It was with Mrs Stewart that I first saw Tennyson. She had, I suppose, asked leave to take me there with her to luncheon, and I was of course glad to go, though a little unwilling, as my manner was. I forget where it was—an ordinary London house, where they were living for the season. Mrs Tennyson lay upon her sofa, as she did always—though able to be taken to the luncheon-table by her excellent son Hallam, whom I knew a little, and who was always kind and pleasant. I have always thought that Tennyson's appearance was too emphatically that of a poet, especially in his photographs: the fine frenzy, the careless picturesqueness, were almost too much. He looked the part too well; but in reality there was a roughness and acrid gloom about the man which saved him from his over romantic appearance. He paid no attention to me, as was very natural. The conversation turned somehow upon his little play of 'The Falcon' —now more forgotten, I think, than any of his others, though it seemed to me much the most effective of them. I said something about its beauty, and that I thought it just the kind of entertainment which a gracious prince might offer to his guests; and he replied, with a sort of indignant sense of grievance, 'And they tell me people won't go to see it.' I am afraid, however, that I did not attract the poet in any way, to Mrs Stewart's great disappointment and annoyance. She was eager to point out to me that he was much occupied by a very old lady—a fair, little, white-haired woman, nearly eighty, the mother of Mr Tom Hughes (Tom Brown),* who was just then going out to America to the settlement in the backwoods which was called Rugby, in Tennessee, where the young Hughes were, and which was going to be the most perfect colony on the face of the earth, filled with nothing but the cardinal virtues. I think the old lady died there, and I know the settlement went sadly to pieces and ruined many hopes. However, feeling I had not been entirely a success,—a feeling very habitual to me,—I was glad of Mrs Stewart's sign of departure, and went up to Mrs Tennyson on the sofa, to which she had returned, to take my leave. I am never good at parting politenesses, and I daresay was very *gauche* in saying that it was so kind of her to ask me; while she graciously responded that she was delighted to have seen me, &c., according to the established ritual in such cases. Tennyson was standing by, lowering over us with his ragged beard and his saturnine look. He eyed us, while these pretty speeches were being made, with cynical eyes. 'What liars you women are!' he said. There could not have been anything more true; but, to be sure, it was not so civil as it was true. I never saw him again till that recent occasion when my Cecco and I went to Farringford when he was Lord Tennyson, and very old and infirm, and his wife was a shrunken old, old lady, laid upon a sofa from which she never moved, and pushed aside into a corner it seemed to me, the flood of life flowing past her but never touching her,—a pathetic sight. It was after Lionel's death, and after my Cyril's death, and I sat by her and cried; but she seemed in her old age as if she could weep no more. That time Lord Tennyson was delightful—kind and friendly and full of stories, talking a great deal, and in the best of humours. He read the 'Funeral Ode' to us after-wards, and one or two shorter poems ('Blow, bugles, blow'); and I was so glad and thankful that Cecco should see him so, and have such a bright recollection of him to carry through his life. Alas! alas! It had always been a regret that he had never seen Carlyle—so little as it matters now!

It is rather a fictitious sort of thing recalling those semi-professional recollections. It is by way of a kind of apology for knowing so few notable people. I met Mr Fawcett* once, the blind politician, a huge mild man, cheerful in talk and amiable in countenance, whom some-body (not me, I am afraid) overheard saying to his wife when she came back to him from another room, to take—the small smiling woman she was—his colossal person in charge, 'Oh, Milly, your step is like music.' He spoke to me very kindly, magnifying my work, though I don't remember how, except the pleasant impression. At the same party was Sir Charles Dilke, who, on being introduced to me, began at once to speak of *his* books and of his publishers, as if he and not I were the literary person. The same thing happened with a great lady I afterwards met in the same house,—a Roman Catholic lady, and a very great personage. There had been several invitations given to her at one time and another by the mistress of the house, but they all failed somehow, and at last the one she could accept fell on a Friday. The great lady took the trouble to write the day before to remind my friend that it *was* Friday, and consequently to her a fast day. This put C. R. on her mettle, as any one who knows her will understand, and we were served with the most exquisite and luxurious meal, I don't know how many *maigre* dishes—fish, eggs, and vegetables, all beautifully cooked and seductive to the last degree, about as little like fasting as the imagination could conceive. I like fish and vegetables better than any other kind of food, and, beguiled by the variety, followed Lady——'s example and kept up with her as long as I could. But it was a vain attempt, and I had to sit and look on for some time while she travelled valiantly through every dish. She, too, chose as the theme of her conversation her own books, their success or rather their relative successes, and the troubles she had with her publishers, and all the rest, while I sat with rueful amusement listening, feeling my little *rôle* taken from me. The worst was, I had never heard she had written anything, and was in mortal terror of betraying my ignorance! What with her literature, and her

beautiful appetite, and our beautiful meal, the occasion was delightful. There were some actor-gentlemen of the party,—I know not if
the great lady had a liking for actors, but there they were, furtively
regaled with beef after the lighter quips and fancies of the feast, and
rather ignored in consequence by us finer people who had fasted on
about twenty of the daintiest dishes in the world.

The year 1875 was an era in my life—a great many things happened
in that year. Frank, my good Frank, my nephew, who had grown the
most trustworthy and satisfactory boy in the world, loving home,
fond of amusement and diversion, but only in the right ways,—such a
one as is a stand-by and tower of strength in a family,—completed his
work at Cooper's Hill very well, taking a high place, and so having
the right to choose what part of India he would go to.* Things had so
developed in the family that this event seemed an occasion for various
other changes, especially as at the same time Cyril was to go to
Oxford. My brother had been getting feeble and less easy to take care
of, and I was anxious that he should live in a doctor's house and be
watched and cared for, as his state seemed to demand; and he was
himself desirous of making a change, although his plan for himself
was quite different, and he preferred the freedom of going off by
himself somewhere as my father had done, and living in his own way,
for which he was evidently not strong enough, though he did not
perceive it himself. We settled, however, that when the elder boys, as
we called them, went away, Frank to India and Cyril to Balliol, this
further move should be decided on; and that the little girls, whose
education ought to be seriously thought of, should go to Germany at
the same time. I think the pressure of my poor brother's illness,
though he was not ill then but only ailing, and of his different way of
looking at things and perhaps unconscious criticism and often dis-
approval of my ways, had become a little too much for me, and he
wanted to be free himself, and when his children were gone would no
longer have had anything to bind him to my house. But all this was
made unnecessary, these plans and arrangements, as often happens in
such a breaking up. Death is often opportune, as Mr Pigott said. I
was trying to make Frank's last summer at home pleasant, and
wanted him within the limitations of our small ways to see and do
everything possible. There is an incident in one of my own books, in
'Kirsteen,' which is a sort of illustration of my feeling about him. It
was not my own invention, but told me by C. R. as the family custom

in the large, poor, proud family which formed the model through her stories of the family in that book,—the bottle of champagne solemnly produced and drunk by the whole party on the night before the boy went away. I wanted Frank to have his bottle of champagne. I had settled to take them all to Switzerland for one thing, and I took them up to an opera for another, and to stay a night or two in London, and to see everything they could see in the small amount of time. There was a match going on at Lord's, I think, which filled the morning, and then we were to dine at Miss Blackwood's, and stay in the same house in Half Moon Street where she was. All was very lively and pleasant for the boys, who went up in the morning all so bright and gay, with their little bows of blue ribbon, and button-holes with a bit of forget-me-not, to serve the same purpose. How often have I come out with them to the door, seeing them off, so spruce, in the bright morning (surely the days were always bright when they went up for that Eton and Harrow match), so full of pleasure. I found one of these little blue bows in my Tiddy's room after—God bless him!—and it lies with other treasures. I can see them now setting out, the little hall full of the little bustle, and I half scolding, telling them they were sure to be late, and so proud—the three of them—all well, not a cloud, the most hopeful youths, Frank tall and strong, my Tids with his beautiful face, my Cecco only a boy and little, straining to keep up with them, all dressed in their best, with that keen regard to the fashion which I laughed at and loved,—but what did I not love in them? They were my all in this world. I was always anxious; but there was not a cloud upon the skies, and what had I to fear?

Next morning we were called back by a telegram. My brother had been taken ill, and the little scheme of pleasure was broken up. I found him very ill, scarcely conscious, when I got home, and in that state he remained, with a few lightenings, till he died. It lasted only a few days. He was not quite sixty, but worn out, and his life withered away to the barest skeleton of living. Often, often have I been vexed with thoughts that I might have been more tender to him. I did all I could for him, grudging nothing, but we had veered far away from each other, and I do not know that I was always kind. But it was not in unkindness, but with a full heart, that I thanked God for his release then. He was taken away from the partings which would have been hard to bear, from the evil to come: he had not to give up his son or to part with his little girls; and I was glad for him. He was delivered just in time, and slept and dreamed away, without any trouble in going so far as any one knew. He had not taken very much part in our life; the children, who were much with him, were too young to mourn except for the moment.

There was one thing that it was a balm to me to think of. At first it was supposed that he might rally and go on for some time, for two years perhaps, the doctor said. I took my own boys into council, and they both said warmly, with all their hearts, that there must be no thought now of any change,—that we could let him go into no stranger's hands now that he was ill. It cost my Cecco something to make such resolutions as that, I knew after, but only long after. To Cyril it cost nothing, but they both agreed cordially, both the boys, as to a thing that could not be gainsaid. But they were not put to the proof—and he was saved seeing them all go away.

Cyril left Eton at the end of that half, a little while after. When he went down to see if the lists were out before we left home, the man at Drakes told him, smiling, that he could not tell him the names, but he could tell him this, that in the first three, two were Oppidans. This was very rare, and there was little doubt that he was one of them. He and Frank came rushing up with this exciting news to tell me. I have had great trouble, but also I have had many joys. I forget who the Colleger was who was first,—I think it was Ryle, or perhaps Harmer, now Bishop; then Farrar, Oliphant. These two went to Balliol, both with scholarships from Eton, Farrar also with a Balliol scholarship, which Tiddy ought to have got too, but did not. Both of them now are, I hope and believe, fulfilling their lives in a better place than this, Farrar very young. He was more regular, more dutiful; he had not the wayward touch in him, the careless heart. He did far better after. At that time there was no better possible,—it was all triumph and anticipation of every good. Eton is very dear, very bright to me in all its recollections. No brighter being than my Cyril ever came from it, a boy unharmed in every way, handsome, winning, clever, gay, the most light-hearted, the most generous in feeling, full of understanding and of tenderness, nothing about him commonplace or dull, looking as if he would not subdue but win the whole world. I used to think that if one could desire to have another personality than one's own, his would have been the thing to dream of at that bright moment. And I used to apply to him the description of the young squire in Chaucer,—

'Singing he was, or flyting, all the day,
He was as fresh as is the month of May.'*

There was no prouder woman in the world than I was with the three. Frank was twenty-two, Cyril nineteen, Cecco sixteen—he doing so well too, with his strange little ways and shyness and close clinging always to his mother. It is just twenty years ago. I think often if all had gone well, as might then have been so confidently expected,—had Frank been a prosperous man in India, perhaps sending home his children to be educated, and Tiddy been a rising lawyer as was hoped, and Cecco, if delicate, still able with care to keep on,—it would all have been so natural, not anything wonderful, just the commonplace of life for which other fathers and mothers would scarcely pause to give special thanks, it being all so usual, exactly what might have been expected. And ah, the difference to me! But, thank God! we did not know what was coming in these days.

We went to Interlaken, Cecco and I and our dear Miss Clifford, 'little Nelly.' The older boys took the little girls to their German school at Arolsen, and joined us after, coming round by the Lake of Constance. We found Annie Thackeray,* attended by Miss Huth, a gentle little soul, very much like my little Nelly, and making great friends with her at Interlaken; and here it was that Annie and I became fast friends. There never was any more fascinating or a more delightful companion, so pleased to please, so ready to see the best of you—a little, perhaps, too ready to perceive a best that might not be in you, yet with a keen observation underneath that was—yet if the report was unfavourable would scarcely permit itself to be—critical. She was always more effusive than myself, delightfully flattering, appreciating. I used to say that if you wanted the moon very much, she would eagerly, and for a moment quite seriously, think how she could help to get it for you, scorning the bounds of the possible. We went to Grindelwald together and were in the same hotel—the old Bear in its homely days—for about a fortnight, and grew intimate. She was joined there by the Leslie Stephens, meaning her sister Minnie and Minnie's husband: The first prettier, smoother, much *less* as was natural than Annie, taking certain little snubs which came to Annie not with indignation as I did but with laughter as if they were a great joke which perhaps was the wiser way, but never commends itself to me. These snubs the dear Annie invited with a naïveté entirely her own and took with a sweetness also peculiar to her as if she did not perceive them or considered them amusing too. I, who had nothing to do with it, sitting fuming in the background. It was Mrs Stephen's last summer in this world, but we did not know that either. She was not strong, but there were reasons for that, and no sort of alarm about her. Little Minnie, her one little girl, was the baby of the party—a little, fragile, quaint thing, whom I remember standing by the great St Bernard, Sultan, with her hands in his deep fur, a curious little picture. She was full of quaint sayings and wondering looks, looking on at the boys and asking solemnly, 'What are they ninking about?' with the gravest observation, and defending her little basket of cakes from Cyril's pretended attacks with a serious discrimination of him as the greedy boy, which became one of our little jokes. It takes but a small matter to make a joke when all is well and one's heart inclined that way.* I made acquaintance with Mr Leslie Stephen* at that time, a man I had some little prejudice against and with whom I had had a slight passage of arms by letters about some literary work, he being the editor of the 'Cornhill', a prosperous magazine in those days. Not an amiable man by any means, not thinking well of his neighbours, given to putting in a keen little stab as of a penknife quietly, a penknife with a fine edge. I fell into a chance talking with him one evening in front of the Bear, when the sky was growing dim over the Wetterhorn, and the shadows of the mountains drawing down as they do when night is coming on, not liking him, nor intending to like him, with a small grievance in my own person and a greater one on another account. I recollect we walked up and down and talked, I have not the smallest remembrance what about. But the end of it was that when I went in we had become friends, or so it was at least on my side. I don't know why. There is no reason in these matters. The reason is if one was to put it in surprising language that the man has a great deal of charm. He is a cantankerous person and has not a good word for anybody, yet he has a fascination which is more effective than any amount of goodness. I don't mean that he is not good. I have always said of him that he is one of the men who are angry with God for not existing, and cannot get that irritation out of their mind or their eyes, but not in himself ungenerous or unnoble, though spoilt by that determined prepossession against the order of things and the course of life. There are some people to whom it seems to be easy enough to be without hope and without God—either by reason of an easy temper which takes any-thing lightly and does not trouble to think, or for other reasons. (Is it perhaps a theory to take into consideration that we are not all intended to be immortal, that some may always stop and cease when this world is over, thinking no more and wishing no more, and being taken by God, as it were, at their word?) But Leslie Stephen, I think, is not one of these. He is angry, always angry for that failure, never satisfied, restless and eager to put out this discontent on anybody or anything. I used to wonder what would be the effect on such a man of dying and finding out that he had been wrong—and think that the wonderful surprise and relief that there was some other Him regulat-ing all things would more than make up to him for any personal suffering he might have to go through on account of his own perver-sity and obtuseness.

Leslie Stephen was kind to the boys, taking them for walks with him up among the mountains; and, egged on by the ladies, he was so far kind to me that he took two of my stories for the 'Cornhill' which meant in each case the bulk of a year's income,* but later when he might have given my Cecco work on the National Biography which he would have done so well he did not do so. I could never imagine why. No one indeed, however good they may have been in profes-sions towards me ever did anything to help me in that chief care of my life, but what does all that matter now?

This expedition was altogether very successful and delightful, the last time the three boys were to spend together, for many years, we thought,—for ever in this world, as it turned out. One thing happened in it on which I look back with a mixture of feeling and amusement. It was the coming to life of the two who were then called the little girls. They had been very unresponsive children, not 'forth-coming' as Mrs Freshfield says; little shy mice, half-shy, half-defiant, as I think children often are whose childhood has been broken up by transplantation to another house. They had not had perhaps so much as they should have had of the petting of the nursery. The household when they came into it was preoccupied by the boys, who were so much older; and though everybody was kind, they missed, no doubt unconsciously, poor little souls, the something more than kindness, the indulgence, the mother. At all events they were very chilly, scared, distrustful little things. They left home with no apparent feeling at all, and much comment among us (most of the bystanders were always rather against these two little impedimenta) at the absence of feeling. Of course they were excited by the prospect of the journey in the care of the two big brothers, and all the novelty. But when they were left in Germany among strange-speaking people, among new ways, in such a strange place, the two little hearts gushed out all at once. They wrote to me the most pathetic, imploring letters. 'Oh, come and take us home; oh come, come and take us home. We will be as good as angels,' said Madge, 'if you will only come and take us home.' It was very hard work refusing. We were in Interlaken, I think, when these letters came, and we made up a basket of all the toys and pictures and cakes that would carry, to console them. Lina* who had scolded and petted and taught in her way, and loved also in her way, with a little roughness and neglect (wholesome) would have started off that moment to bring them—but that of course would not do. And they soon got over their first home-sickness. But they never relapsed into those chills and mists of their childhood, but have always been since my true children, the unquestioned daughters of the house, and with no further cloud upon the completeness of their adoption—they of me, as well as I of them. The first is often the more difficult of the two.

With that year began a new life, one of which I cannot speak much. That was the burden and heat of the day: my anxieties were sometimes almost more than I could bear. I had gone through many trials, as I thought, and God knows many of them had been hard enough, but then I knew to the depths of my heart what the yoke was and how heavy. Many times I have woke in the morning feeling in myself that image of Shelley's 'Prometheus,' which in my youth I had vexed my husband by not appreciating, except in what seemed to me the picture rather than the poem, the man chained on the rock, with the vultures swooping down upon him. Their cruel beaks I seemed to feel in my heart the moment I awoke. Ah me, alas! pain ever, for ever, God alone knows what was the anguish of these years. And yet now I think of *ces beaux jours quand j'étais si malheureuse*,* the moments of relief were so great and so sweet that they seemed compensation for the pain,—I remembered no more the anguish. Lately in my many sad musings it has been brought very clearly before my mind how often all the horrible tension, the dread, the anxiety which there are no words strong enough to describe,—which devoured me, but which I had to conceal often behind a smiling face,—would yield in a moment, in the twinkling of an eye, at the sound of a voice, at the first look, into an ineffable ease and the overwhelming happiness of relief from pain, which is, I think, our highest human sensation, higher and more exquisite than any positive enjoyment in this world. It used to sweep over me like a wave, sometimes when I opened a door, sometimes in a letter,—in all simple ways. I cannot explain, but if this should ever come to the eye of any woman in the passion and agony of motherhood, she will more or less understand. I was thinking lately, or rather, as sometimes happens, there was suddenly presented to my mind, like a suggestion from some one else, the recollection of these ineffable happinesses, and it seemed to me that it meant that which would be when one pushed through that last door and was met—oh, by what, by whom?—by instant relief. The wave of sudden ease and warmth and peace and joy. I felt, to tell the truth, that it was one of them who brought that to my mind, and I said to myself, 'I will not want any explanation, I will not ask any question,—the first touch, the first look, will be enough, as of old, yet better than of old.'

I do injustice to those whom I love above all things by speaking thus, and yet what can I say? My dearest, bright, delightful boy missed somehow his footing, how can I tell how? I often think that I had to do with it, as well as what people call inherited tendencies, and, alas! the perversity of youth, which he never outgrew. He had done everything too easily in the beginning of his boyish career, by natural impulse and that kind of genius which is so often deceptive in youth, and when he came to that stage in which hard work was necessary against the competition of the hard working, he could not believe how much more effort was necessary. Notwithstanding all distractions he took a second-class at Oxford,—a great disappointment, yet not disgraceful after all. And I will not say that, except at the first keen moment of pain, I was in any way bitterly disappointed. *Tout peut se réparer.** I always felt so to the end, and perhaps he thought I took it lightly, and that it did not so much matter. Then it was one of my foolish ways to take my own work very lightly, and not to let them know how hard pressed I was sometimes, so that he never, I am sure, was convinced how serious it was in that way, and certainly never was convinced that he could not, when the moment came, right himself and recover lost way. But only the moment, God bless him! did not come till God took it in His own hands. Another theory I have thought of with many tears lately. I had another foolish way of laughing at the superior people, the people who took themselves too seriously,—the boys of pretension, and all the strong intellectualisms. This gave him, perhaps, or helped him to form, a prejudice against the good and reading men, who have so many affectations, poor boys, and led him towards those so often inferior, all inferior to himself, who had the naturalness along with the folly of youth. Why should I try to explain? He went out of the world, leaving a love-song or two behind him and the little volume of 'De Musset,' of which much was so well done, and yet some so badly done, and nothing more to show for his life. And I to watch it all going on day by day and year by year!

My Cecco took the first steps in the same way; but, thanks be to God, righted himself and overcame—not in time enough to save his career at Oxford, but so as to be all that I had hoped,—always my very own, my dearest companion, choosing me before all others. What a companion he was, everybody who knew us knows: full of knowledge, full of humour—a most accomplished man, though to me always a boy. He did not make friends easily, and he had few; but those whom he had were very fond of him, and all our immediate surroundings looked up to him with an affectionate admiration which I cannot describe. 'I don't know, but I will ask Cecco,' was what we all said. He had not much more than emerged from the desert of temptation and trial, bringing balm and healing to me, when he fell ill. When his illness first was declared, it seemed to me that my misery was more than I could bear. I remember that we all went to the Holy Communion together the Sunday before we left for Pau, and that as I went up to kneel at the altar I was so nearly overcome, that Cyril put his hand on my arm and gripped it almost roughly to recall me to myself. And then the whole world seemed to come back again into the sun after a time; he got so much better, and the warm summer of the Queen's Jubilee year seemed to complete what Pau had begun. And he passed his examination for the British Museum, coming out first, and his life seemed now to be ordered in a safe place—in the work he loved. Alas! Then Sir Andrew Clark* would not pass him, but other doctors gave the best of hopes. And he did a great deal of good work, and finally went to the Library here;* and we had many blinks of happiness, both in the winter on the Riviera and at home. I cannot tell what he was to me—consulting me about everything, desiring to have me with him, to walk with me and talk to me, only put out of humour when I was drawn away or occupied by other things. When he was absent he wrote to me every day. I never went out but he was there to give me his arm. I seem to feel it now—the dear, thin, but firm arm. In the last four years after Cyril was taken from us, we were nearer and nearer. I can hear myself saying 'Cecco and I.' It was the constant phrase. But all through he was getting weaker; and I knew it, and tried not to know.

And now here I am all alone.

I cannot write any more.

APPENDIX A: Diary entry for Christmas night, 1887

This year have kept no record of any kind and do so now only because it is a kind of leisure moment and I have a headache and am indisposed to do anything else. This is a very dull Christmas day, nothing pleasant present, nothing to look forward to—my prospects very bad. The boys nil. In short, if I were to give myself up to thought of that, nothing could be darker, nor more dreary. I am writing a little story, 'Mr Sandford',* chiefly to give a little outlet to the miserable sensations which I must not express otherwise, for why trouble the children with these who can do nothing, who cannot tell that my heart is not always down in the depths but has unreasonable risings and revolts against despair and really is not miserable except by moments. It is dreadful in the morning when I wake and try to keep the vultures off.

All the things I seem to want are material things. I want money. I want work, work that will pay, enough to keep this house going which there is no-one to provide for but me. I don't know how to stop, to change, to make another way of living, everything is so perplexed and hard. When I try another place it is always more expensive, and there are all the helpless young people, boys who ought to be earning their own living, girls who can't, but would somehow if I was out of the way, servants, dependents—all accustomed to have anything that is wanted and only me to supply all, and I will be sixty in a few months and my work is failing, whether my strength is or not. What a situation to contemplate if one did face it fairly. I do, but I don't dwell upon it. What is the good? I keep my eyes open on any way of finding a new opening, always hoping, always praying—and yet sometimes feeling as if prayers which are only for material good were poor sort of things with which to importune God. Poor—and yet it is not only that he may have a settled place and income that I try everything for T, but that he may have his chance—a way of doing well. Oh, if that might but be that I

see something come to him that is happy and good before I die. My
heart is so much easier for C. who will do well one way or other,
thank God for that assurance, though all is dark now.

[The writing resumes two pages later in a different ink.]

It is very difficult for me to realise what I have done during the
year. I have written, I suppose, the greater part of *The Second Son* and
the greater part of *Joyce*, Old Saloon articles, some of Venice, various
miscellaneous matters.* Beginning of the year very miserable about
Cecco and his illness and went off with him to Pau at about a week's
notice, where, thanks for ever be to God for his goodness, he mended
at once and never has fallen back. We were there more than two
months and then had three weeks in Spain. In Pau one chief solace
was Mlle de Castelbaque and her uncle, very quaint, French and
friendly, an immense thing for Cecco. English people very indifferent—took no notice, as why should they, seeing we were neither
amusing nor attractive? Cecco really too silent for anything and
myself not particularly lively. My chief pleasure and comfort the
French people upstairs and my nice young Jesuit, the flowers, especially enormous, which I wasted many evenings on, sending them
off to people at home. Walked a great deal with C., but did not mend
of my bad back, as one might have hoped. The journey to Spain very
agreeable, but our Spanish forsook us as soon as we got over the
frontier. Came home to all the row and commotion of the Jubilee.
House full, Coghills a large party, Windsor en fête the whole week.
Feeling really touched and sensitive and extremely sympathetic with
her, sent the Queen some verses to which she responded by sending
her medal. I think on the whole H. M. had the best of the bargain, for
the verses were not bad of their kind* and the medal was! We went to
the Lake country in August and ought not to have done so, being very
short of money, but, on the other hand, it was recommended for
Cecco—or at least mountain air was recommended and that would do
very well Dr M. said. N.B. it is not mountain air at all as the houses,
views, etc. are low down in the valleys and by lakesides. Switzerland
much better in point of mountain air, where you really can live high
up. However, Borrowdale was delightful and Patterdale also. I
walked alone a good deal, little walks, while the young ones took big
ones, and liked it. Not thinking, but that soothing sense of a great

benign presence by, which has come upon me of recent years and carries such a sense of solace with it—God walking in the cool of the garden.* The little cares seemed to drop away and calm and satisfaction comes—like a true companionship, when nothing needs to be said, where all is knowledge and comprehension. The feeling is so strong that I have got to permit myself to entertain it. At first it seemed too much to hope. At the sea in St Andrews, when I thought my heart would break after the Ceylon episode, this feeling came upon me like dew. I wanted solace if ever woman did and the great Father, without appearing to answer my prayer, leaving me so nothing changed, yet stilled and comforted to the bottom of my heart. One does not talk with any readiness on such subjects, but I wonder if others have felt so, probably with more confidence and assurance than me.

Came back very poor, oh very poor, nothing but struggles to make ends meet. The struggle scarcely seems to relax at any time, though I forget how bad it has been, but somehow always the seams with dreadfully ragged edges and gaps and unevenness do pull together. I have been very low many times in the end of the year. No work, that is the dreadful thing and the consciousness that I am old and that no new spring of imagery is at all to be looked for, or that the public should change its always very mild approval into something more warm. *That* is never at all likely to come now. And it does not seem God's will for me that I should ever know any very marked success. I suppose I did have in the Carlingford days, but never had any such prices as Trollope and many others. H. and Black.* would have three times as much as I—Mrs Craik, a great deal more, George Elliot (sic) of course ten times and Miss Braddon's books* go on selling as well as ever now they say. Queer!—I don't understand it—not in all their cases at least. And now I suspect the stream is ebbing away from me all together, and yet I have nothing before me but to work till I die. But God opens new ways in which getting on is possible and joins the pieces in the most wonderful way and I hope I shall not live too long. If only the children were somehow settled. This year has been full of disappointment in this way. In Sept. full of hope. Cecco passed the exam with flying colours.

1st—Tids recommended by the Queen herself to the Education department. For a little while I thought that my reproach was to [be] taken away* and all go well with both.

Then came the downfall. C. rejected by Sir A. Clark for health. T. for no reason but because he had not taken a first class—but, he must reason, no doubt undeservedly, that valid or not so. And so the hopes collapsed and we were as before.

Oh, that the Lord would take away my reproach and establish my boys! If that were but so, what could I desire more? Nothing, nothing, any struggle would be welcome.

Very sad ending to the year. All these hopes gone. Tids ill, not without fault of his own. Cecco ordered off, and nothing opening for me. Wrote 'Mr Sandford' in a sort of cheerful despair, still hoping that the way would open—that it has done so wonderfully so far as my work is concerned, but that belongs to 1888.

APPENDIX B: 1888 Diary

Begun the year amid great anxiety. Cecco left for the Riviera on the 14th. January, very unwilling and feeling the loneliness very much. His letters always were delightful and original, but sometimes quite heartbreaking to me, especially at first, saying witty things which I was most deeply happy and thankful for, though often making me rather wretched with the thought of his solitude and depression.

In great trouble otherwise, pecuniary chiefly. Mr Macmillan came to my aid. And Mr Craik and he, evidently anxious to do what they could, arranged for me, really by their own invitation a book upon Edinburgh* after the fashion of the others, which I have not been able to begin yet (end of May). I don't really know what I have done during the beginning of this year, except the Principal's memoir, which has been very troublesome work: a world of letters to read.

[Resumed in different ink.]

Finished Memoir before going off to Scotland in September and various other things. St. James's came to an end to my great sorrow. During summer wrote for Longman, to clear off debt with them, *Lady Car*, one volume. During September wrote a short story, two numbers, for Blackwood (pot boiler), called *Sons and Daughters** and began *Kristine*. Things much as usual, good and bad. Sorry to have gone to Scotland, but gravitated in spite of myself. Always much more expensive than I expect.

Principal's Life published October—sold 1250 edition. Nov 20: another edition proposed, but letter accompanying to say that the publisher's profit on first edition was very minute and that, instead of giving me, as I asked, £200 for small second and larger 3rd edition cheap, they would only give £50 for next edition, and will not take the others into consideration. I have written to refuse.

APPENDIX C: 1896 Diary

[French diary, leather bound, gold tooling, metal clasp and pencil. At the front of the diary are a few jotted worknotes.]

64 pages, 32 sheets my writing. 4 sheets each part.
Go to London Library to look up National Biography on Charles Lamb.

Janvier 14 Mardi

Just a little note of this night. I had been working very hard and came to my room very late and tired, but took up a book, the *Fortunes of Nigel** and read on and on till it was three o'clock in the morning. I was blaming myself bitterly then, that I could so occupy myself instead of going to bed and talking to Him as I sometimes find it out a comfort to do, of myself so loving and truthful and of *them*. It seemed such a miserable thing to go on reading the old book which I about know by heart, instead of this, the only privilege that remains to me, shortening it for the sake of that mere listless amusement. When I was thus blaming myself I felt almost as if I was suddenly surrounded by a soft atmosphere of tender love and almost laughter, such as sometimes was when I would blame myself for some of my familiar little faults, which they rather liked in me than blamed. It was only a moment, a kind of delightful humorous derision of boys, and I could almost think I felt Cecco touch my forehead as he used to do and say 'Poor Mamma' with the musing I know so well. 'Poor Mamma' as if she might not know her little folly and be indulgent in it. It gave me a great feeling of comfort. It seemed to imply that the Father in heaven would so regard it too, not blaming, pitiful and so indulgent. Poor soul praying.

Oh my God—and oh my children.

Notes

3 *the turning point*: Oliphant's sense of this episode as pivotal in her career is demonstrated by the frequency with which she retells it. Cf. p. 90 and *Annals of a Publishing House: William Blackwood and His Sons* (2 vols., Edinburgh and London, 1897), ii. 486. John Blackwood, assisted by his elder brother Major William, were then in charge of the Edinburgh publishing company and became Oliphant's friends and, on occasion, bankers.

He left the mountain breeze to dry: W. Scott, *The Lady of the Lake* (1810), Canto III, xix.

3–4 *the giant who . . . touched the earth*: Alcyoneus, son of Earth and Sky in Greek myth.

4 *no harm to speak of*: this page of musing over the decision to face life as a single woman seems to offer corroboration to speculations that Oliphant received and rejected a proposal from the Revd Robert Herbert Story (see note to p. 93) at about this time.

my darling, in her father's grave: Margaret Wilson Oliphant died on 27 January 1864, aged ten.

my ewe-lamb: 2 Samuel 12: 3.

many mansions: John 14.

5 *Testaccio*: the Protestant cemetery in Rome, at the foot of Monte Testaccio, where her husband Frank was also buried.

softly all the days of my life: cf. Isaiah 38: 15.

6 *The Principal*: John Tulloch (1823–86), Principal of St. Mary's college, University of St. Andrews and a liberal theologian in the Church of Scotland. Oliphant had escorted Tulloch's wife to Rome where she was to meet the Principal who had been travelling in Europe to cure his depression (see p. 106) Their presence at this tragedy cemented the bonds of a close and lasting friendship between the two families. Tulloch and Oliphant were to dedicate books to one another and she became his biographer.

6 *'In Memoriam'*: for Oliphant's growing appreciation of Tennyson's *In Memoriam A. H. H.* (1850) see the introductory essay.

7 *neither marry nor give in marriage*: Matthew 22: 30.

   the trial of faith which is precious: cf. 1 Peter 1: 7.

8 *God is more merciful than man*: probably an echo of Effie Deans's famous courtroom speech in W. Scott's *The Heart of Midlothian* (1818), ch. 24.

   He hateth nothing he has made: cf. the collect for Ash Wednesday in *The Book of Common Prayer*.

   knows her no more: cf. Psalm 103: 16.

9 *go to Frank*: Francis Wilson Oliphant (1818–59), her husband.

10 *and W. is entirely dependent . . . upon me*: William Wilson, 'Willie', had early in life become Oliphant's especial responsibility, although he was ten years her senior. During his ministerial training in London for the Free Church of Scotland Maggie joined him to guard him from his besetting sins of drink and debt (1849, see p. 26). His ministerial appointment only lasted eighteen months before alcoholism set in again; his family removed him speedily so that he should not be publicly disgraced by the church authorities (1852, see p. 32). He lived with his parents until his mother's death in 1854 and occupied himself copying out the manuscripts of his sister's novels, four of which she allowed to be attributed to him. He wrote five further novels himself, one of which, *Andrew Ramsay of Errol* (3 vols., 1865) includes an admiring portrait of his sister as a girl. In the early 1860s Oliphant found Willie a permanent home with the Macphersons (see note to p. 73) in Italy, where he acted as an assistant in their photographic business in between recurrent bouts of alcoholism. Oliphant contributed to his upkeep for the next quarter of a century.

   as a father his children: Psalm 103: 13.

10 *a fuller conception of life*: Oliphant had been reading E. C. Gaskell's *The Life of Charlotte Brontë* (1857), a biography she later claimed had started the trend for laying bare the unsavoury aspects of writers' private lives. From her first review (*Blackwood's Edinburgh Magazine*, May 1855) to her last study ('The Sisters Brontë', *Women Novelists of Queen Victoria's Reign*, 1897), Oliphant maintained the historical importance of Charlotte's novels as revolutionary fiction in the passionate strength with which they pleaded woman's right to consideration as an independent being with needs and desires as strong as any male's.

11 *Mr Maurice*: Frederick Denison Maurice (1805–72). Oliphant had reviewed Maurice's controversial *Theological Essays* (1853) in 'Modern Light Literature and Theology', *Blackwood's*, July 1855. In this book he had revealed unorthodox views on eternal punishment, a concept which he believed to be incompatible with a loving God. Oliphant's personal acquaintance with Maurice sprang from her friendship with his sister (see p. 96). She continued to admire

him as 'pre-eminently Christian', though remaining sceptical as to the benefits of liberal theology for the laity at large. M. Oliphant and F. R. Oliphant, *The Victorian Age of English Literature* (2 vols., 1892), ii. 23–9.

12 *those on whom the tower fell*: Luke 13: 4.

13 *Mrs Somerville*: Mary Somerville (1780–1872), the Scottish naturalist and scientist after whom Somerville College, Oxford, was named. Oliphant had reviewed *Personal Recollections of Mary Somerville by her Daughter Martha Somerville* in 'New Books', *Blackwood's*, April 1874.

14 *pangs . . . beyond description*: in 1876 her son Cyril's behaviour as an undergraduate at Oxford had first given her serious cause for concern.

Sara: Sara Tarver, *née* Tulloch, oldest daughter of Principal Tulloch, had met Frank Tarver, a French master at Eton, when staying with Oliphant. Their son, Wladimir, had died in 1883, aged ten, an event which was to inspire Oliphant's tale, 'The Little Pilgrim in the Seen and the Unseen', *The Land of Darkness* (1888).

Pains and sacrifices too: see notes to pp. 45 and 151.

'Werena my heart licht I wad dee': this favourite refrain of Oliphant's comes from *Orpheus Caled* (1733), i. 88, by Lady Grizel Baillie, *née* Hume (1665–1746), a Scottish heroine and poet.

George Eliot's life: Oliphant had reviewed *George Eliot's Life as Related in her Letters and Journals*, ed. J. W. Cross (3 vols., Edinburgh and London, 1883) in the *Edinburgh Review* 161 (1885), 514–53.

Trollope's talk about . . . his books: Anthony Trollope's *Autobiography* had been posthumously published in 1883.

15 *Mrs Carlyle*: Jane Baillie Welsh Carlyle (1801–66). Mrs Carlyle's swift overtures of friendship and resemblance to her own dead mother won her an impassioned supporter in Oliphant. Oliphant played a leading part in the controversy which ensued when J. A. Froude published Carlyle's *Reminiscences* (1881), containing a memoir of his wife, only three weeks after his death and, subsequently, his *Life of Carlyle* (4 vols., 1882–4). Oliphant's views on Froude's betrayal and traducement of both the Carlyles can be found in detail in 'Mrs Carlyle', *Contemporary Review* 43 (1883), 609–28 and 'The Ethics of Biography', *Contemporary Review* 44 (1883), 76–93; for the rest of her life Oliphant never passed up an opportunity to set the record, as she saw it, straight.

Browning's Andrea: R. Browning's 'Andrea del Sarto', *Men and Women* (2 vols., 1855), was a favourite poem of Oliphant to which she alluded elsewhere in her work; e.g. in *At His Gates* (3 vols., 1872), vol. i, ch. 2, and *The Curate in Charge* (2 vols., 1876), vol. i, ch. 6.

the Laurence Oliphants: Laurence Oliphant (1829–88). Laurence's blend of philosophical scepticism and spiritual idealism attracted Margaret to him on their first meeting in the House of Commons during the Reform Bill debates. An M P in 1867, he had already tried the roles of barrister, travel writer, and diplomat. In 1867 he threw up everthing to become a labourer in an American religious community tyrannized over by its spiritual leader, Thomas Lake Harris. Harris continued to direct Laurence's life and family relationships for many years, although he encouraged Laurence himself to re-enter society. Eventually Laurence became disillusioned by Harris's leadership and emigrated in 1882, accompanied by his wife Alice, by then also a close friend of Margaret's, to Haifa to found a Zionist community. In her biography, *Memoirs of the Life of Laurence Oliphant, and Alice Oliphant, his Wife* (Edinburgh and London, 1890), Margaret drew a sympathetic but discerning picture of an eccentric who craved the excitement which his various idealist ventures seemed to provide.

16 *my poor brother's family fell upon my hands*: in 1868. For a fuller account see p. 128.

17 *hideous . . . as his previous story was*: in her review of Cross's *Life of George Eliot* (see note to p. 14). Oliphant hints that G. H. Lewes had been a roué, familiar with 'all the lowest scenes of London life', before he embarked upon bourgeois 'domestic bliss' in his liaison with George Eliot. She also comments at length upon the irony of a woman who had offended in a way not permitted to a duchess or a dressmaker adopting the role of 'a great moral teacher'.

George Eliot and George Sand: this pairing is not simply a matter of euphony. Oliphant had once based an article upon a comparison of the two authors: 'Two Cities: Two Books', *Blackwood's*, July 1874.

'by none am I enough beloved': this seems to be a free adaptation of *Antony and Cleopatra*, I. ii. 24, possibly prompted by memory of a line in C. Patmore's *The Unknown Eros* (1877), I. iii. 1.

19 *like Absalom*: 2 Samuel 14: 26.

the Reform Bill: Lord Brougham (1778–1868), a Scots Whig and founder member of the *Edinburgh Review*, made a celebrated speech on the second reading of the Reform Bill in 1831 and was involved in many reform movements, especially in the fields of education and the abolition of slavery. As Prime Minister in a Whig administration Lord Grey introduced and finally carried the Great Reform Bill.

20 *taking him to Glasgow*: in Glasgow her father took up a post as clerk at the Royal Bank.

21 *a brown front!*: False curls worn over the forehead.

fallen into poverty and obscurity: this note was probably added after research into the Oliphant genealogy for her biography of Laurence Oliphant; the material was then turned to fictional account in the short story, 'The Heirs of Kellie', *Blackwood's*, March 1896.

22 *Sir Walter attributes to Queen Mary*: W. Scott, *The Abbot* (1820).

22–3 *an office in the Custom-house*: her father worked as a clerk in the export department of the Excise Office in the Customs House.

25 *published . . . by W. on his own account*: *Christian Melville*, written around 1845 and published under William Wilson's name in 1856.

26 *history of Mrs . . . Maitland*: *Passages in the Life of Mrs Margaret Maitland, of Sunnyside, written by Herself* (1849).

27 *of Edward Irving's wife*: see p. 93.

that never was on sea and shore:

> Ah, then, if mine had been the Painter's hand,
> To express what then I saw; and add the gleam,
> The light that never was, on sea or land,
> The consecration, and the Poet's dream.

W. Wordsworth, 'Elegiac Stanzas on a picture of Peele Castle in a storm', (1807).

28 *Wordsworth's little boy . . . at Kilve*: 'Anecdote for Fathers', *Lyrical Ballads* (1798).

middle-aged and stout!: the 1899 editors commented, 'Probably under Thirty'.

29 *the 'Athenæum*: *Athenaeum*, 24 November 1849.

why the book succeeded so well: the novel received sufficient publicity for Dickens to parody its title in a letter to Miss Coutts of 4 February 1850. *The Letters of Charles Dickens*, eds. G. Storey, K. Tillotson and N. Burgis (6 vols., 1965–88), vi. 28.

an abashed gratitude: the long and detailed letter of critical appreciation from Francis, Lord Jeffrey (1773–1850), for many years a feared but respected critic in the *Edinburgh Review*, is reproduced in *Autobiography and Letters of Mrs M. O. W. Oliphant*, ed. Mrs H. Coghill (1899), 153–5.

the date of her marriage!: Oliphant was correct in recalling 1849 as the date.

30 *'Caleb Field'*: *Caleb Field: A Tale of the Puritans* (1851).

31 *seceders of 1661*: the year 1661 saw the first part of the 'Clarendon Code' enacted and in 1662 the passing of the Act of Uniformity resulted in 1,603, roughly a fifth, of the Anglican clergy being ejected from their livings.

34 *George Wilson*: (1818–59) a chemist and writer on religious matters. In 1853 he was created Regius Professor of Technology at Edinburgh University. He also became President of the Royal Scottish Society for the Arts. He supported the young Oliphant's novel-writing with a series of letters of praise and encouragement.

Sir Daniel in the end of his life: Daniel Wilson (1816–92), archaeologist and educational reformer, emigrated in 1853.

34 *Dr Moir of Musselburgh*: Dr David Macbeth Moir (1798–1851) took a keen interest in the young Oliphant's work. In a letter of critical appreciation of her novel *Merkland* (1851) he seems to have given her the germ of her first novel to be serialized in *Blackwood's*, *Katie Stewart*. He suggested that she should use some national event such as a threatened invasion or the horrors of the Press gangs (17 January 1851, National Library of Scotland, Acc. 5793/5).

à la Galt: John Galt (1779–1839), essayist and author of novels about Lowland Scots rural life.

35 *a Mr Cupples*: George Cupples (1822–91), author of *The Green Hand*, which began as a 'short yarn' (*Blackwood's*, December 1848) and continued intermittently for thirteen episodes (concluded October 1850).

a very effective contributor twenty years before: Michael Scott (1789–1835). *Tom Cringle's Log* ran for seventeen instalments (*Blackwood's*, June 1831–August 1833).

a pleasant homely house: an editorial note in 1899 editions of the *Autobiography* read, 'This house is the scene of the story of "Isabel Dysart", reprinted since Mrs Oliphant's death'.

my story 'Katie Stewart': *Katie Stewart: A True Story*, *Blackwood's* July–November 1852.

38 *'A little while and ye shall not see me'*: John 16: 16.

39 *Several times in words*: her sensations, this world of minor literary talents and their lionizers, are all exploited in *The Athelings, or the Three Gifts* (3 vols., Edinburgh and London, 1857).

Mr Laing: probably Revd David Laing, then Perpetual Curate of Holy Trinity, St. Pancras, London.

in 'Zaidee' I think: George Lance (1802–64) was a pupil of Benjamin Haydon. The portrait she alludes to is presumably that of Mr Steele in *Zaidee: A Romance* (3 vols., 1856), vol. III, ch. 8. Lance is also the name of the artist brother in *The Three Brothers* (3 vols., 1870).

40 *the sort of thing one expected*: Samuel Carter Hall (1800–89), was an energetic but financially inept editor of a series of newspapers and periodicals. His chief publishing success was the *Art Union Monthly Journal*, founded in 1839, which he edited for the next fifty years. The fact that Hall failed to include Oliphant among the many far less successful people mentioned in his *A Book of Memoirs of Great Men and Women of the Age from personal acquaintance* (1871) may well confirm her self-image as a reticent social presence at this period. Anna Maria Hall (1800–81) was a far more prolific author than Oliphant suggests, writing some fifty books, nine novels, and fifty short stories.

the Howitts: William Howitt (1792–1879), author. Mary Howitt (1799–1888) began her prolific career as a poet and, after her marriage, collaborated with her husband as an essayist. Having learnt Swedish and Danish she became an early translator of Hans Christian Andersen and herself wrote children's books.

41 *full of enthusiasm about*: the Halls and the Howitts were promoters, in the 1850s, of the notorious American spiritualist, Daniel D. Home.

a literary person . . . the book which she wrote when she got back: Sara Jane Lippincott (*née* Clarke), poet and journalist. Her account of this encounter appeared in *Haps and Mishaps of a Tour in Europe* (1854), pp. 57–8. Recalling this event prompted Oliphant to include an unflattering reference to 'Grace Greenwood' in *Effie Ogilvie* (1886), ch. 6.

Mr Frost, the academician: William Edward Frost (1810–77), RA, gold medallist, two of whose pictures were purchased by Queen Victoria.

Gavan Duffy: Sir Charles Gavan Duffy (1816–1903). In the early 1840s he had been briefly imprisoned along with other Young Irelanders who supported Daniel O'Connell in his campaign for the repeal of the Union between Great Britain and Ireland. After the collapse of the Repeal Association Duffy helped to found the Irish Confederation which fell foul of the British government in 1848, during the period of European revolutions, when Duffy was again arrested, tried and acquitted four times. In 1852 Duffy became an MP and founder member of the Independent Irish Party, campaigning for tenant rights. With the collapse of this party he emigrated to Australia and became Governor General of Victoria. His entrée to the Hall's literary set was presumably secured by his authorship of *The Ballad Poetry of Young Ireland* (1845), which reached fifty editions.

42 *Rosa Bonheur*: (Marie Rosalie) (1822–99). A French painter of animal and rural scenes whose work sold particularly well in England. Her devotion to her art led her to the dissection of animals in slaughterhouses; she finally settled near Fontainebleau with a menagerie of animals on her estate. As to her character, a contemporary critic wrote, 'It is scarcely more unusual to find talent like hers than to find a woman who can preserve her good name, and enjoy the absolute freedom from conventionalities necessary to such an artistic career as that of Rosa Bonheur; her studies having placed her in contact with men and circumstances not often met by artists of her sex.' Her work won from George Eliot the exclamation, 'What power! That is the way women should assert their rights.' (letter of 19 August 1857). *The George Eliot Letters*, ed. G. S. Haight (9 vols., 1954–78), ii. 377.

42 *Miss Mulock*: Dinah Maria Mulock (1826–87) was a prolific essayist, novelist, short-story writer, poet, translator from the French, and author of children's books. Oliphant effected the introduction between Mulock and Henry Blackett, of Hurst and Blackett, who was to publish Mulock's best-seller, *John Halifax, Gentleman* (1856), a classic Victorian middle-class morality tale. Her financial success, which Oliphant frankly envied, enabled her to donate her Civil List pension (1864) to less fortunate writers. In the same year she married George Lillie Craik, fifteen years her junior, and already known to Oliphant

through her work for the publishing house of Macmillan of which he was a senior member. Their friendship survived mutually critical appraisal of each other's work. Having extracted an apology from an acquaintance who spoke slightingly of Oliphant's *Agnes* (1866), Mulock wrote, 'Nevertheless, I dare say to *you* what I would not say to the world—I think you will yet be sorry for having written *Agnes*—the reason being that it does *not* "justify the ways of God to men"—and its doubts may trouble weaker souls long after you have conquered them and lived to see that His ways are right—and His mercy endureth for ever.' 2 November 1865, National Library of Scotland Acc. 5793/5. Oliphant was invited to write the obituary tribute to Mrs Craik in *Macmillan's Magazine*, 57 (1887), 81–5.

43 *Mrs Browning . . . I met her*: Oliphant had met Elizabeth Barrett Browning in 1859 in Italy, while she was nursing her husband through his final illness.

a Mr Smedley: Francis Edward Smedley (1818–64).

that sober city man: George William Lovell (1804–78), Secretary of the Phoenix Insurance Company, enjoyed considerable success as a dramatist and was paid £400 in advance by the actor-manager Kean for *The Wife's Secret* (first performed in New York in 1846).

44 *Alexander Johnstone's house*: Alexander Johnston (1815–?), RA, like Frank Oliphant had trained in Edinburgh. He had begun to exhibit portraits and historical figures in 1835 and was still exhibiting in the late 1870s.

done evil in thy sight: cf. Psalm 51: 4.

45 *Strathtyrum*: the hill-top country-house, entirely surrounded by trees, located about a mile from St Andrews, owned by John Blackwood.

Pattern of memorial: cf. Exodus 12: 14.

46 *because they are not*: cf. Jeremiah 31: 15.

and Frank with him: Frank Wilson, her nephew, who had died in 1879.

47 *reading the service*: Revd James John Hornby, Headmaster of Eton, 1868–84; Revd Stuart Alexander Donaldson, now Assistant Master at Eton; and Lionel Eardley Blake.

as he is known: cf. 1 Corinthians 13: 12.

his little book: C. F. Oliphant. *Alfred de Musset* (Edinburgh, 1890). It had Cyril eight years to fulfil this contract and even then his mother had to ed work severely before it could appear in Blackwood's Foreign Classic English Readers, a series for which she was the general editor.

48 *the former occasion*: in January 1889 Cyril had a violent fit on a railway statio. in Paris when accompanying his mother and brother on an expedition to the South of France. She had twice feared him dead in the ensuing hours of unconsciousness.

49 *my son, my son*: cf. 2 Samuel 18: 33.

'let me die': 'The Song of Love and Death', from Tennyson's 'Lancelot and Elaine', 11. 1000–1011, *Idylls of the King*.

51 *the speaking dress*: annually, on 4 June, parents would attend to hear sixth formers attired in freshly pressed Etonian uniform and sporting carnations, recite speeches before the cricket match, boat races and fireworks which rounded off the day.

my good dear girls: 'Madge ' and 'Denny', the nieces who had lived with her since 1870.

52 *it will be done for them*: cf. Matthew 7: 7 and 18: 19.

53 *the peace that passeth all understanding*: Philippians 4: 7. The intensity of the spiritual experience at St Andrews in 1884 was occasionally repeated; see p. 157. She drew upon the experience in one of her most autobiographical tales: 'Mr Sandford', *Cornhill Magazine*, April–May 1888.

the battle that was against him: cf. Psalm 55: 18.

a little poem of Swinburne: Swinburne's elegy for the purblind young poet and pre-Raphaelite disciple, Philip Bourke Marston, was first published in the *Athenaeum*, 13 December 1890.

54 *performed in him now*: cf. Colossians 4: 12.

longing so for her home: Madge had stayed behind in England when the others had left for Switzerland a week after Cyril's funeral.

55 *a volume in twelve days*: Scott's *Journal* had been published in 1890.

56 *non recuso laborem*: 'I am not unwilling to work.'

in the way of every harm: such references suggest that it may have been more than ill health that terminated Cyril's brief spell as private secretary to Sir Arthur Gordon, Governor of Ceylon.

dear Anne Ritchie: see note to p. 135.

oh vain repetitions: Matthew 6: 7.

58 *chiefly upon Newman*: probably a reference to the lengthy section on Newman in *The Victorian Age of English Literature*, vol. ii, ch. 1., although it is possibly a reference to some as yet unidentified obituary article, since Newman had died in 1890.

the Pickersgills: a family of artists: Frederick Richard (1820–1900), a historical painter, successful in the Houses of Parliament competition, nephew of Henry William (1782–1875), fashionable portrait painter and father of Henry Hall (d. 1861), also a painter of historical scenes.

gleaming ornaments and dusky faces: glimpses swiftly worked up into a brief article for *Blackwood's*: 'A New Una', October 1856.

65 *Robert Macpherson*: see note to p. 73.

66 *good Jane*: Jane Hockey, the nursemaid who stayed in Oliphant's employ until 1866 and provided the model for a devoted serving-girl in *The Last of the Mortimers* (1862).

67 *full of ex-votos*: offerings made in fulfilment of vows.

68 *by diligence*: public stage-coach.

   'the awful rose of dawn': A. Tennyson, 'The Vision of Sin', 1. 50.

   vettura: carriage.

70 *anch' io pittore*: 'I too am a painter.'

71 *confraternita*: 'Brotherhood': white-robed monks.

   misericordia: a lay brotherhood who gave aid to the sick.

   the revolution occurred: on 27 April 1859, a revolution that was to bring about the end of the Grand Duke of Tuscany's despotic rule and see the province of Florence entrusted to the protection of Victor Emmanuel II of Sardinia. In 1861 the province was incorporated in the kingdom of Italy.

72 *a dolce*: 'a sweet'.

73 *Robert Macpherson*: (1811–72). Oliphant's husband had met Macpherson in Edinburgh where he trained as a surgeon, a fact that may help explain why Frank wanted to be near him and why Oliphant subsequently entrusted her alcoholic brother Willie's care to him. In 1840 he emigrated to Rome where he painted Roman and Italian scenes. In about 1851 he gave up painting in favour of photography and became well known for his views of Rome and Roman antiquities.

   'Felicita': *Blackwood's*, August–September 1859. Oliphant's pro-revolutionary sympathies were unlikely to make her commentary on contemporary political events welcome to *Blackwood's* Tory editor.

   must have written something . . . I cannot recollect: one of Oliphant's worst novels, *The House on the Moor* (3 vols., 1861), published by Hurst and Blackett, bears the following Prefatory Note: 'This book was overshadowed and interrupted by the heaviest grief. The author says so, not to deprecate criticism, but to crave the tender forbearance of her unknown friends.'

74 *Nero*: the old church party of the Guelfs.

75 *Geraldine Bate*: Geraldine Macpherson, *née* Bate (1829–78), met Robert in 1847 when she was travelling in Europe with her aunt Anna Brownell Jameson (1794–1860), a well-known literary and art critic. The two tragedies through which the Macphersons helped Oliphant cemented this friendship and Geraldine adopted the habit of signing her letters to Oliphant, 'Ever your loving sister, Geddie'. Geddie supplemented the family income by helping out with the business, undertaking translation work, writing—she was to be her aunt's biographer—and art work. Oliphant endeavoured to help her place her work and Geddie illustrated at least one of Oliphant's novels: *Madonna Mary*,

serialized in *Good Words*, January–December 1866. When her friend died Oliphant edited and reviewed her *Memoirs of the Life of Anna Jameson* (1878), and, according to another friend's account, helped out with the upbringing of the younger Macpherson children (J. L. Story, *Later Reminiscences*, Glasgow, 1913).

76 *villeggiatura*: 'holiday retreat'.

or some such title: 'The Seaside in the Papal States', *Blackwood's*, October 1859.

78 *Mr Blackett wrote*: for her close friendship with the Blacketts see p. 100. Oliphant's novel, *Agnes* (1866) was dedicated to Mrs Blackett.

79 *indulgence and extravagance*: many of Oliphant's acquaintance felt that she had been an over-devoted mother. Robert Story's wife, whose husband's previous fondness for Oliphant was perhaps inclined to make her a little acid in her observations, later wrote of the boys: 'They were being educated at Eton, a great mistake, as they would have been much better at a more ordinary school. But their mother thought an Eton education the only one suitable for a gentleman, and was prepared for any sacrifice on her part for what she fondly imagined the good of her boys' (Story, *Later Reminiscences*, 49).

81 *are to me as brass*: cf. Leviticus 26: 19.

in an unfortunate way: at the age of thirty Madge had married William Valentine, a partner in a jute manufacturing firm in Dundee, in July 1893. After Madge's long and expensive training as an engraver Oliphant was dissatisfied with her 'matter of fact' decision to marry a man with whom she was not in love and who was unfamiliar with the artistic milieu in which she had been raised. Moreover, despite her own humble upbringing, Oliphant was immensely proud of her breeding, and Valentine's work, demeanour, and bourgeois establishment attracted that genteel Victorian prejudice against 'trade' which had often manifested itself in her novels. In the months after her marriage Madge had implored 'the person I love best by far in the world' to come and stay, but Oliphant had wisely refrained from laying such strains upon the marriage as her own had suffered. (National Library of Scotland, Accs. 593/1 and 5678/6.)

82 *about Tiddy*: see above, p. 49.

depart in peace: Luke 2: 29.

83 *Mr Hutton*: Richard Holt Hutton (1826–97), theologian, literary critic, and journalist: editor of the *Spectator* for whom Oliphant had contributed a series of weekly articles from December 1889 to November 1890 under the heading 'A Commentary from an Easy-Chair'.

84 *'beholding the glory of God'*: cf. 2 Corinthians 3: 18.

Fanny: Fanny Tulloch, Principal Tulloch's second daughter, by now middle-aged, had spent long periods of time with Oliphant since her childhood, including a year immediately after Maggie Oliphant's death.

84 *Archbishop Tait*: Archibald Campbell Tait (1811–82) was Archbishop of Canterbury from 1869. During an outbreak of scarlet fever in 1856 five of his seven children died in just over a month. His only surviving son, Craufurd, died in 1878, swiftly followed by his wife. Oliphant had been reading *The Life of Archibald Campbell Tait* by R. T. Davidson and W. Benham (2 vols., 1891).

a sense of common suffering: the Archbishop had approved and contributed to *Catherine and Craufurd Tait; A Memoir* by W. Benham (1879).

85 *after his boy*: Davidson and Benham, *Life of A. C. Tait*, ii. 328.

86 *I know not what I say*: cf. Luke 23: 34.

87 *tale of the Cæsarini*: 'The Romance of Agostini: a true story of Modern Rome', *Blackwood's*, September–December 1860.

Dr Kennedy of Shrewsbury: Benjamin Hall Kennedy (1804–89), Headmaster of Shrewsbury and author of the famous Latin primer that became the standard school text for the next century.

the rapide: 'fast train'.

88 *Mr Pentland*: Joseph Barclay Pentland (1797–1873).

Mr Laing: see note to p. 39.

Monks of the West: her authorized translation ran to seven volumes (1861–79), Charles, Comte de Montalembert (1810–70), orator, politician and historian, was born in London where his father was exiled. He swiftly became a leader of liberal Catholic opinion in France, opposing the state monopoly on teaching, but submitted when, in 1831, the Pope condemned liberalism. During the 1848 Revolution Montalembert, fearing the return of mob rule, swung the Catholic party behind Louis Napoleon but, as the Second Empire's dictatorial tendencies emerged, once again fought for civil and religious liberties, despite the inevitable collision with Rome. Oliphant published *Memoir of Count de Montalembert: a Chapter of Recent French History* (2 vols., Edinburgh, 1872).

91 *'noise and glee'*: the significance, perhaps, lies in the suppression of the opening words of this quotation: 'To meet their Dada, wi'flichterin noise and glee' (Robert Burns, *The Cotter's Saturday Night*, 3).

first of the Carlingford series: 'The Executor', *Blackwood's*, May 1861. The lawyer in this tale was in fact named John Brown. John Brownlow, also a lawyer, appeared in a later novel, *The Brownlows*, *Blackwood's*, January 1867–February 1868. 'The Chronicles of Carlingford' eventually included *The Executor*, *The Rector* and *The Doctor's Family* (*Blackwood's*, September 1861–January 1862), *Salem Chapel* (*Blackwood's*, February 1862–January 1863), *The Perpetual Curate* (*Blackwood's*, June 1863–September 1864), *Miss Marjoribanks* (*Blackwood's*, February 1865–May 1866), and *Phoebe Junior: A Last Chronicle of Carlingford* (1876).

that of Mrs Humphry Ward: Mrs Humphry Ward's *Robert Elsmere* (1888) achieved three editions by 1891, selling 70,500 copies before 'hundreds of thousands' of cheap editions were published.

Professor Aytoun: William Edmondstoune Aytoun (1813–65), lawyer, poet, and mainstay of *Blackwood's*, had been professor of rhetoric and literature at Edinburgh since 1845. He was co-author of the parodic *Bon Gaultier* ballads (1845) and a noted humorist. This encounter unfortunately took place while Aytoun was suffering from depression after his first wife's death.

92 *'Come hither, Evan Cameron'*: the first line of a 216-line poem 'The Execution of Montrose', one of Aytoun's *Lays of the Scottish Cavaliers*. It was first published in *Blackwood's*, September 1844.

93 *old Mrs Wilson*: see p. 33.

the Storys: Robert Herbert Story (1835–1907) had become minister at Rosneath in 1860 on his father's death and was subsequently to become Moderator of the Church Assembly and Principal of Glasgow University. Oliphant erected a memorial window to her daughter Maggie at Rosneath. Its loch-side setting and recent religious history provided the germ of her Scottish novel, *The Minister's Wife* (1869).

before we went to Italy: 'Edward Irving', *Blackwood's*, November 1858; *The Life of Edward Irving* (1862).

Mr Drummond: Henry Drummond (1786–1860), businessman and politician, largely financed the emergence of the Holy Catholic Apostolic Church which, in preparation for the imminent Second Coming of Christ, reinstituted the offices of the primitive church. Drummond himself became 'angel' (bishop) for Scotland.

94 *his father's long intimacy with Irving*: Robert Story (1795–1860) was a friend of both Carlyle and the millenarian preacher Edward Irving. He exposed the female parishioner whose alleged 'gift of tongues' was to bring about Irving's rejection by the sect he had created, when it emerged that he lacked the very gift he had done so much to encourage.

'a field to bury strangers in': cf. Matthew 27: 7.

Mr Campbell of Row: McLeod Campbell of Row was deposed from his ministry in 1831 by the General Assembly for his views on the Atonement.

96 *Dr Carlyle*: John Aitken Carlyle (1801–79), younger brother of Thomas, who had supported him throughout his medical training. After a series of posts as travelling physician to the nobility John turned to the literary life with a particular interest in Icelandic language and literature.

97 *he could tell me little himself*: Thomas Carlyle did not commit his own memories of Irving to paper until the autumn of 1866 (*Reminiscences*, 1881) when he paid generous tribute to Oliphant's biography.

98 *Lady Cloncurry*: Elizabeth, Lady Cloncurry (1815?–95). Oliphant became a

close friend of hers in her old age and published a charming extended obituary of her, entitled 'A Noble Lady', *New Review* 14 (1896), 241–7.

99 *Mr Symonds*: John Addington Symonds (1840–93), historian of the Renaissance, poet, and translator, was admired by his intimates for his energetic struggle against ill-health. His memoirs and letters, by contrast, give the impression of paralysing nervous debility and morbid introspection. Oliphant was now preparing a review of Symond's biography to appear in 'Men and Women', *Blackwood's*, April 1895.

invidiosa non fui: 'I have not been envious.' Oliphant compares herself with the avaricious and prodigal suffering in circle 4 of Hell in Dante's *Inferno*, Canto VII. She had written a guide to Dante's work in 1877 for the Foreign Classics for English Readers series published by Blackwoods.

102 *Mr Simpson*: manager of the Edinburgh end of the publishing house.

104 *tirée à quatre épingles*: meticulously apparelled.

105 *Farmer Flamborough and his daughters*: characters from Oliver Goldsmith's *The Vicar of Wakefield* (1766).

108 *fauteuil*: 'armchair'.

donna da faccenda: 'housemaid'.

110 *'Life on an Island'*: 'Life in an Island', *Blackwood's*, January 1865.

111 *Prévost-Paradol*: Lucien-Anatole Prévost-Paradol (1829–70), French academician, journalist, and littérateur was well-known for his mordant political satire. Sent as a government minister to America in 1870, he died shortly after his arrival there.

112 *all but Iona*: from his monastery in Iona, St Columba had sent missionaries throughout Scotland in the sixth century. Subsequently the island became the burial place for Scots, Irish, and Norse kings and was regarded as a holy place.

Lamennais: Félicite Lamenais (1782–1854), French priest and writer on philosophy and politics. His advocacy of papal authority as a curb upon the French bishops and his support for the separation of church and state resulted in his final estrangement from the church. In his last years he pointed to the common man rather than the church as the source of social regeneration.

113 *Père Félix*: Célestin-Joseph Félix (1810–91), a noted Jesuit preacher, whose series of Easter sermons, delivered in Notre Dame, were first published in 1872. Described in 'Madame Saint-Ange', *Good Cheer*, December 1867. For Mrs Craven see note to p. 127.

the sound of many waters: Revelation 1: 15.

'Dix soldats—et un petit bon homme en blouse': 'Ten soldiers and a good little fellow in an overall'.

grande dame au bout des ongles: 'a great lady to the tips of her fingers'.

114 *'fired'*: cauterized.

Ruffini: John Ruffini (1807–81) also gains a mention in *The Victorian Age of English Literature*, ii. 194–5.

115 (*. . . or O'Mahony, as he called himself*): Francis Sylvester Mahony (1804–66), one-time Jesuit and Catholic priest, had abandoned the religious life by the mid-1830s. As poet, parodist, and essayist he had helped to establish the tone of *Fraser's Magazine* before moving to Paris in 1848. S. C. Hall may have given Oliphant an introduction to this now reclusive man, who retired to a monastery shortly before his death in 1866.

garniture de cheminée: set of mantelpiece ornaments.

116 *bonne à tout faire*: maid of all work.

beloved cousin Annie: Annie Louisa Walker. Recently returned from Canada and orphaned, Annie gravitated to Oliphant for help. In 1866 she became a part of Oliphant's household, acting as housekeeper and secretary. In 1884 she married a rich and elderly widower, becoming the Mrs Harry Coghill who first edited this autobiography.

118 *Jeanie Deans*: the heroine of W. Scott's *The Heart of Midlothian*.

shandrydan: any sort of rickety old conveyance.

119 *a carriole*: lightly covered cart or trap.

120 *bateau de poissage*: ferry-boat.

Fête Dieu: Corpus Christi day.

121 *en robe de chambre*: cooked in their skins.

122 *vetturino*: carriage driver; see p. 68.

123 *a little perhaps of Pecksniff*: an allusion to the character in C. Dicken's *Martin Chuzzlewit*, who was 'fuller of virtuous precept than a copy-book. Some people likened him to a direction-post, which is always telling the way to a place, and never goes there.'

ben trovato: a good story.

124 *the Gaelic song*: 'The Solitary Reaper'.

Aunt Nelly: Ellen Clifford (1824–82), travelled abroad with Oliphant in 1875.

Miss Lawless: the Honourable Emily Lawless (1845–1913), daughter of Lady Cloncurry (see above, note to p. 98), was a poet and novelist in whose career Oliphant had taken an interest. *Hurrish* (1886) and *Grania* (1892), two novels with Irish settings, achieved popularity.

127 *goes all the way*: an allusion to Autolycus's song in *The Winter's Tale*, IV. ii. 134.

> 'A merry heart goes all the day,
> Your sad tires in a mile-a'.

that Mrs Craven speaks of: Oliphant had been much impressed by the interesting mixture of worldliness and religious piety in the *journal intime* of Mrs Craven, the French wife of a minor English diplomat ('A Memoir of Mrs Augusta Craven', *Edinburgh Review* 181 (1895), 315–45).

127 *attempted any performance myself*: although she did not care to act, Oliphant had written 'little drawing-room plays' for her guests even before her own children were old enough to perform. (*Autobiography and Letters*, 184, 213). One such comic melodrama, *The Elderly Lover*, was printed for private circulation in 1885.

133 *of good report*: cf. Philippians 4: 8.

134 *George Smith*: (1824–1901), publisher and owner of the *Cornhill Magazine* and the *Pall Mall Gazette*.

'*Innocent*': *Innocent, A Tale of Modern Life*, appeared in the *Graphic*, 4 January– 28 June 1873. The curious, unawakened moral and emotional life of the orphaned heroine, brought back from Italy to live with English relatives, seems to have been prompted by the 'absence of feeling' Oliphant's little nieces so shockingly manifested (see p. 150).

135 *I never had any help from outside*: although a Civil List pension of £100 a year was granted to her in 1868.

136 *yet so as by fire*: 1 Corinthians 3: 12–15.

137 *my 'Beleaguered City'*: *A Beleaguered City, being the Narrative of certain Recent Events in the City of Semur* (1880), the first of Oliphant's tales of the unseen.

138 *Mrs Duncan Stewart*: *Née* Harriet Everlida Gore (1804–84). Hare's sketch for *Good Words* (1892) was republished in his *Biographical Sketches* (1895), where a picture of her in her 'peculiar head-dress' is included. Henry James's *Notebooks* suggest that he too found Mrs Duncan Stewart and her daughter a rewarding study and they were to provide the germ of two short stories: *Brooksmith* and *A London Life*: see *The Notebooks of Henry James*, ed. F. O. Matthiessen and K. B. Murdock (New York, 1961) entries for 19 June 1884 and 20 June 1887.

139 *Pour rire*: to make one laugh.

affublés: grotesquely rigged out.

'*La pièce m'intéresse*': 'A room full of people who interest me.'

Christina Rogerson: Christina Rogerson's first husband, an elderly, alcoholically inclined Scotsman, with whom she had not been in love, had died in 1884. She then became embroiled in the notorious Victorian scandal surrounding Sir Charles Dilke. In July 1885 it was Christina who broke the news of an impending divorce suit, in which he was to figure as co-respondent, to Dilke. Her brother was acting as solicitor to the aggrieved husband, Donald Crawford, while she became the confidante of the wife, Kitty Crawford. Kitty subsequently claimed that Christina had hoped to marry Dilke, allegedly an ex-lover, and that acting out of pique she had written an anonymous letter to Crawford alerting him to his wife's adultery. When the matter came to court Christina's own brother testified against her. By that time she had had a mental breakdown and had been temporarily placed under restraint and was described in open court as 'an hysterical woman'. Henry James remarked that 'if she had been beautiful and sane she would have been one of the world's great wicked women' (L. Edel, *Henry James: The Conquest of London, 1870–1883* (1962)), p. 335.

141 *the excellent Sir Theodore*: Sir Theodore Martin (1816–1909), parliamentary lawyer, essayist, theatre critic, and translator, collaborated with Aytoun in writing the *Bon Gaultier* ballads (1845). After a ten-year courtship he had married the famous actress Helen Faucit, who had continued to act until 1871. Against this passage on the Martins Oliphant had written the marginal comment, 'Not to be printed unless they have died'.

142 *the son-in-Law of a friend of ours*: Christina Rogerson's daughter Harriet Kingscote and her husband took Crawford's side in the Dilke affair.

143 *(Tom Brown)*: Thomas Hughes (1822–96), always best known as the author of *Tom Brown's Schooldays* (1857), which drew heavily on his memories of Rugby.

144 *Mr Fawcett*: Henry Fawcett (1833–84), Cambridge Professor of Political Economy and Radical politician.

145 *what part of India he would go to*: Francis Wilson attended the Royal Indian Engineering College.

148 *'singing he was . . . month of May'*: as so often in Oliphant's work this is a slight misquotation, as is the phrase 'And, ah the difference to me!', which occurs at the end of the following paragraph and is an allusion to Wordsworth's poem 'She dwelt among the untrodden ways'.

Annie Thackeray: Anne Isabella Thackeray Ritchie (1837–1919), the elder daughter of William Thackeray and herself a novelist and writer of memoirs. Oliphant became her closest friend, associated as she was with some of the most intense moments in Ritchie's life. Oliphant had given her the first review which so pleased her father; it was with Oliphant that she was staying on the night her sister Minnie died in childbirth, and Oliphant facilitated a number of her literary activities. Two years after this meeting Annie married an Eton contemporary of Oliphant's nephew Frank, seventeen years her junior. Ritchie's memoir of Oliphant is to be found in *From the Porch* (1913).

149 *one's heart inclined that way*: by the time Oliphant wrote this passage she was aware that Laura Makepeace Stephen (1870–1946) had inherited the mental weakness of her maternal grandmother's family.

Leslie Stephen: (1832–1904), an agnostic who had resigned his orders and earned his living as literary critic, philosopher, and editor of the *Cornhill* (1871–82) and then of the *Dictionary of National Biography*. Oliphant had reviewed his literary accounts of Alpine expeditions in 'New Books', *Blackwood's* October 1871.

150 *the bulk of a year's income*: Oliphant in fact published a number of essays and stories in the *Cornhill* during Stephen's editorship, but presumably here refers to longer serials which later appeared as three-deckers (*Carita, Cornhill* June

1876–August 1877 and *Within the Precincts, Cornhill* February 1878–April 1879).

151 *Lina*: Oliphant's maid.

ces beaux jours quand j'étais si malheureuse: 'those blessed days when I was so unhappy', an allusion to a line from a poem by Claude de Rulhiere (1735–91), 'Oh c'était le bon temps, j'étais bien malheureuse.'

152 *Tout peut se réparer*: 'There's a remedy for everything.'

153 *Sir Andrew Clark*: (1826–93), the most celebrated physician of the day.

the Library here: for five years Cecco had a part-time post at the Royal Library in Windsor.

155 *'Mr Sandford'*: when this tale was reissued in *The Ways of Life* (1897) Oliphant publicly acknowledged its autobiographical impulse.

156 *various miscellaneous matters*: the two novels both feature young adults who survive on their inner resources when their natural expectations are disappointed. A series of review articles she had begun for *Blackwood's* that year were entitled 'The Old Saloon' because they purported to come from Maga's Library or Saloon, where over the years so many literary reputations had been weighed. *The Makers of Venice: Doges, Conquerors, Painters and Men of Letters* had also appeared that year.

not bad of their kind: these verses appear in *Autobiography and Letters*, pp. 435–6.

157 *in the cool of the garden*: cf. Genesis 3: 8.

H. and Black: Hurst and Blackett.

Miss Braddon's books: Mary Elizabeth Braddon (1837–1915), chiefly remembered now as the author *of Lady Audley's Secret* (1862), a sensational novel including bigamy, child desertion, murder, and insanity, published seventy-five novels. In 'Novels', *Blackwood's*, September 1867, Oliphant had attacked her work for plagiarism and immorality, and stigmatized her as 'the inventor of the fair-haired demon of modern fiction'.

my reproach . . . taken away: cf. Genesis 30: 23 and Luke 1: 25.

159 *a book upon Edinburgh*: a letter of 13 February 1888 (British Library, MSS. 54919, Macmillan Archive) to Craik (see n. 71) refers to a recent visit Oliphant had paid to Macmillan, her publisher, who 'thought I wanted him to supply my wants which was what I did not expect nor ask', The commission resulted in *Royal Edinburgh: Her Saints, Kings, Prophets and Poets* (1890).

Sons and Daughters: *Blackwood's*, March–April 1890.

160 *Fortunes of Nigel*: W. Scott, *The Fortunes of Nigel* (1822).

Select Bibliography

A Select List of M. O. W. Oliphant's Fiction

This list has been compiled by the editor to represent a chronological spectrum of Oliphant's finest or most interesting fiction.

The Athelings, or The Three Gifts (3 vols., Edinburgh and London: W. Blackwood and Sons, 1857).

The Rector and The Doctor's Family (Edinburgh and London: W. Blackwood and Sons, 1863).

The Perpetual Curate. (3 vols., Edinburgh and London: W. Blackwood and Sons, 1864).

Agnes (3 vols., London: Hurst and Blackett, 1865).

Miss Marjoribanks (3 vols., Edinburgh and London: W. Blackwood and Sons, 1866).

A Son of the Soil (2 vols., London: Macmillan and Co., 1866).

At His Gates: A Novel (3 vols., London: Tinsley Brothers, 1872).

A Rose in June (2 vols., London: Hurst and Blackett, 1874).

The Curate in Charge (2 vols., London: Macmillan and Co., 1876).

Phoebe Junior: A Last Chronicle of Carlingford (3 vols., London: Hurst and Blackett, 1876.

A Beleaguered City: Being a Narrative of certain Recent Events in the City of Semur (London: Macmillan and Co., 1880).

Hester: A Story of Contemporary Life (3 vols., London: Macmillan and Co., 1883).

The Ladies Lindores (3 vols., Edinburgh and London: W. Blackwood and Sons, 1883).

Sir Tom (3 vols., London: Macmillan and Co., 1884).

The Wizard's Son (3 vols., London: Macmillan and Co., 1884).

A Country Gentleman and his Family (3 vols., London: Macmillan and Co., 1886).

The Land of Darkness, along with some Further Chapters in the Experiences of the Little Pilgrim (London: Macmillan and Co., 1888).

Kirsteen: The Story of a Scotch Family Seventy Years Ago (London: Macmillan and Co., 1890).

The Railwayman and His Children (3 vols., London: Macmillan and Co., 1891).

The Marriage of Elinor (3 vols., London: Macmillan and Co., 1892).

The Cuckoo in the Nest (3 vols., London: Hutchinson and Co., 1892).

Old Mr Tredgold (3 vols., London: Longman, 1896).

The Ways of Life: Two Stories (London: Smith, Elder and Co., 1897).

A Widow's Tale, and Other Stories, with an Introductory Note by J. M. Barrie (Edinburgh: W. Blackwood and Sons, 1898).

Stories of the Seen and the Unseen (Edinburgh and London: W. Blackwood and Sons, 1902).

Criticism

Colby, V. and R. A., *The Equivocal Virtue: Mrs Oliphant and the Victorian Literary Market Place* (New York: Archon Books, 1966).

Davis, P. M., *Memory and Writing: From Wordsworth to Lawrence* (Liverpool: Liverpool University Press, 1983).

Fleishman, A., *Figures of Autobiography: The Language of Self-Writing in Victorian and Modern England* (Berkeley and London: University of California Press, 1983).

Jelinek, E. C. (ed.), *Women's Autobiography: Essays in Criticism* (Bloomington and London: Indiana University Press, 1980).

Johnson, B., *A World of Difference* (Baltimore and London: Johns Hopkins University Press, 1987).

Landow, G. P. (ed.), *Approaches to Victorian Autobiography* (Ohio: Ohio University Press, 1979).

Olsen, T., *Silences* (New York: Delacorte Press, 1978).

Showalter, E., *A Literature of their Own: British Women Novelists from Brontë to Lessing* (Princeton: Princeton University Press, 1977).

Index